Constructivist Teacher Education

Constructivist Teacher Education:
Building New Understandings

Edited by

Virginia Richardson

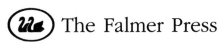 The Falmer Press

(A member of the Taylor & Francis Group)
London • Washington, D.C.

UK   The Falmer Press, 1 Gunpowder Square, London, EC4A 3DE
USA   The Falmer Press, Taylor & Francis Inc., 1900 Frost Road, Suite 101,
Bristol, PA 19007

First published in 1997

**A catalogue record for this book is available from the British
Library**

**Library of Congress Cataloging-in-Publication Data are
available on request**

ISBN 0 7507 0615 5 cased
ISBN 0 7507 0616 3 paper

Jacket design by Caroline Archer

Typeset in 10/12pt Garamond by
Graphicraft Typesetters Ltd., Hong Kong.

*Printed in Great Britain by Biddles Ltd, Guildford and King's Lynn on
paper which has a specified pH value on final paper manufacture
of not less than 7.5 and is therefore 'acid free'.*

Contents

Contents

Foreword

For the past half dozen years, school reformers have admonished us that K-12 students must learn more at higher levels of understanding. They urge that students acquire concepts and routines that lead to deeper understanding of content. Attention has turned to ways of promoting thinking and reasoning with the goal of creating schools where students are deeply engaged in problematic situations that matter to them. Those admonitions prompt many questions and concerns about teacher education. The basic question is, of course, how preservice teacher education programs can or ought to respond to these expectations.

At an annual meeting of the American Educational Research Association I visited with Virginia Richardson, on whom, over a 20-year friendship, I have come to rely heavily for insights into teacher education issues. On this occasion, my questions pertained to how these new efforts for building knowledge were different from those advocated by John Dewey a half century before and what new meaning they held for teacher education. I admitted to Virginia that I simply didn't know enough about constructivism to be able to answer my own questions.

Wonderful teacher that she is, Virginia talked to me of the roots of constructivism in the writings of Dewey and Piaget, Bruner and Vygotsky. She pointed to the promise of constructivism and compared it with behavioristic and cognitive theories. She noted that it is based on the assumption that knowledge is constructed by learners as they attempt to make sense of their experiences. Virginia drew my attention to Bruner's description of education as needing 'to be conceived as aiding young humans in learning to use the tools of meaning making and reality construction, to better adapt to the world in which they find themselves and to help in the process of changing it as required.'

Virginia also helped me to see connections with various work that AACTE had engaged in over the preceding decade and pointed to chapters in *The Teacher Educator's Handbook* that would be helpful to my understanding. She drew connections to work in critical thinking and learning communities and other thinking activities. We talked of the work of the University of Arizona colleagues to build a constructivist pedagogy and what the dimensions of such an approach might represent.

At a meeting of the AACTE Board of Directors, a spirited discussion about constructivism and its application to teacher education reinforced, for me, the need to sponsor this monograph. If knowledge is constructed by students in a more independent manner, what implications does this hold for teacher education? If the reformers' ideal teacher is one who centers his or her work on depth of understanding, refinement of skills, and the application of knowledge, how do we fashion preservice preparation programs that enable beginning teachers to accomplish this? How do teacher educators ensure that teacher candidates experience such inquiry-based teaching in courses outside the realm of teacher education? Students from one set of socioeconomic experiences present enormous challenges to teachers with other backgrounds and experiences. If the goal is to understand 'where children are at,' with regard to their thinking and understanding, how can this best be accomplished? Similarly, preparing young people for a world that sees knowledge as merely facts and figures presents challenges for teachers using constructivist principles. What obligations do we have to address these concerns in preservice preparation programs? How do we equip prospective teachers for the breadth vs. depth arguments that they encounter in school curriculum committees and local school boards? How should situated learning and authentic instruction be emphasized in environments that traditionally value other forms of learning? I struggled to reconcile these competing claims when I began my discussion with Virginia.

I was pleased, therefore, when the AACTE Committee on Publications agreed to sponsor this work and am indebted to Virginia Richardson for undertaking this project while editing the massive *Handbook of Research on Teaching*. In the thoughtful chapters that follow, teacher educators can sort through these issues and find solutions to where we should set our sights. It is a significant contribution to AACTE's ongoing work in enhancing the quality of beginning teachers and meeting the challenges of their schools.

David G. Imig
Chief Executive Officer, AACTE
Washington, DC
April 9, 1997

Preface

The major contribution of this book written by US, Canadian, and Australian teacher educators is that it will help push the field to think more deeply and critically than has been the case to date about the implications for teacher education of recent developments in constructivist thinking and practices. While a great deal has been written in recent years about constructivist learning theories and their applications to elementary and secondary school classrooms, much less has been said about the implications of these ideas and practices for teacher education. This volume explores the possibilities and limitations of constructivist learning theories in a variety of teacher education contexts such as methods courses, field experiences and a study group for experienced teachers.

While all of the authors of this book reject a transmission approach to teaching as a dominant approach and are generally supportive of the assumptions, beliefs and practices associated with constructivism as a way of thinking about the formation of knowledge and understanding, they clearly reject the idea of constructivism as a monolithic and agreed-upon concept that leads to prescriptions and recipes for teaching practice. The diversity of theoretical approaches to constructivism (e.g., Piagetian, situated cognition, sociocultural, and emancipatory approaches) and the diversity of practices in teaching and teacher education that are associated with these various approaches are thoroughly examined in this text, both in their contemporary forms and in terms of an examination of the historical evolution of contemporary approaches. The authors raise many important philosophical and practical questions associated with adopting some version of a constructivist philosophy in teacher education and candidly share some of their most serious concerns about the ways in which constructivist approaches have been presented to prospective teachers and in turn interpreted by them in the current 'bandwagon' climate surrounding constructivism in education.

The authors of this volume represent a diverse group of perspectives on constructivism even though they are committed to the same set of general ideas about learning. For example, some of the authors focus primarily on the cognitive development of individuals, while others emphasize the connections between constructivist ideas and issues of equity and social transformation.

Constructivism in teacher education is examined in this volume in several different senses. First, with regard to the practice of teacher education, there is the idea of teaching teachers to teach according to a particular constructivist approach. On the other hand, constructivist teacher education is defined as working with teachers in a constructivist way, helping them to reexamine and reflect about the tacit ideas they bring to their education for teaching. The bias in this book is toward an approach to constructivism in teacher education which encourages constructivist teaching practice by modelling it in the teacher education classroom, and which also maintains recognition of the diversity of theoretical approaches to constructivism. Constructivism is also discussed in the book as a lens through which we can understand the process of learning to teach and there is discussion in a few of the chapters of constructivist based research methodologies that can and have been used to understand and document how teachers construct knowledge and develop over time.

All of the authors of this book are practicing teacher educators and several of the chapters in this book represent thoughtful analyses of the authors' own attempts to implement a constructivist philosophy either in a preservice teacher education program or in a professional development program for practicing teachers. These self-studies of the complexities of translating ideas associated with a set of descriptive theories about learning to practices in teacher education and teaching illuminate many of the dilemmas (e.g., concerning power and authority) that have been faced by those who have attempted to translate constructivist ideas into practice. These studies are encouraging because the authors do not oversimplify or romanticize about the benefits of adopting a constructivist approach. They openly face the complexities of the task and the result is a series of discussions and reflections about constructivism in teaching and teacher education that is both challenging and useful to those of us who work in teacher education programs.

If we are to make progress in developing and improving the ways in which we make use of the ideas and practices associated with constructivism in the education of teachers, then practicing teacher educator/researchers, like those represented in this volume, must play a major part in testing out and discovering how to do this. This well written book is very informative about the different possibilities for constructivism in educating teachers. This is a much needed volume that should help teacher educators, researchers and policy makers make more intelligent decisions about the ways in which constructivism can enhance the education of teachers to benefit all students.

Ken Zeichner
Madison, Wisconsin
October, 1996

I *Theory*

1   Constructivist Teaching and Teacher Education: Theory and Practice[1]

Virginia Richardson

Constructivist teaching and teacher education has clearly arrived. Discussions of these topics dominate scholarly and practitioner journals in most subject matter areas (for example, *Educational Researcher*, **23**, 4; and *Journal of Teacher Education*, **43**, 5). Further, constructivist approaches are reflected in national and state level policy documents designed to influence the curriculum and pedagogy of American classrooms (for example, the National Council on Teachers of Mathematics Standards), and in state and local policies. The Tucson, Arizona Unified School District, for example, is contemplating asking early elementary school teachers to throw away their mathematics textbooks and teach mathematics primarily through a constructivist approach using manipulatives.

One cannot think of constructivist teaching, however, as a monolithic, agreed-upon concept. The extent of the agreement among the various constructivist approaches is that constructivism is a learning or meaning-making theory. It suggests that individuals create their own new understandings, based upon the interaction of what they already know and believe, and the phenomena or ideas with which they come into contact. Constructivism is a descriptive theory of learning (this is the way people learn or develop); it is not a prescriptive theory of learning (this is the way people *should* learn).

Most constructivists would also agree that the traditional approach to teaching — the transmission model — promotes neither the interaction between prior and new knowledge nor the conversations that are necessary for internalization and deep understanding. The information acquired from traditional teaching, if acquired at all, is usually not well integrated with other knowledge held by the students. Thus, new knowledge is often only brought forth for school-like activities such as exams, and ignored at all other times.

While these are important common understandings, there are also considerable disagreements. In part, these conflicts relate to the difficulty in translating a descriptive theory of learning into the practice of teaching. As we have learned in the past, this translation is not a direct procedure, both because teaching takes place in a social milieu and is not just a psychological process, and because of the myriad of individual and contextual diversities that characterize our classrooms. Further, learning does not always require a formal, educational process. There are, however, other fundamental theoretical differences in the various constructivist approaches. One area of disagreement concerns the focus of attention in a constructivist teaching environment. There are those who focus on the individual acting as sole agent in the process of constructing and reconstructing meaning. Others focus on the sociocultural context in which an individual lives, and still others on both the individual and social by suggesting that it is not useful to separate the two analytically. The second disagreement concerns the role of formal knowledge in the education of students. Is formal (or academic) knowledge acquisition a goal to which the teacher and students should aspire, or is it simply a tool in classroom discourse leading to shared understandings?

These disagreements may be found between and within two quite different constructivist approaches — the psychological Piagetian approach to constructivism; and the situated social constructivist approach. The questions that I address are whether the disagreements make a difference in practice, and how we should approach theory and practice in constructivist teaching and teacher education. But first, I will place this inquiry within a concrete issue of practice.

A dilemma in constructivist teaching and teacher education may be demonstrated by a question of practice that so many practitioners — teachers and teacher educators — ask about constructivism. What is the place of formal knowledge in a constructivist classroom, and how should it be introduced? By formal knowledge, I am referring to concepts, premises and understandings that have been debated and pretty well agreed upon within discourse communities that are considerably larger than the classroom: The communities of scientists, mathematicians, or teacher educators, for example. This formal knowledge is represented in textbooks, standards, testing programs, the teacher's understandings, etc. It is the unanswered questions about formal knowledge that help to produce the dilemmas that many practitioners confront as they seek to create constructivist classrooms. These relate to questions about the 'correct answer', 'teacher telling', and other concerns about both traditional and constructivist teaching (see, for example, Chazan and Ball, 1995). Cobb (1994) provides a quote from Deborah Ball who presents this dilemma:

> *How* do I create experiences for my students that connect with what they now know and care about but that also transcend the present? *How* do I value their interests and also connect them to ideas and traditions growing out of centuries of mathematical exploration and invention? (Ball, 1993, p. 375)

Why is the use of formal knowledge an issue for constructivist practitioners? The following are questions related to this issue that I have encountered both as a person working with teachers in elementary and secondary schools, and as a teacher educator attempting to develop a constructivist teacher education program. If we accept that meaning is formed and reformed on the basis of an interaction (or transaction) between prior meaning and new experiences, an individual's understandings will be more or less idiosyncratic. This says that formal knowledge as represented in a textbook and read by thirty different students will be understood in thirty different ways if the students engage in a transformative process. What, then, *is* formal knowledge? How can formal knowledge be agreed upon in a formal discourse community if each person has an idiosyncratic understanding of it? We are asked to create learning environments in which 'shared' meanings can develop, and individual meanings can be challenged. How can there be 'shared' meanings when all meanings are unique to an individual? And what if the shared meanings that are developed are at odds with formal disciplinary knowledge? Who or what is the authority in judging the meanings and understandings developed within the classroom? And what should the teacher 'know' to help facilitate the process?

Constructivist teacher educators are often faced with a further dilemma. How can I introduce constructivist theory and practice to my students without 'telling' them about it? In a constructivist environment, should my goal be to 'get' the students to understand and believe in constructivist theory and practice? And in my telling, am I not forcing them into a studenting role in which they will simply store the knowledge in a place easily accessible for the next exam and lose soon after?

These questions would be answered in different ways by those who subscribe to the Piagetian, psychological approach, or to the situated social constructivist approach. The answers depend, in part, on the views of the goals of education, and on the degree to which we allow understandings of the social aspects of learning — particularly those related to power and control — enter into our theoretical constructions of constructivism.

Piagetian Psychological Constructivism

The Piagetian, psychological proponents of constructivism see the meaning-making process as individualistic with the purpose of constructivist teaching being to lead toward higher levels of understanding and analytic capabilities. For example, Schifter and Simon (1992) describe the goals of constructivist mathematics instruction as teaching the 'nature of mathematics inquiry and the modes of generating knowledge that are characteristic of the discipline' (p. 187). In order to reach these higher levels, students must be actively engaged in reconstructing their existing understandings by restructuring their cognitive maps. The teacher encourages this in two ways: facilitating an environment in which students undergo a certain amount of cognitive dissonance, and devising tasks that hopefully lead to a reorganization of existing cognitive maps. By and large, this has been translated into instructional practices such as hands-on activities (for example, the use of manipulables); the engagement of students in tasks that are meant to challenge their concepts and thinking processes; and certain forms of questioning that dig deeply into students' beliefs, turn the beliefs into hypotheses, and provide a non-threatening atmosphere in which those beliefs may be examined.

But the teaching and learning that we are examining, here, takes place in schools and colleges — which means a particular form of social milieu. The social milieu also provides a context for the learning processes in the class-room. However, this context has never been a favorite focus of psychologists. Recently, however, the Piagetian/psychologists have allowed the social to enter into their constructivist frameworks. Schifter and Simon (1992), for example, suggest that the negotiation of shared meaning within social interaction often provides a source of cognitive dissonance that allows individual students to restructure their concepts. Bereiter (1994), on the other hand, advocates the creation of progressive discourse communities in classrooms that mirror the ways in which knowledge is created and advanced in disciplinary fields. Bereiter suggests that it is through continual critique of work within a research com-munity that progress in a discipline takes place. The disciplines are the subject matters, such as science, mathematics, and art that are taught in schools. He suggests that these discourse communities be replicated within the classrooms to allow subject matter progress to take place within the classroom context.

Issues of power, authority and the place of formal knowledge are seldom directly addressed by psychological constructivists. An exception is Bereiter's (1994) recent response to the postmodernist critique. He feels that 'what stu-dents learn in science will come from authoritative sources — teachers and texts, mainly' (p. 10), regardless of the curriculum or mode of instruction. A text should therefore be seen as one form of evidence in the classroom progressive discourse process. And since the same text may be used in many classrooms, it becomes a common input to local classroom processes. Teachers play an authoritative role in selecting the most appropriate texts for the students.

It is the emphasis on, or reification of, the cognitive as separate from action, and the lack of attention to power issues — particularly those related to knowledge — that form the basis of the postmodernist critiques of the psychological approach (see, for example, O'Loughlin, 1992b). As long as the teacher and text are seen as authoritative, students will, to a certain degree, accept it without question. Authoritative knowledge will be transmitted whether we want it to be or not — particularly within a system that values grades. Students will continue to try to figure out what they think the teacher wants them to learn from the tasks.

This controlled teaching, says the critique, leads to the maintenance of the status quo — that is the maintenance of social and class differences that exist in our society today. How does this happen? Several studies demonstrate how this takes place in classrooms. Edwards and Mercer's (1987) studies of element-ary classrooms indicated the degree to which teachers controlled the learning outcomes of supposedly constructivist and discovery tasks. The tasks were structured with predetermined learning outcomes in mind. In these classrooms, the teacher, on the one hand, attempted to encourage 'discovery', and on the other hand, had a clear notion about exactly what the students should discover.

These mixed messages are particularly debilitating for students who do not understand the power relationships that undergird the middle-class con-text of the school. In these constructivist classrooms, the power relationships are masked, making it even more difficult for students of color and ethnic and linguistic minority students to figure out the game. This problem has been well described by Delpit (1988) and Reyes (1992). In this form of classroom, if the student takes the teacher's word that the student should construct and own the knowledge while the teacher is still really in control, it could lead to serious but often unspoken misunderstandings with social, political and cognitive consequences.

It is difficult for the teacher who is intent upon creating a constructivist environment to get around the problems of authority and control in a setting in which grades are important. In my teacher education classes, I devise new and intuitively exciting tasks in which the students may engage. However, I am not clear at all about what the outcomes will be, at least the first time I employ the task. Will I like what the students develop? Will some be better than others? I will only know when I see the direction in which the students are going, and the final product. This is not exactly fair to the students. They ask how it will be graded. I try to bring them in on the discovery process with me, and suggest that I will not grade the project. This drives them even crazier! After all, they know I will give a grade at the end of the semester, and that grade is important for their GPA and future activities in life.

This approach to constructivism, then, focuses on the individual meaning-making process. There is an assumption that students, such as those in preservice teacher education, bring understandings into the classroom that need to be adjusted, added to, or completely altered. The teacher's role is to facilitate this cognitive alteration through designing tasks and questions that create dilemmas for students. The critique of this form of constructivism focuses on the importance of the social elements of learning, and on the power relationships among the teacher, students and formal knowledge.

Social Cognition

If one rejects the individualistic, psychological view of learning that separates the individual from the social, thought from action, and the knower from the known, but still believes in a constructivist view of learning, what are the alternatives? One is the general theoretical approach called social constructivism. Social constructivists have a very different view of the process of the construction of knowledge than Piagetians. They do not focus, primarily, on the individual, but view the social as instrumental, if not essential, in both the construction and appropriation of knowledge. There are two forms of this conception, each of which contains its own approaches and scholarly traditions: situated cognition and sociocultural.

The situated cognition form of this approach suggests that knowledge is constructed by a person in transaction with the environment; that is, both the individual and environment change as a result of this learning process. In terms of school learning, the environment is thought of as a social milieu that affects the actions taken by students and the learning that occurs and is

7

affected by those actions. Knowledge is socially constructed, because meaning can only be constructed through the use of language in a social context. Dewey (1916) suggested that:

> . . . the use of language to convey and acquire ideas is an extension and refinement of the principle that things gain meaning by being used in a shared experience or joint action . . . When words do not enter as factors into a shared situation, whether overtly or imaginatively, they operate as pure physical stimuli, not as having a meaning or intellectual value. (pp. 15–16, quoted in Bredo, 1994, p. 30)

In this constructivist view, learning cannot be separated from action: perception and action work together in a dialogical manner. And there is no representation of reality that is privileged, or 'correct'. There are, instead, a variety of interpretations that are useful for different purposes in differing contexts. Knowledge is not thought of as a received, static entity that is separate from the individual. Neither is it separable from the activities within which knowledge was constructed, nor from the community of people with whom one communicates about the ideas.

The sociocultural form of this conception derives primarily from L.S. Vygotsky (see Davydov, 1995; Moll, 1990; Wertsch, 1991). Within this framework, the development of an individual relies on social interactions. It is within this social interaction that cultural meanings are shared within the group, and then internalized by the individual. Further, the child is seen as a unity. Davydov (1995) describes Vygotsky's approach in the following way:

> Developmental upbringing and teaching deals with the entire child, the child's entire activity, which reproduces in the individual socially created needs, capabilities, knowledge, and ways of behavior. This activity, if we see it as a special object of study, includes social, logical, pedagogical, psychological, and physiological aspects in its unity. (Davydov, 1995, p. 19)

Formal knowledge, as understood in signs and symbols, enters the learning situation as tools within the social interaction, and affects development or learning through activity engaged in by the learner. Moll suggests that school learning or development is coming 'to use essential "cultural tools", such as reading, writing, mathematics, or certain modes of discourse, within the activities that constitute classroom life' (1992, p. 21).

One can see, from this framework, how 'school subjects' and school knowledge may become separated from, and perhaps quite useless in everyday life. School is the sociocultural setting, and the meaning that is constructed within that social milieu is useful for schooling and similar situations (see Lave, 1988; Civil, 1995). Of course, many of us have continued our work within the schooling context as teachers and professors, and use that knowledge on a daily basis; however, many, many others do not work within such contexts.

How these social theories of construction and development are translated into teaching and schooling remains a puzzle. While the Vygotskian concepts of scaffolding and the zone of proximal development are useful in the consideration of teaching (see, for example, Newman, Griffin and Cole, 1989), questions remain. What, exactly, is the role of the teacher? When does 'formal knowledge' (if such a term is allowable) fit into the curriculum? Do different content areas (or disciplines) engender different forms of constructivist classrooms? Does the situated nature of knowing not suggest that school knowing is useful primarily for school-like activities?

Several people have contributed insights into these questions. Moll (1992), for example, has worked with schools and communities in the Tucson area to help teachers and working-class students understand the funds of knowledge within their communities. Teachers and students interview parents to understand how their knowledge grows out of the activities in which they are engaged, and how this knowledge is shared within the community. Teachers often bring parents and others into the classroom to indicate, for example, the way in which the builder of houses thinks about mathematics. Newman, Griffin and Cole's (1989) work in schools — particularly their after school program — is based on Vygotsky's sociohistorical learning theory and represents attempts to develop tasks that are everyday (such as cooking) in which subject matters such as mathematics are embedded. O'Loughlin (1992a) has attempted to develop teacher education classes in which multiple perspectives are respected, presented and worked through.

Subject Matter in Constructivist Classrooms

What is clear from an analysis of the literature is that there are different approaches to the formation of constructivist classrooms. Two factors seem to affect the approach taken by teachers. One relates to the degree to which the 'social' is acknowledged as integral to the individual learning/development process, and the second relates to the particular content or subject matter. While I have addressed the individual/social issue above, the subject matter focus has not been examined.

Mathematics, for example, as a content or discipline, has very different characteristics than other subject matter areas such as science, reading, history or writing. Arithmetic problems may be thought of by teachers as having 'correct' or at least 'more appropriate' answers. The discipline is bounded by a relatively concise symbol system the meaning of which is generally agreed upon within the mathematician community. On the other hand, reading comprehension is understood within the constructivist community as highly interpretive and based on individual or cultural meanings of concepts and ideas. Thus, it is less bounded than mathematics, and there is an understanding that while some interpretations of text may be more appropriate than others, there are probably none that are 'wrong'. Thus, the way in which subject matter, or formal knowledge, enters the constructivist classroom is very different depending upon the subject matter.

One may examine written descriptions of 'good' constructivist teachers to discern these differences in approach. For example, an article by Cobb, Wood, Yaekel and McNeal's (1992) compares two mathematics teachers, one traditional and the other constructivist, by focusing on relatively micro interactions about mathematics. Among other factors, they examined the degree to which the students were encouraged to explain and justify their answers to problems set by the teacher. The mathematical tasks and problems were carefully developed by the constructivist teacher to reflect understandings in the mathematical discipline. On the other hand, Freedman (1994), who was comparing two teachers' approaches to the teaching of writing, described the constructivist writing teacher's curriculum planning: 'Fiona had no set activities; nothing in the curriculum was pre-planned. Her theoretical framework told her that activities must be planned anew with each class to meet their particular needs' (p. 81). It would appear in these two descriptions of practice that the two constructivist teachers differed in the degree to which and manner in which they consciously brought their subject matter areas into curriculum planning and implementation. Thus, the culture of the subject matter area impacts strongly on the constructivist classroom. Since teacher education also has its own particular content, it is probably the case that the constructivist teacher education classroom differs considerably from those of other subject matter areas.

The Challenge for Teacher Education

Two quite different forms of constructivist teacher education are being advocated today. One form attempts to teach students how to teach in a particular constructivist manner (for example, Black and Ammon, 1992). Often these approaches apply to the teaching of particular subject matters (Mosenthal and Ball, 1992; Schifter and Simon, 1992), and are usually Piagetian. Another form of constructivist teacher education involves working with teachers and preservice students to help them understand their own tacit understandings, how these have developed, and the effects of these understandings on their actions; and to introduce new conceptions and premises as potential alternatives to those held by the students (Harrington, 1995; O'Loughlin, 1992a; Richardson, 1992 and 1994). The first form often involves considerable direct instruction in theory and practice. The second attempts to model a manner of involving students in investigations of premises and perspectives that it is thought may be used by the preservice students when they begin to teach.

Both forms of constructivist teacher education could present problems. When the teacher educator directly instructs teacher education students in Piagetian and constructivist theory and has in mind a particular approach to teaching, he or she models an approach to teaching that is contrary to the one that it is hoped the students will employ when they are teaching. On the other hand, the second form — the investigation of beliefs and presentation of alternative conceptions of teaching — models an approach to constructivist teaching that may not be appropriate for the teaching of certain subject matters such as science and mathematics. The content of teacher education is teaching — a subject matter area with very different characteristics than content such as mathematics. It is less bounded, for example, than mathematics or science, and there is less agreement on an important aspect of its content — that is, the nature of good teaching practice. The introduction of formal knowledge in constructivist teacher education happens in quite different ways than in the teaching of subject matter areas in which the students will eventually be engaged. This is particularly the case in the 'generic' teaching courses, or those that introduce the concept of teaching to the students. Thus, the modelling of a constructivist classroom by a teacher educator when the content is, for example, classroom organization, may not be a model that is appropriate to the constructivist teaching of high school mathematics.

The challenge for constructivist teacher educators is to develop an approach to teaching that does not contradict the content of the course — that is, constructivist teaching — but acknowledges differences in the nature of constructivist teaching depending on the subject matter that is being taught. I believe that this challenge will require considerable inquiry into the nature of constructivist teacher education and the effects on the way students think about teaching and eventually teach.

Conclusion

I am attracted to the critique of the Piagetian approach that relates to hegemony of knowledge and the exclusion of certain students from the conversation. Within a school context as it operates today, one can see how the Piagetian framework of constructivism — particularly corruptions of it — is able to develop and even thrive. The emphasis on individualization, the separation of thought and action, and the masking of power relationships continue to allow schools to perform a function in maintaining the economic and social class status quo. At the same time, I am aware that the social constructivist alternatives have not yet been well developed or described. Perhaps the reason for this is that such programs could not really be developed within schools as they exist today. Thinking of learning as a sociocultural process and teaching with conscious moral intent would require our rethinking the nature of the communities within and outside the school, as well as radically altering power relationships. This would be the case, also, in higher education institutions. For example, the concept of 'grades' would have to be reconceptualized.

In any event, it is essential that the alternatives not be worked out at academic meetings, but, rather, these ideas and practices should be debated, developed and tested within the context of schools, colleges, and classrooms. As I was working on this chapter, I was reading a book by Amy Kelly called

Eleanor of Aquitaine and the Four Kings. She was describing Paris of the mid-twelfth century, and how the focus of all attention was on the intellectual. She quoted Auguste Berthaud who described the concerns around which the society of Paris swirled at that time: 'When we speak in universal terms of class and category, do these terms correspond to realities existing outside the mind? . . . do they correspond to realities, what is their nature? . . . Do they have their being outside the sensual domains, that is, outside the individual, or do they lodge within?' (Kelly, 1950, p. 12). These concerns were argued in public disputations that were attended by royalty and common people. At the same time as these yeasty debates were going on, feudal wars were breaking out on a daily basis in the rest of France, and a crusade was being planned that taxed people to starvation in France, and spread destruction in its wake. The intellectual debates seemed to bear little on what was going on in practice.

While I do not feel that the intellectual discussions that we have around the issues of constructivism are in quite the same league as those in twelfth-century Paris (kings and queens do not attend our conferences), I would like to suggest that we do our best to constantly stay tuned to how these disputations relate to teaching practice and to the educational goals we hold dear. We have a tendency to attempt to work out the complexities of our theories in the hallowed halls of academia and academic conferences. And then, quite cavalierly, we turn it over to the practitioners to work out the practices. 'Here's a neat idea,' we say, 'its called constructivist teaching. You should be doing it in your classrooms.' We don't mention the theoretical disagreements, nor do we admit that turning a theory of learning into a theory of teaching is an inexact process, at best. We often come up with a type of five step process, and then wonder why it is not being implemented as we had expected.

I would urge us not to approach constructivist teaching and teacher education in a similar manner. Instead, the place to develop constructivist praxis is in classrooms, with teachers and teacher educators who are interested in pushing theory and practice ahead. I am impressed with the work of teacher educator-researchers such as those writing chapters in this book. These are practicing teacher educators who examine constructivist theory and practice in their own classroom and programs. The relatively new and extremely popular American Educational Research Association Self-Study Special Interest Group attests to the interest of teacher educators in such inquiry. I believe that there is no better way to develop and bring together constructivist theory and practice in a way that works to the benefit of all students.

Note

1　This chapter was originally presented at the annual meeting of the American Educational Research Association, New Orleans, 1994, and a version appeared in Richardson, V. (1994) 'Constructivist teaching: Theory and practice,' *Teaching Thinking and Problem Solving*, **16**, 6, pp. 1–7.

References

BALL, D.L. (1993) 'With an eye on the mathematical horizon: Dilemmas of teaching elementary school mathematics', *Elementary School Journal*, **93**, pp. 373–97.

BEREITER, C. (1994) 'Implications of postmodernism for science, or, science as progressive discourse', *Educational Psychologist*, **29**, 1, pp. 3–12.

BLACK, A. and AMMON, P. (1992) 'A developmental-constructivist approach to teacher education', *Journal of Teacher Education*, **43**, 5, pp. 323–35.

BREDO, E. (1994) 'Reconstructing educational psychology: Situated cognition and Deweyan pragmatism', *Educational Psychologist*, **29**, 1, pp. 23–36.

CHAZAN, D. and BALL, D.L. (1995) *Beyond Exhortations not to Tell: The Teacher's Role in Discussion-intensive Pedagogy* (Craft Paper 95–2), East Lansing, Michigan State University, National Center for Research on Teacher Learning.

CIVIL, M. (1995) 'Everyday mathematics, mathematicians' mathematics, and school mathematics', Paper presented at the annual meeting of the American Educational Research Association, San Francisco.

COBB, P. (1994) 'Where is the mind? Constructivist and sociocultural perspectives on mathematical development', *Educational Researcher*, **23**, 7, pp. 13–20.

COBB, P., WOOD, T., YAEKEL, E. and MCNEAL, B. (1992) 'Characteristics of classroom mathematics traditions: An interactional analysis', *American Educational Research Journal*, **29**, 3, pp. 573–604.

DAVYDOV, V.V. (1995) 'The influence of L.A. Vygotsky on education theory, research, and practice', *Educational Researcher*, **24**, 3, pp. 12–21.

DELPIT, L. (1988) 'The silenced dialogue: Power and pedagogy in educating other people's children', *Harvard Educational Review*, **58**, pp. 280–98.

DEWEY, J. (1916) *Democracy and Education*, New York, MacMillan.

EDWARDS, D. and MERCER, N. (1987) *Common Knowledge: The Development of Understanding in the Classroom*, London, Methuen.

FREEDMAN, S.W. (1994) *Exchanging Writing, Exchanging Cultures*, Cambridge, MA, Harvard University Press.

HARRINGTON, H.L. (1995) 'Fostering reasoned decisions: Case-based pedagogy and the professional development of teachers', *Teaching and Teacher Education*, **11**, 3, pp. 203–14.

KELLY, A. (1950) *Eleanor of Aquitaine and the Four Kings*, Cambridge, MA, Harvard University Press.

LAVE, J. (1988) *Cognition in Practice*, Cambridge, UK, Cambridge University Press.

MOLL, L. (Ed) (1990) *Vygotsky and Education: Instructional Implications and Applications of Sociohistorical Psychology*, Cambridge, Cambridge University Press.

MOLL, L. (1992) 'Bilingual classroom studies and community analysis', *Educational Researcher*, **21**, 2, pp. 20–4.

MOSENTHAL, J. and BALL, D. (1992) 'Constructing new forms of teaching: Subject matter knowledge in inservice teacher education', *Journal of Teacher Education*, **43**, 5, pp. 347–56.

NEWMAN, D., GRIFFIN, P. and COLE, M. (1989) *The Construction Zone: Working for Cognitive Change in Schools*, Cambridge, UK, Cambridge University Press.

O'LOUGHLIN, M. (1992a) 'Engaging teachers in emancipatory knowledge construction', *Journal of Teacher Education*, **43**, 5, pp. 336–47.

O'Loughlin, M. (1992b) 'Rethinking science education: Beyond Piagetian constructivism toward a sociocultural model of teaching and learning', *Journal of Research in Science Teaching,* **29**, pp. 791–820.

Reyes, M. de la Luz (1992) 'Challenging venerable assumptions: Literacy instruction for linguistically different students', *Harvard Educational Review,* **62**, 4, pp. 427–46.

Richardson, V. (1992) 'The agenda-setting dilemma in a constructivist staff development process', *Journal of Teaching and Teacher Education,* **8**, 3, pp. 287–300.

Richardson, V. (Ed) (1994) *Teacher Change and the Staff Development Process: A Case in Reading Instruction,* New York, Teachers College Press.

Schifter, D. and Simon, M. (1992) 'Assessing teachers' development of a constructivist view of mathematics learning', *Teaching and Teacher Education,* **8**, 2, pp. 187–97.

Wertsch, J.V. (1991) *Voices of the Mind: A Sociocultural Approach to Mediated Action,* Cambridge, MA, Harvard University Press.

2 Child Development and the Purpose of Education: A Historical Context for Constructivism in Teacher Education

Jennifer A. Vadeboncoeur

Throughout the twentieth century, two competing views of child development and the purpose of education have framed the teaching of pedagogy in teacher education. In the first view, the purpose of education is to educate the individual child in a manner which supports the child's interests and needs. The principles which guide this educational prescription are based on a theory of cognitive development that identifies the individual as the subject of study. In the second view, the purpose of education is social transformation and the reconstruction of society aligned with democratic ideals. This view is based on a theory of human development which locates the individual within a cultural milieu and identifies the subject of study as the dialectical relationship between the two. These two themes are also central to the current discussion of constructivisms: Piagetian constructivism is aligned with an emphasis on education for individual cognitive development while forms of Vygotskian constructivism are aligned with an emphasis on education for social transformation.

These initial organizing statements, however, belie the complexity of developing constructivist pedagogical approaches. Constructivisms are epistemologies, or theories about the nature of knowledge and how knowledge develops, with multiple interpretations. In addition, while pedagogical approaches that are 'constructivist' may be derived from one particular interpretation of constructivist epistemology, these approaches may take various forms. An unfortunate consequence of multiple interpretations and variable approaches is that the connections between the theory of knowledge and the way it is put into practice in education become blurred. As options for pedagogy and practice are developed from different epistemologies, it is essential to deconstruct the cultural assumptions upon which certain interpretations of constructivism rest in order to expose the way social beliefs have influenced both the production of theory and the ensuing pedagogical practices.

The purpose of this chapter is to frame the discussion among Piagetian and Vygotskian constructivist theorists within a historical debate about whether education should be for individual cognitive development or for social transformation. Given the current demographic reports, teacher education programs need to take seriously the task of preparing preservice teachers for diverse classrooms (Hodgkinson, 1985; Pallas, Natriello, and McDill, 1989). Providing preservice teachers with the awareness, knowledge, and skills they need to effectively teach all of their students should be a central concern for teacher educators. Now more than ever we need to examine constructivist epistemologies with a lens sensitive to social inequalities and forms of oppression. Constructivist pedagogical approaches must consider the larger social climate in order to develop in a manner that is culturally relevant and socially just.

This chapter is divided into four sections which, taken together, represent an argument for incorporating one form of constructivism, emancipatory constructivism, in teacher education programs. In the first section, I will describe development and educational practices as socially and historically constructed processes that reflect certain assumptions specific to the time and culture within which they are produced. Next, I will discuss the reform movements that developed at the turn of the century in the United States as a historical context within which to situate constructivist pedagogical approaches. In the third section, I will briefly identify three main strands of constructivist epistemologies: Piagetian, sociocultural, and emancipatory. And finally, I will outline a position for emancipatory constructivism in teacher education. Each section will revisit a dominant theme in developmental psychology: Development as a process which follows the 'nature' of the 'individual' child.

Development and Education in Context

For human beings, development is the sequence of psychological and physical changes that we undergo as we grow older, from conception to the end of life. Cognitive development is one aspect of human development and it reflects age-related changes that occur in mental activities or processes. Studies of child development are developed within a social and historical framework and they are therefore, bounded by the dominant paradigms of the culture or the popularized and accepted examples of scientific theory (Kuhn, 1970). Science is contextualized by cultural beliefs and ideologies that sensitize and constrain even the scientist. Theories about development, in general, and cognitive development, in particular, are influenced by dominant cultural assumptions. As a result, if theories are not situated within the history and culture of the society that gives rise to them, they function to obscure our understandings of development rather than to foster them. For example, two theories about child development that are dominant in western culture propose that development follows a course in keeping with the 'true nature' of the 'individual' child. The social and historical construction of the concept of development as a process that occurs according to 'nature' in the 'individual' child and the accompanying educational practices will be discussed in this section.

French philosopher Jean-Jacques Rousseau argued that social differentiation and stratification were a function of the different experiences shaping a child's development and were not determined at birth. In *Émile*, Rousseau

(1762/1911) described the development and education of two children: a boy, Émile and a girl, Sophy. He proposed that children were born with innate goodness and were corrupted by civilization. In a natural world, uncorrupted by the rise of industry and property, all people were born equal; inequality appeared only as society imposed its will on people. The ideal environment for the child was one in which the natural self could be encouraged and supported without adult influence and social regulation. Rousseau (1762/1911) argued that a caretaker should provide children with protection from the pressures of adult society. Émile was perceived not as an incomplete person whose deficiencies should be remedied by instruction, but as a whole human being who functioned with capabilities appropriate for his age. During development Émile passed through several natural stages and, guided by a caretaker, his activities were well matched to his needs at the time.

It is interesting to note that Rousseau would not offer the same education he prescribed for Émile to Sophy; a cultural assumption that influenced his thinking proposed that boys and girls were to be educated differently in keeping with their 'nature'. Rousseau (1762/1911) argued that 'Sophy should be as truly a woman as Émile is a man, i.e., she must possess all those characters of her sex which are required to enable her to play her part in the physical and moral order' (p. 321). Therefore, he proposed that a woman's education be designed in relation to man:

> To be pleasing in his sight, to win his respect and love, to train him in childhood, to tend him in manhood, to counsel and console, to make his life pleasant and happy, these are the duties of woman for all time, and this is what she should be taught while she is young. (Rousseau, 1762/1911, p. 328)

Rousseau's ideas as noted here reflect more than just a treatise on education. Rather, Rousseau himself, and his ideas, are bounded by cultural assumptions about gender that were popular and well accepted in eighteenth-century France. And more important to note, these dominant cultural assumptions of appropriate gender roles were thought by Rousseau to originate from nature and not from societal beliefs. Looking back, however, we can see that Rousseau's theories about development were socially constructed and reflected assumptions about natural gender differences — rather than 'truths' — which prescribed a different education for boys than for girls.

Our position in the twentieth century allows us much clarity when looking back on theories that were taken to be 'true' and representative of 'nature'. However, we struggle with the same issues today when we disregard the social and historical context within which ideas about development are promulgated. A more current example is reflected in the work of Deyhle and LeCompte (1994) who found that the design of middle schools, and the middle school philosophy upon which the design is based, are informed by an Anglo view of development and one which differs markedly from the Navajo view in the community they studied. For example, children in grades 6–8 (11- to

15-year-olds) according to the Anglo view, need time to grow in a protected environment, away from the pressures of adult sexuality and competition. They need more time to be children and should not be rushed into adulthood. The definition of middle school as a protective environment, however, contradicts the Navajo conception of development and cultural practices. According to the Navajo view, 11- to 15-year-old children are capable of certain kinds of adult behaviour and should be treated as such under most circumstances. Their behaviour should not be completely controlled by adults. The mismatch between Anglo and Navajo conceptions of development and educational practices are, for Navajo children and parents, a source of considerable conflict.

Theories of child development and appropriate schooling are influenced by cultural assumptions and reflect certain dominant views about the nature of development and how schooling should be constructed. While the commonly accepted theories represent the prevailing view in this country, there are many people and groups of people whose ideas and beliefs are excluded by this discourse. In order to create pedagogy which is culturally relevant, we need to design ways to include different views of development and educational practices and, at the same time, recognize that dominant theories are culturally bounded and reflect belief systems rather than 'truths'.

Historical Context

During the early twentieth century several reform movements surfaced in American education. Two reform movements, in particular, provide a historical context for the current debate among Piagetian constructivists and the various Vygotskian constructivist interpretations. The first and most varied perspective was represented by the Progressive Education Association and arose in opposition to the social efficiency theorists who focused their educational reform efforts on scientific management and 'time studies' modelled after industrial efficiency. Instead, the progressive movement focused on identifying the needs of the individual child and constructing educational contexts which supported development. The second reform movement, represented by the social reconstructionists, identified schools as a principal force in social change and argued for education to be guided by a social orientation based upon democratic ideals. George S. Counts (1932), a social reconstructionist, noted the failure of the Progressive Education Association to articulate a social orientation for the progressive movement. This debate foregrounds the importance of an articulated social orientation for constructivist epistemologies and pedagogical approaches, and an inclusive discussion of what constitutes constructivist theories and practices. In this section, I will describe the purpose of education defined by the progressives and the social reconstructionists and the assumptions underlying their respective positions. Within this discussion, the most salient feature is Counts' critique of the progressive view of development as a process that occurs according to the 'nature' of the 'individual' child.

The Progressive Education Association began as a small group of teachers and administrators associated with private and experimental schools and reform minded lay people. Founded in 1919 as the Association for the Advancement of Experimental Schools, the membership grew rapidly and reflected many complementary viewpoints. The main group within the Progressive Education Association adhered to developmentalist principles which evolved under, most notably, G. Stanley Hall, at the turn of the century. Hall and others 'led the drive for a curriculum reformed along the lines of a natural order of development in the child' (Kliebard, 1986, p. 28). The developmentalists pushed for more accurate scientific data in order to better understand the stages of child and adolescent development and also to explore the nature of learning. From this information, a curriculum emerged which complemented and built upon the child's interests and ways of learning. For the developmentalists, and reminiscent of Rousseau, the appropriate curriculum could unlock the child's natural curiosity and desire to learn and to know. The curriculum was not to be imposed by adults but was to originate from the child and reflected the child's interests and curiosity at particular stages in development.

In 1920, the Seven Principles of Progressive Education were adopted and represented the vision statement of the organization. These principles clearly indicated the child-centered orientation that the organization promoted. Early issues of *Progressive Education* arrived with a summary of the principles on the front inside cover: 'The aim of Progressive Education is the freest and fullest development of the individual, based upon the scientific study of his physical, mental, spiritual, and social characteristics and needs' (Kliebard, 1986, p. 191). For the developmentalists, the purpose of education was to ascertain the natural course of development through scientific study and to create a curriculum that supported each individual child.

John Dewey (1916), perhaps the most prominent of all American educators, was a member of the Progressive Education Association and a proponent of child-centered pedagogy. Like the developmentalists he advocated that the learning environment be shaped to fit the development of the individual child and that the subject matter be integrated and connected to the students' lives. He argued that

> learning is active. It involves reaching out of the mind. It involves organic assimilation starting from within. Literally, we must take our stand with the child and our departure from him. It is he and not the subject-matter which determines both quality and quantity of learning. (Dewey, 1916, p. 9)

However, his views differed in at least one important way. He saw a wider social purpose for education: to prepare students to be critical thinkers in order to participate in democracy. Dewey (1916) and other progressives argued that schooling should not amount to social control and vocational training. Instead, schooling should lead to lifelong learning and a lifetime of citizenship.

The second reform movement discussed here, social reconstructionism, was established by the 1930s as a result of discontent about the American economic and social system. The work of George S. Counts in the 1920s called attention to what he saw as an 'American school system oriented not to a new and better social order, but to preserving and stratifying existing social conditions.' (Kliebard, 1986, pp. 185–6). This movement, which was strengthened by the economic depression and by massive social unrest, 'stressed the role of the school, allied with other progressive forces, in planning for an intelligent reconstruction of US society where there would be a more just and equitable distribution of the nation's wealth and the "common good" would take precedence over individual gain' (Liston and Zeichner, 1991, p. 26). Increasing contradictions between the ideals of democracy and the economics of capitalism clearly highlighted economic, social and political inequality for a growing population. Counts (1932) wrote compassionately about the effects of inequality on children when he noted that, 'Breakfastless children march to school past bankrupt shops laden with rich foods gathered from the ends of the earth' (p. 30). For Counts, these inequities had to be addressed and he proposed that schools become the public forum for the message of social reconstruction.

At the annual meeting of the Progressive Education Association in 1932, Counts argued that a progressive curriculum that was directed and organized according to the child was focused on individual needs and interests rather than on democratic ideals such as equality and social justice. The social reconstructionist curriculum, on the other hand, offered a method for inculcating democratic ideals which were being compromised by the economic structure of capitalism. The values of social responsibility, equality, and community were being lost in the struggle to produce and to profit. Counts called upon teachers to transform their role in the classroom from transmitters of cultural ideology to agents of change working toward social reconstruction. Teachers could be change agents if they taught democratic values rather than assuming that these values would surface in children by nature or by an act of divine will (Counts, 1932). Leaving it up to the child to develop and generate interests appropriate for dealing with current societal concerns and issues was inappropriate and naive. Counts (1932) asserted that 'the weakness of Progressive Education thus lies in the fact that it has elaborated no theory of social welfare, unless it be that of anarchy or extreme individualism' (pp. 4–5). He continued to define progressivism as a mere reflection of the liberal minded upper classes rather than a truly 'progressive' pedagogy. He proposed that,

> If Progressive Education is to be genuinely progressive, it must emancipate itself from the influence of this class, face squarely and courageously every social issue, come to grips with life in all of its stark reality, establish an organic relation with the community, develop a realistic and comprehensive theory of welfare, fashion a compelling and challenging vision of human destiny . . . (Counts, 1932, p. 7)

According to Counts, the progressives disregarded a crucial part of the purpose of education by denying the importance of a collective social construction of, and commitment to, democracy.

Two assumptions particular to the general progressive position were considered false by Counts: First, it was a fallacy to assume that individual children exist in society free and unconstrained; and second, that development, likewise, followed a course which was determined by nature and unfettered. Counts argued that ideas about development and the education of children were bounded by the culture within which they were described, the language by which they were articulated, the beliefs, customs and traditions that defined the cultural context, and the social and economic lives of the children they were supposed to represent. For example, the socioeconomic class that a child was born into afforded certain possibilities; more opportunities for children from the upper classes and fewer for the children of the working classes. When teachers assumed that schooling was isolated from the larger economic context of the nation, or unaffected by the economic reality of the local community, they tended to reproduce inequalities rather than providing methods for the examination and elimination of oppression. While the progressive teaching style and learning context reflected the belief that each individual exists in a social context, the context was assumed to be democratic and there was no structural analysis of the constraints on democracy caused by classism and social stratification. Even Dewey's (1899/1969) emphasis on the importance of educating children to become participants in our democracy lacked an analysis of the politics of knowledge production and the internal politics of knowledge producing communities (Phillips, 1995). Therefore, while students may have been exposed to social issues such as classism given their personal histories, the issue of social stratification remained incidental to the experiences of each child; if left unproblematized by the teacher and unexamined by the students, social inequalities would go unchallenged.

Counts (1932) was criticized for imposing beliefs on students though he insisted that there must be 'no deliberate distortion or suppression of facts to support any theory or point of view' (p. 10). Of necessity, the curriculum made inequitable social conditions explicit so that they could be ameliorated. Counts (1932) argued that:

> all education contains a large element of imposition, that in the very nature of the case this is inevitable, that the existence and evolution of society depend upon it, that it is consequently eminently desirable, and that the frank acceptance of this fact by the educator is a major professional obligation. (Counts, 1932, p. 12)

His point was that we need to feel more comfortable with the idea of teaching the rules and skills necessary for living in a democracy — what Barber (1992) calls 'an apprenticeship in liberty' — and he found the reluctance to address social issues was a tremendous problem within progressivism. Although the progressives were willing to consider the inadequacies of progressive education in terms of social reform, and the discussion continued for two more decades, no clear social orientation was articulated (Karier, 1986).

To summarize, Counts proposed that we articulate a social orientation for schooling and pedagogy which is liberatory for all students and his position introduced a structural critique into the discussion of the purpose of education: Though we live in a democracy, the critical question remains, does the social context we live in operate democratically, and is the purpose of education aligned with facilitating the development of a democratic citizenry? Perhaps a distinction needs to be made between the ideal of democracy and the democracy we live in as compromised by capitalism. In some ways, Counts was willing to articulate ideas that were, and still are, unpopular. His call for collective social responsibility still seems to contradict our nation's ideology of independence. While his beliefs were firmly grounded within a democratic framework, even today they tend to make nervous those who choose to emphasize rugged individualism.

Piagetian and Vygotskian Constructivisms

The current debate among Piagetian and Vygotskian constructivists is reminiscent of the historical debate between the progressives and George S. Counts (1932), and the prioritization of education for individuals over education for social transformation. The objective of the following section is to connect the current debate to the historical context outlined earlier. Piagetian and Vygotskian constructivisms are discussed and three main strands are briefly described: Piagetian, sociocultural, and emancipatory constructivism. These strands represent a spectrum of forms of constructivism that differ in terms of:

1   the subject of study;
2   the development of cognitive forms; and
3   the liberatory power of pedagogical approaches derived.

The aim is to describe each in terms of the three dimensions mentioned above and locate each form of constructivism within a sociohistorical discourse.

However, before beginning, a definition of 'liberatory power' is in order. For a pedagogy to have the capacity to liberate students means that it affords possibility to all students in a way that uncovers and reduces inequality. For some students, this may mean exposing and examining institutional structures that exert an oppressive force. For other students it may entail making explicit certain rules that exist within the classroom context; helping these students understand what is expected of them and how they should participate. Ultimately, though, the idea of liberatory power implies not only a new awareness of the way in which cultural beliefs and assumptions influence both theory and practice, but also thoughtful and transformative action.

Piagetian Constructivism

Piagetian constructivism originates within the developmental framework established by Piaget. For Piaget (1972), the study of development follows from a biological analysis of the laws of nature. Piagetian constructivists focus on individual cognitive development through co-constructed learning environments with rational, decontextualized thinking as the goal of development.

Subject of study

The subject of study is the individual child and his or her cognitive forms as he or she actively builds systems of meaning and understanding about reality through experiences (von Glasersfeld, 1989). Piagetian constructivists focus on the development of autonomous cognitive forms *within* the individual, culminating in rational thought that is decentered from the individual. While experience plays a role in the development of cognitive structures, the lived experience and situatedness of the individual only plays a minor role (Venn and Walkerdine, 1977).

The decision to create as a subject of study an individual separated from the surrounding social context is not without consequences. Vygotsky (1986) notes that Piaget's fundamental problem is that 'reality and the relations between a child and reality' are missed in his theory (pp. 51–2). Indeed, Murray (1983) notes that Piaget's 'epistemic subject has no social class, sex, nationality, culture, or personality' (p. 231).

Development of cognitive forms

Cognitive growth occurs naturally and follows organized and progressively hierarchical developmental patterns. Development occurs as the individual adapts logical and stable mental operations to external reality. The world is not directly known rather, knowledge about the world is created out of adaptive activities. For Piaget, 'the structure of the mind is the source of our understanding of the world' (Venn and Walkerdine, 1977, p. 73). The child is perceived as a solitary scientist who continually constructs more accurate theories of the world as a result of using logical tools. Learners construct ways to make sense of experiences and will continue to use these constructions as long as they work.

Piaget (1972) conceptualized cognitive tools as logico-mathematical operations that are universal and do not vary across cultures and social contexts. Applying these operations by acting on objects in the environment, the child is able to construct knowledge about his world. Certain very simple operations are present from birth and they gradually become differentiated and organized into systems of increasing complexity. At specific points in development, these systems become stable and four stages can be identified, each representing a qualitatively different and more complex understanding of the world. Development concludes when 'formal' or abstract operations emerge and the individual is able to decenter and perceive from an objective vantage point his or her own actions. This marks the endpoint of cognitive development for Piaget in decentered and rational thought.[1]

While meaning and understanding are constructed through the use of language, meanings themselves are not given to us by society (von Glasersfeld, 1993). Social interaction and the social nature of language merely shape the meanings that we abstract from our own experiences. The meanings that we develop individually gravitate toward compatibility with the meanings developed by others. However, meanings themselves are not shared, only constrained. For Piaget, the emphasis is on the 'formal properties of action without regard for the situatedness of actions in a sociohistorically articulated web of meanings' (Saxe, 1991, p. 6). The individual acts alone when constructing meaning based on past experience and present interpretation; the influence of history, subjectivity, and social collaboration on the formation of knowledge are systematically excluded (O'Loughlin, 1993).

Liberatory power of pedagogical approaches derived from Piagetian constructivism

In order to explore whether pedagogical approaches derived from Piagetian constructivism have the potential to be liberating, according to Walkerdine (1984), we must first deconstruct the assumptions upon which developmental psychology and progressive child centered pedagogy are founded. She notes that within this arena, 'children are to be enabled to develop at their own pace, to work individually, to be free and to grow up into rational adults' (Walkerdine, 1984, p. 153). If this is liberating, Walkerdine (1984) asks, why 'do so many children fail and what part does developmental psychology play in all this?' (p. 153).

Walkerdine examines the historical conditions which create the possibility for developmental psychology and progressive pedagogy to form a set of taken for granted practices which exist today in education. She notes that:

> the understanding of the 'real' of child development is not a matter of uncovering a set of empirical facts or epistemological truths which stand outside, or prior to, the conditions of their production. In this sense developmental psychology is productive: its positive effects lie in its production of practices of science and pedagogy. (Walkerdine, 1984, p. 162)

Her analysis exposes the productive rather than objective effects of theories which, over time, create an unquestioned and impenetrable structure that continues to produce the 'evidence' through which it is itself maintained. Unless the original cultural beliefs and assumptions are exposed, and the historical conditions which made them possible deconstructed, theories are taken for granted as 'objective truths' and limit the way we think about development.

All human beings exist within a certain historical setting, within a specific culture with social beliefs, ideologies, and constructions such as language. Characteristics or qualities — such as our social class, race, gender, physical ability, and sexual orientation — provide us with greater or fewer possibilities in life, given the value our historical setting places on them, and position us in relation to the standards or norms set by the dominant culture. Our ability to participate within the dominant culture, and whether our position affords us more or less power, significantly relates to our chance for economic success and human fulfillment. Whether or not our cultural environment leads us to speak a language that is privileged, and whether our mode of discourse represents that which is valued in schools, in part determines our success in or alienation from the process of schooling. Piagetian constructivism exists within this set of socially constructed 'truths' and not outside of it, yet these factors are not recognized as important influences within the paradigm.

In order for Piagetian constructivism to liberate, to afford possibility and reduce inequality, the derived pedagogical approaches must offer possibility to all learners equally. However, when 'natural development' is assumed, the options for appropriate behavior reflect socially constructed stereotypes rather than the 'true nature' of the child. For example, Clark (1989) notes that when teachers act to challenge stereotypical beliefs about masculinity and femininity which are dominant in the school, their efforts to change the gendered behavior of children, especially boys, are often seen by other staff members to be unnatural or impossible. This example highlights how easy it is for socially constructed types of behavior, in this case aggressive behavior for boys and quiet behavior for girls, to be identified as innate qualities. Cultural assumptions about the 'nature' of girls' and boys' behavior reproduce rather than expose inequality and work against young women in schools while supporting gendered stereotypes in society.

Clark (1989) also argues that beliefs about 'individualism' which are assumed to be 'true' obfuscate and promote highly gendered attitudes. She notes that

> the belief that children should be treated as individuals might seem at first glance to be more sophisticated than the natural difference belief. It is after all one of the cornerstones of child-centred education and could be seen as a framework for a liberating education by not straitjacketing children into fixed sex-role stereotypes. (Clark, 1989, p. 249)

However, in practice this belief tends to be used to mask gendered attitudes because appropriate types of behavior remain predetermined by what is considered to be socially acceptable for girls and for boys. Individual differences which happen to conform to the dominant ideas about appropriate gender roles obscure the central role of classroom practices in producing those gendered behaviors.

While Piagetian constructivists may desire to develop liberatory pedagogical approaches, the cultural assumptions that provide the foundation for developmental and child centered pedagogy, in particular naturalism and individualism, serve to reproduce inequity and maintain the status quo by concealing the influence of the classroom culture and the broader social context in the production of stereotypical differences. The examples used in this section highlight the reproduction of socially constructed gendered behavior, however, it is possible to expand this discussion to include the production of differences which conform to stereotypes of other kinds, such as race, sexual orientation, and linguistic diversity. By using the view of development as a process that occurs according to the 'nature' of the 'individual' child, the liberatory power of pedagogical approaches derived from Piagetian constructivism is weak; and may even be considered exclusionary.

Vygotskian Constructivisms

There are currently two distinct interpretations of Vygotsky's sociohistorical approach in the literature. The first is a sociocultural interpretation which tends to focus on a microlevel analysis of social interaction within the zone of proximal development.[2] Theorists interested in this interpretation are most concerned about learning, development, and language; the larger social picture is not neglected, 'but they tend to treat social considerations in general and beneficent terms' (Burgess, 1993, p. 4) resembling the progressives. Meanwhile, the second group of theorists extend the context to include a macrolevel analysis of the cultural politics of development as a context for social interaction. This emancipatory interpretation is ultimately concerned with both micro and macrolevel analyses; 'resistance and deconstruction as well as internalization and individual construction' (Burgess, 1993, p. 6) similar to the social reconstructionists. Both interpretations reflect Vygotsky's ideas; what distinguishes them is the extent to which Vygotsky's methodology is employed and the depth of contextualization. These two interpretations, taken as sociocultural constructivism and emancipatory constructivism, will be discussed following a brief discussion of Vygotsky's methodology.[3]

Working within the materialist history of Marx and Engels (1846/1970), Vygotsky used a historical analysis, rather than a biological analysis like Piaget, to study the development of higher cognitive forms. His methodology lays out four levels of historical movement or development. The first level is microgenesis or the development of mental processes. Second, ontogenesis, is the subject's individual developmental history. The third level, phylogenesis, is biological evolution. And the final level is sociohistorical development or the development of socially organized activities. The first two levels — microgenesis and ontogenesis — refer to the microlevel. The final two levels within Vygotsky's methodology — phylogenesis and sociohistorical development — are taken as the macrolevel. For Vygotsky, in order to understand human development, a multilevel analysis using all four levels of history must be employed.

Sociocultural constructivism

Sociocultural constructivists emphasize a microlevel analysis and, as noted earlier, are inclined to defer to a general macrolevel situating microgenesis and ontogenesis. In a manner similar to the progressives, the larger social and historical context is considered but only in broad and beneficent terms; it tends to be taken for granted rather than analysed with regard to the influences of politics and power relations and their effect on the production of knowledge and the types of knowledge which are legitimized.

Subject of study

The subject of study is the contextualized individual, embedded within a society and formed through a dialectical relationship with the cultural milieu. Vygotsky (1986) argued that individual development cannot be understood without reference to the interpersonal and institutional surround which situates the child. The social context is mediated through sign systems, such as language and number classifications, which are historically produced artifacts. While for Piaget the direction of cognitive development moves from the individual to the social, the direction for Vygotsky is from the social to the individual.

Development of cognitive forms

While Piaget talked about the active construction of knowledge through *action on* the world of objects, for Vygotsky, the construction of knowledge occurs through *interaction* in the social world. Thus, for Vygotsky (1978), the development of cognitive forms occurs by means of the dialectical relationship between the individual and the social context. The situated individual actively builds knowledge through the process of internalizing social knowledge; knowledge moves from the *intermental* plane to the *intramental* plane, from the social to the psychological. According to Vygotsky (1978),

> any function in the child's cultural development appears twice or on two planes. First, it appears on the social plane, and then on the psychological plane. First, it appears between people as an *interpsychological* category, and then within the child as an *intrapsychological* category. (Vygotsky, 1978, p. 57)

The transformation of the intermental plane to the intramental plane occurs within the zone of proximal or potential development: the distance between the lower level, where the student or child works independently, and the upper level, where the child completes the task with assistance by an adult or more experienced peer. Vygotsky expanded the notion of development by conceptualizing it as not only tasks which are independently completed but also assisted tasks, and argued that this conception would better inform pedagogical approaches.

Studies of the zone of proximal development are based on social interaction in a dyad, where the role of the adult, teacher or more experienced peer is to guide or provide scaffolding for the child, student, or less experienced peer. Vygotsky (1986) describes children as active in their own development and as creating knowledge of the world through activity. The active role of the child allows for the transformation of knowledge: knowledge is dynamic and is created, examined, and transformed rather than merely transmitted, whole, from the adult to the child.

Cognitive functions emerge from situated actions and are therefore dependent upon and, to some extent, determined by the social context surrounding the individual. Culture influences the development of cognitive forms by providing regulative information that falls within the zone of proximal development (Laboratory of Comparative Human Cognition, 1983). Therefore, human development is never totally free of cultural influence and human beings are not autonomous with respect to societal forces. Instead,

> even an individual functioning in isolation will draw upon the socially organized cultural values and tools, since any functioning at the intramental plane is derivative of that which is previously established on the intermental plane. (Rahm, 1994, p. 7)

Cultural symbols, tools, and values surface in social processes and Vygotsky notes that these processes underpin the emergence of the child's cognitive forms.

Liberatory power of pedagogical approaches derived from sociocultural constructivism

Two areas of concern arise when analysing the liberatory power of pedagogical approaches derived from sociocultural constructivism; both are linked to the de-emphasis of a macrolevel analysis with regard to the influences of politics and power relations on knowledge production. First, the assumption of a beneficent social context is quite problematic. Without a structural critique of the larger sociohistorical context at the macrolevel, we cannot ask the questions Counts implored us to ask: What is the social orientation of this setting, classroom, or institution? Does it operate democratically? Again, we lack an articulated social orientation to frame the construction of knowledge. Our capacity to alter the cycle of the reproduction of inequality is connected to the ability to transform rather than merely absorb cultural knowledge. As noted in the earlier discussion of progressive pedagogy, if the teacher does not problematize and question existing knowledge and social structures, and it does not occur to the child to do so, it is quite possible that cultural assumptions and beliefs, as taken for granted 'truths', will be appropriated by the child unchallenged.

Second, when the macrolevel *is* recognized as an important influence but is not analyzed with regard to the politics of knowledge production, social discourses of power and privilege cannot be exposed and examined. Each culture's historical development includes many voices and represents the growth of current beliefs about characteristics or qualities of people which are considered to be valuable; over time, certain voices and beliefs become dominant while others are silenced or excluded from the outset. For example, a myth in the United States that is still persistent links wealth with morality and poverty with immorality. This cultural understanding can be traced back to our roots in ascetic Protestantism and the value of laboring in God's name in exchange for the visible 'blessing' of wealth (Weber, 1972). In order to understand current beliefs and cultural myths, the macrolevel analysis is essential; it is here that we can fully situate ourselves with the development of our social history.

Emancipatory constructivism

Recent support for the infusion of discussions of class, race, and gender within pedagogy and practice, as well as an exploration of relationships of power within society, necessitate the development of a constructivist epistemology with a method for exposing inequality. Emancipatory constructivism is based on Vygotsky's complete multilevel methodology; therefore, all four levels of development — microgenesis, ontogenesis, phylogenesis, and cultural and historical development — are analyzed together and in relation to each other. The development of the subject of study is situated within cultural and historical development to examine larger social myths and beliefs which influence our behavior in, and understanding of, our world. Consequently, this method permits an analysis of epistemological and pedagogical approaches in terms of current cultural beliefs and fully locates the subject of study within the development of social history.

Subject of study

The subject of study for emancipatory constructivism is the dialectical relationship between the situated individual and the cultural milieu embedded within the larger sociohistorical context. Discourses of power and privilege, which have developed over time, reflect the behaviors, qualities, and characteristics of individuals that are considered to be valuable and legitimate within the culture. The individual, the cultural context, and the meaning or interpretation of the larger sociohistorical context are integrated. For example, as noted by Delpit (1988), progressive, child centered pedagogy meets with variable success for black children because they may interpret the classroom context and the role of the teacher differently than white children. This is due to the differences between their home environment and the expectations of schools and/or the history of oppressive social conditions which are reflected and institutionalized in schools. Whether children feel included or excluded by the process of schooling effects their understanding of their role, the roles of others, and their needs in the classroom context. And the context of schooling is embedded in the larger cultural context of our social history: A country that legalized slavery for over 200 years and segregation for 100 more years.

Development of cognitive forms

Given that emancipatory constructivism is based on an epistemology rooted in the work of Vygotsky, the development of cognitive forms follows the process of internalization from the social to the individual as discussed under sociocultural constructivism. But by also extending the analysis to include the macrolevel, this process invites not only the transformation of knowledge but, in addition, a recognition of the effects of social discourses of power and privilege.

For Vygotsky, based on the work of Marx and Engels (1846/1970), productive activities such as labor, speech, and other forms of communication allow the human species to free itself from biological determination; culture supplants nature. The important issue to remember is that we produce social discourses and can, therefore, change and transform them to reflect a more just distribution of resources.

Liberatory power of pedagogical approaches derived from emancipatory constructivism

O'Loughlin (1993) notes that the purpose of emancipatory knowledge construction is a commitment to social change, justice, and responsibility, the reduction of inequality, and the exposure of relationships of exploitation and oppression. The pedagogical approaches derived foster the development of critical thinkers who are able to recognize their position in relation to others in a way that also makes them aware of their participation in discourses contributing to inequality and privilege. In an important sense, students are able to explore their own situatedness, as well as to deconstruct social factors that influence them by affording them with the opportunities that exist given our social stratification. In order for students to learn to question and explore, this behavior must be modelled by the teacher. When teachers recognize their own biases and model this struggle to their students, they develop — with the students — a pedagogy which is inclusive of both students' voices and experiences and aimed at exposing, examining and reducing the constraints of the traditional transmission model of pedagogy. Developing an awareness in students to cultural constraints which are mirrored in textbooks and instructional materials is dependent upon a teacher creating an emancipatory social context within the classroom; one within which the teacher respects, guides, and takes leadership from the students involved.

Teachers can construct and act on emancipatory conceptions of knowledge, yet the effects of these conceptions may be confined to their own classrooms. The movement of knowledge from the classroom context to the larger community will be limited unless an action component is also emphasized. In addition, the ability to expose students to this pedagogy is highly dependent, though not restricted to, the pedagogy appropriated by the teacher during his or her teacher education. Teachers can experience a change in beliefs and practices after they have entered the workforce. However, teachers tend to be isolated within their classroom or school community and may not have access to new ways of thinking about teaching. In addition, the ability of teachers to become agents of change and to empower their students is dependent on support; teachers need to learn how to do this. If we engage preservice teachers in processes of emancipatory knowledge construction, we have an obligation to prepare them to work toward the political changes necessary to allow them to incorporate these practices in their future classrooms. It is to this process of emancipatory knowledge construction for preservice teachers that I now turn.

Emancipatory Constructivist Pedagogy for Teachers and Teacher Educators

As noted earlier, the necessity for teacher education programs to take seriously the task of preparing preservice teachers for diverse classrooms is reflected in current demographic reports. While the pattern of white, middle and upper-middle class women entering teacher education programs continues, the population of school-aged children in this country has become more culturally and linguistically diverse over the last decade, a trend that will persist through the twenty-first century (Hodgkinson, 1985; Pallas, Natriello and McDill, 1989). Complicating matters further, LeCompte (1985) found that when some teachers were forced to accommodate culturally diverse students for prolonged periods of time, feelings of fear and hostility developed. The need for emancipatory constructivism in teacher education is urgent if we are to attempt to teach all of our children.

Implementing emancipatory constructivism in classrooms is in the hands of teachers, who are in turn, in the hands of teacher educators. Emancipatory constructivist pedagogical approaches are dependent upon teachers who are prepared with particular attention paid to the content and form of their teacher education program. The groundwork of an emancipatory teacher education program begins with content that:

1 foregrounds cognitive development as sociohistorically situated and attends to the merging of everyday and academic concepts;
2 defines knowledge as partial and positional rather than foundationalist; and
3 provides for the awareness and examination of discourses of power and privilege.

In addition, the form of an emancipatory pedagogical approach stresses critical analysis and reflection. Suggestions for the content and form of teacher education programs that are appropriate for emancipatory knowledge production will be the subject of this final section.

An emancipatory constructivist teacher education program begins with content that foregrounds cognitive development as sociohistorically situated and based upon merging everyday and academic concepts. For example, in place of Piaget's traditional model of individualist, relatively autonomous development, Lemke (1991) offers an ecosocial model of development which is non-linear, non-hierarchical, and supports the idea of development as opportunistic or 'patchy' with sensitivity toward both the particularity of individual subjectivities and the influence of the social, historical, and political setting within which the development occurs. When subjectivity is situated — recognizing alternative experiences due to class, race, gender, sexual orientation, linguistic diversity, and other differences — the everyday lived experiences of students and teachers may be used as a base upon which *to develop* academic knowledge rather than *to be replaced* by academic knowledge. Vygotsky (1986) argued that everyday concepts are rich but limited to personal experiences. Thus, by using them as the foundation for academic concepts — that are hollow but extensive — the development of higher mental processes begins. Finding a way to recognize and value the everyday lived experiences of students dramatically alters the options for pedagogical approaches.

An emancipatory constructivist teacher education program begins with a view of knowledge as partial and positional. For example, in contrast to the foundationalist view which assumes the existence of a single, definable, objective standard of truth that can be known, emancipatory constructivism views knowledge as partial and positional because it is grounded in personal experience and an individual's interpretation of the world. LeCompte (1993) notes that all acts of knowing are acts of interpretation. Each student constructs knowledge from multiple perspectives and frames of reference, each perspective, in turn, is flavored by their background, their class, race and gender, the language they use and the language they feel most comfortable using, their sexual orientation, and their physical abilities (Ellsworth, 1992). The potential for emancipatory knowledge construction depends almost completely on the way that teachers and school administrators respond to the students as they approach schooling from these diverse frames of reference. Emancipatory knowledge construction will occur only within settings that view knowledge as both partial and positional and encourage an awareness of the use of discourses within society to privilege certain forms of knowledge and communication over others (Lather, 1991).

Inherent in the goals of emancipatory constructivist pedagogy is the awareness of discourses of power and privilege. Whether or not we choose to continue with traditional pedagogical methods in teacher education programs or use methods that expose inequity in a manner that empowers teachers to become agents of change is not a minor issue. Indeed, who makes the choice of the type of pedagogy used in teacher education programs? In whose interest is this choice made? Whose social position is privileged? Which students benefit? Bernstein (1990) notes that pedagogies advocated by constructivists and other progressives that do not explicitly work to expose and redistribute the power relations inherent in schooling tend to mask the power relations. In doing so, he argues that these types of pedagogies make it even more difficult for students who are not already well versed in the white, middle class, values of schooling to negotiate the power relations extant in schooling. He maintains that despite our good intentions, our actions often disadvantage those who are already 'disadvantaged' in schools that privilege white, middle class values.

The main goal of emancipatory pedagogical approaches is to question extant power relationships which are embedded in academic discourses and to search for ways to redistribute power. This way students can gain ownership over the discourses of schooling — mathematics, science, history — without invalidating their own cultural voices and understand power relationships so that they may act to transform their world (O'Loughlin, 1993). This is a moral issue and not merely a philosophic or scientific issue. We must identify our fundamental purpose as teacher educators, our beliefs about the nature of teaching and learning within social contexts that reflect the politics of knowledge production, and identify the social orientation which informs our pedagogy as well. For what purposes are we educating teachers? What drives and motivates our social orientation? Are we creating teachers who will lead as agents of change in the development of a democratic citizenry? Or, are we creating teachers who, themselves disempowered, will create classroom contexts in the fashion of factories and workhouses, with students who follow directions and do not ask questions?

In addition to the changes in teacher education content just mentioned, changes in the pedagogical form used in teacher education are required as well. In particular, emancipatory pedagogical approaches highlight the significance of critical analysis and structured reflection on both academic knowledge from the course content, and everyday knowledge from practical experience. Critical analysis consciously engages students in constructive and deconstructive inquiry about academic discourses and personal experiences, and the way in which they are linked through the construction of meaning. Preservice teachers develop working theories about practical situations based on academic content and then test them with experiences in service learning, in practicums, or in student teaching (Cumbo, 1996). Practical experiences in these settings allow teacher education students to challenge or affirm theory based course materials. In addition, if the settings in which practice takes place are diverse — in terms of class, race, ethnicity, language, ability, gendered experience, etc. — structured reflection and analysis will provide a site for understanding the sociohistorical forces that affect the lives of different students, such as economic oppression, racial discrimination, and privilege (Vadeboncoeur *et al.*, 1996; Zeichner, 1992).

Several suggestions about teacher education reform pertaining to the content and form of teacher education programs have been noted here. All of these changes reflect certain beliefs about the context within which learning occurs and the best way to teach teachers how to construct effective learning environments. In addition, these changes represent my understanding of the current state of teacher education programs and my belief that somehow we need to foster in preservice teachers — through an understanding of the sociohistorical construction of knowledge about teaching and learning — an ability to reach out to the students they teach in a critical and culturally relevant manner.

Conclusion

The debate between advocates of education for individuals and education for social transformation has a long history. In this country the focus of developmental psychology and progressive, child centered pedagogy has historically been on the decontextualized individual who develops through natural and autonomous processes. The analysis in this chapter identifies the need to define the subject of study as the dialectical relationship between the individual and the cultural milieu and, in addition, to fully situate this development in a macrolevel analysis of cultural and historical development and the ways in which it is influenced by politics, power, and privilege.

Three main strands of constructivist epistemologies and the pedagogical approaches derived are discussed in this chapter: Piagetian, sociocultural, and emancipatory constructivism. Further dialogue requires that we first define the epistemological interpretation we are employing in order to make inferences about pedagogical approaches. Indeed, as argued here, epistemology provides the foundation for pedagogical approaches and therefore, an analysis of the epistemology is essential prior to making assumptions about the possible liberatory power of the ensuing pedagogy and practice.

While Piagetian constructivism may offer relatively new and exciting ideas about epistemology and pedagogical approaches, it is based on socially constructed and biased assumptions about development and education. This does not mean that we should disregard the work of Piagetian constructivists, but we must recognize its limitations. Pedagogies derived from Piagetian constructivism do not offer the liberatory power to expose or reduce the discourses that reproduce inequity within our society. Indeed, the pedagogical approaches support the development of individuals who are able to transcend the context and think abstractly, rather than remain situated in the social context. In order to be liberatory for all children, the underlying assumptions of constructivist theories — epistemology and derived pedagogical approaches — must be deconstructed and reframed with a social orientation.

The first interpretation of Vygotsky's sociohistorical approach, sociocultural constructivism, falls dangerously short of its full potential by emphasizing a microlevel analysis rather than the full multilevel analysis of development as suggested by Vygotsky. While sociocultural constructivists recognize the importance of the situated subject of study they are inclined to assume that the larger social and historical levels of development provide a general and rather beneficent atmosphere; similar to the progressives, there is no structural analysis of the larger social context. For even the most focused studies, for example studies which concentrate on learning as it occurs within the zone of proximal development, it is essential to provide a social and historical analysis of the roles of the student and teacher as well as the academic knowledge. The background and current position of each person, their interpretations of the task and learning context, and the meaning and legitimacy of the knowledge within the institution and the society at large must be considered in order to fully understand what is taking place.

Emancipatory constructivism permits students to deconstruct and reconstruct cultural assumptions that have been taken for granted, thereby allowing for the possibility of social transformation. For social reconstructionists, who emphasized the necessity of exploring inequality and power relations over sixty years ago, and for theorists today who are concerned with critical issues and cultural relevance in teaching and learning, emancipatory constructivism is the only form which addresses the macrolevel analysis of a sociohistorical critique. Pedagogical approaches derived from emancipatory constructivism foster an understanding of position in relation to others and in relation to social institutions such that the root causes of inequality are exposed and examined.

In teacher education emancipatory knowledge construction is crucial; teacher educators must be able to teach in a manner that models the attitudes and behaviors that they would like their preservice teachers to manifest in future classrooms. Pedagogical approaches derived from emancipatory constructivism should begin with content that:

1 foregrounds cognitive development as sociohistorically situated and based upon merging academic and everyday concepts;
2 defines knowledge as partial and positional; and
3 provides for the awareness and examination of discourses of power and privilege.

In addition, emancipatory pedagogical approaches stress critical analysis and reflection.

The current social climate in this country mirrors a conservative ideology which maintains the status quo in schools and in teacher education programs marked by inequality for some students and privilege for others. Current demographic reports reflect the urgency of developing pedagogical practices which are culturally relevant. Somehow constructivists must work to ensure that the epistemology upon which their pedagogical approaches are based interrupts and challenges the status quo and facilitates a critical analysis of inequality. Discourses of power and privilege can not be ignored by constructivists if we truly hope to understand how all children develop and learn.

Notes

1 During the last decade of his career, Piaget's conception of these stages tended to be more flexible although he continued to privilege decontextualized thought over situated thinking.
2 Vygotsky usually spoke of his ideas as the 'sociohistorical' or 'cultural historical' approach. As noted in Wertsch, del Rio and Alvarez (1995) 'sociocultural' is a term that recognizes the distinction between Vygotsky's ideas and how they have been appropriated in the West.
3 'Emancipatory' constructivism is used by O'Loughlin (1992, 1993) to introduce a critical and culturally relevant analysis into the discourse: an analysis that recognizes positionality in terms of class, race, gender, sexual orientation, and other characteristics that have historically been used to discriminate against people.

References

BARBER, B. (1992) *An Aristocracy of Everyone*, New York, Ballantine.

BERNSTEIN, B. (1990) *The Structuring of Pedagogic Discourse: Vol. IV, Class, Codes, and Control*, New York, Routledge.

BURGESS, T. (1993) 'Reading Vygotsky,' in DANIELS, H. (Ed) *Charting the Agenda: Educational Activity after Vygotsky*, New York, Routledge.

CLARK, M. (1989) 'Anastasia is a normal developer because she is unique,' *Oxford Review of Education*, **15**, 3, pp. 243–55.

COUNTS, G.S. (1932) *Dare the Schools Build a New Social Order*, New York, Scribner and Sons.

CUMBO, K. (1996) 'Critical multicultural teacher education: An apprenticeship in liberty,' Paper presented at the University of Colorado, Boulder, March.

DEHYLE, D. and LECOMPTE, M.D. (1994) 'Differences in culture in child development: Navajo adolescents in public middle schools,' *Theory into Practice*, **33**, 3, Summer.

DELPIT, L. (1988) 'The silenced dialogue: Power and pedagogy in educating other peoples' children,' *Harvard Educational Review*, **58**, 3, pp. 280–98.

DEWEY, J. (1899/1969) *The School and Society. The Child and the Curriculum*, Chicago, University of Chicago Press.

DEWEY, J. (1916) *Democracy and Education*, New York, Macmillan.

ELLSWORTH, E. (1992) 'Why doesn't that feel empowering? Working through the repressive myths of critical pedagogy,' in LUKE, C. and GORE, J. (Eds) *Feminisms and Critical Pedagogy*, New York, Routledge.

HODGKINSON, H.L. (1985) *All One System: Demographics of Education*, Denver, CO, Institute for Educational Leadership.

KARIER, C.J. (1986) *The Individual, Society, and Education: A History of American Educational Ideas (2nd Ed)*, Chicago, University of Illinois Press.

KLIEBARD, H.M. (1986) *The Struggle for the American Curriculum, 1893–1958*, New York, Routledge.

KUHN, T. (1970) *The Structure of Scientific Revolutions*, Chicago, University of Chicago Press.

LABORATORY OF HUMAN COGNITION (1983) 'Culture and cognitive development,' in KESSEN, W. (Ed) *History, Theory, and Methods*, Vol. 1 of MUSSEN, P.H. (Ed) *Handbook of Child Psychology*, New York, Wiley.

LATHER, P. (1991) *Getting Smart: Feminist Research and Pedagogy with/in the Postmodern*, New York, Routledge.

LECOMPTE, M.D. (1985) 'Defining the differences: Cultural subgroups within the educational mainstream,' *The Urban Review*, **17**, 2, pp. 111–27.

LECOMPTE, M.D. (1993) 'A framework for hearing silence: What does telling stories mean when we are supposed to be doing science?,' in MCLAUGHLIN, D. and TIERNEY, W. (Eds) *Naming Silenced Lives*, New York, Routledge.

LEMKE, J. (1991) 'Science, semantics, and social change,' Paper presented at the annual meeting of the American Educational Research Association, Chicago, IL, April.

LISTON, D.P. and ZEICHNER, K.M. (1991) *Teacher Education and the Social Conditions of Schooling*, New York, Routledge, Chapman and Hall, Inc.

MARX, K. and ENGELS, F. (1846/1970) *The German Ideology*, New York, International Publishers.

MURRAY, F.B. (1983) 'Learning and development through social interaction and conflict: A challenge to social learning theory,' in LIBEN, L. (Ed) *Piaget and the Foundations of Knowledge*, Hillsdale, NJ, Erlbaum.

O'LOUGHLIN, M. (1992) 'Engaging teachers in emancipatory knowledge construction,' *Journal of Teacher Education*, **43**, 5, pp. 336–46.

O'LOUGHLIN, M. (1993) *Developing a Rationale for Emancipatory Knowledge Construction: Five Questions for Constructivists*, Presented at the annual meeting of the American Educational Research Association, Atlanta, GA, April.

PALLAS, A.M., NATRIELLO, G. and McDILL, E.L. (1989) 'The changing nature of the disadvantaged population: Current dimensions and future trend,' *Educational Researcher*, **18**, 5, pp. 16–22.

PHILLIPS, D.C. (1995) 'The good, the bad, and the ugly: The many faces of constructivism,' *Educational Researcher*, **24**, 7, pp. 5–12.

PIAGET, J. (1972) *Insights and Illusions of Philosophy*, New York, Routledge and Kegan Paul.

RAHM, J. (1994) 'The usefulness of a sociocultural approach to mind: A critique of radical educational issues,' Paper presented at the University of Colorado, Boulder, January.

ROUSSEAU, J.J. (1762, 1911) *Émile*, Barbara Foxley (Trans.), New York, Dutton and Co. Inc.

SAXE, G. (1991) *Culture and Cognitive Development: Studies in Mathematical Understanding*, Hillsdale, NJ, Lawrence Erlbaum.

VADEBONCOEUR, J.A., RAHM, J., AGUILERA, D. and LeCOMPTE, M.D. (1996) 'Building democratic character through community experiences in teacher education,' *Education and Urban Society*, **28**, 2, pp. 189–207.

VENN, C. and WALKERDINE, V. (1977) 'The acquisition and production of knowledge,' *Ideology and Consciousness*, **3**, pp. 67–94.

VON GLASERSFELD, E. (1989) 'Constructivism in education,' in HUSEN, T. and POSTLETHWAITE, T.N. (Eds) *International Encyclopedia of Education: Supplementary Vol. 1. Research and Studies*, Oxford, England, Pergamon.

VON GLASERSFELD, E. (1993) 'Notes for AERA Talk, Atlanta, April 12th, 1993,' Notes from presentation at the annual meeting of the American Educational Research Association, Atlanta, GA.

VYGOTSKY, L.S. (1978) *Mind in Society: The Development of Higher Psychological Processes*, Cambridge, MA, Harvard University Press.

VYGOTSKY, L.S. (1986) *Thought and Language*, Cambridge, MA, The MIT Press.

WALKERDINE, V. (1984) 'Developmental psychology and the child-centred pedagogy,' in HENRIQUES, J., HOLLWAY, W., URWIN, C., VENN, C. and WALKERDINE, V. (Eds) *Changing the Subject: Psychology, Social Regulation and Subjectivity*, New York, Methuen.

WEBER, M. (1972) 'Protestantism and the rise of modern capitalism,' in WRONG, D.H. and GRACEY, H.L. (Eds) *Readings in Introductory Sociology, Second Edition*, New York, The Macmillan Co.

WERTSCH, J.V., DEL RIO, P. and ALVAREZ, A. (1995) 'Sociocultural studies: History, action, and mediation,' in WERTSCH, J.V., DEL RIO, P. and ALVAREZ, A. (Eds) *Sociocultural Studies of Mind*, Cambridge University Press.

ZEICHNER, K.M. (1992) *Educating Teachers for Cultural Diversity*, East Lansing, MI, Michigan State University, National Center for Research on Teacher Learning.

3 Constructivism: Contradictions and Confusions in Teacher Education

Allan MacKinnon and Carol Scarff-Seatter

Introduction

While constructivism has received tremendous fanfare in the educational community through the 1980s and early 1990s, recent criticisms question its foundation (Millar, 1989; Ormell, 1993; Solomon, 1994). This chapter focuses on typical representations and illustrations of constructivism to ask whether it is, in fact, a warranted perspective on teaching and learning. Constructivism has become a major orienting framework in curriculum reform projects around the world.[1] Yet, there remain great contradictions and confusions when, for example, teachers and researchers are heard speaking of 'the constructivist *method* of teaching'.[2]

Virginia Richardson comments in the introductory chapter of this volume about how constructivism may appear differently in various subject areas and within different psychological traditions. In the present chapter, we develop our ideas in the contexts of science education and science teacher education. For us, this invites the philosophy of science as a special informant about the nature of constructivism. For example, we understand a central tenet of constructivism to be what philosophers of science have argued for decades — that facts and processes of observation are 'theory laden' (Hanson, 1958) and, therefore, cannot be taken as self-evident in classrooms. Much of scientific knowledge consists not merely of the phenomena of nature, but also of constructs advanced by the scientific community to interpret and explain nature. A constructivist perspective on meaning-making is useful if it develops in individuals a disposition for inquiring into problems of perception and cognition, and therefore pedagogy, in classrooms. We attempt to illustrate such a disposition by presenting two analyses of science learning drawn from vignettes of teacher education students' work with children. We focus on illustrating both individual and social dimensions of constructivist thinking.

While we are generally supportive of a constructivist perspective on teaching and learning, we find that some rhetoric associated with constructivism unfortunately masks — if not distorts — the pedagogical issues at hand. We shall also attempt to show how this rhetoric is evident in some of our experiences in teacher education programs over the past several years. But we do not dismiss constructivism. The point of this paper is to become clear on the epistemological underpinnings of a constructivist perspective, and to show the pedagogical limitations of a teaching practice emanating from misguided attempts to honour students' understandings at the expense of 'right answers'.

It is useful to begin by revisiting ideas about knowledge, teaching, and learning that are inherent in the 'discovery learning' movement in science education. These notions became popular some thirty years ago and they are still very prevalent today. We believe they are significant historically to the development of constructivism, though there are also important epistemological differences that we address later in the paper.

Discovery Learning Revisited

'Discovery learning' is a child-centered approach to the teaching and learning of science that had its 'heyday' in the 1960s and 1970s. In its formative years, it was as much a reaction against rote memorization of factual information as it was an attempt to embed within science curriculum a 'structure of science' emphasis (Roberts, 1988), designed in part to increase the stock of potential scientists in North America. With the belief that children are naturally curious, strong proponents of discovery learning insist on children's ownership of ideas and investigations, and sometimes adamantly refuse to 'tell' them any factual or theoretical information. Rather, 'discovery learning teachers' hone the art of guiding inquiry by creating learning environments and asking questions.

We see the 'hope' of discovery learning to be similar, if not identical, to that of constructivists. There is a hope to facilitate meaningful, 'active' engagement of learners. Curiosity and purpose are seen to be paramount in determining the direction and substance of the learner's engagement. Even in our own teaching practices, we find there can be so much concern for the genuine engagement of students that we hesitate to provide any information or rendering of phenomena by our own account.

The epistemological underpinnings of discovery learning seem to be clear and simple. Although it is difficult, if not deceptive, to translate conceptual frameworks to teaching practices, discovery learning seems to imply a realist, or empiricist epistemology. The term 'discovery' implies that knowledge builds up inductively from observable events. As Matthews (1992) suggests, 'any epistemology which formulates the problem of knowledge in terms of a subject looking at an object and asking how well what they see reflects the nature or essence of the object is quintessentially . . . empiricist' (p. 6). Moreover, the empiricist epistemology of 'discovery learning' has obvious pedagogical implications. Hanson, for example, characterizes the 'dust-bowl empiricist' as one who will 'tinker, roam, and ruminate at random, giving the world . . . every opportunity to express itself' (1971, p. 25).

Constructivism

Traditionally, the role of the teacher has been to impart knowledge to students. In science teaching, where the subject matter consists in ways of representing and explaining nature, there is a long-standing ritual engaging students in experience with nature through text, films, stories, or laboratory experiences. Although this simplified view of teaching is sometimes evident in the discussions of educators, most would agree that pedagogical problems do arise in conveying concepts, principles, models, purposes, and criteria for interpreting the events of nature. Part of the problem is in learning how to perceive nature like a scientist. For example, we can speak in 'pedestrian' ways about cold entering the kitchen from the refrigerator, or the sun setting over the horizon. It is a very different accomplishment to *perceive* thermal energy being exchanged in the kitchen, or the earth rotating easterly on its axis. Here we have the sort of problems facing teachers, as documented in a rather extensive literature pertaining to 'children's science'.

Certainly, teachers rely on various strategies to overcome such problems of perception and cognition in their classrooms. It is almost a moot point nowadays to suggest that students' ideas must be taken into consideration in order to provide a foundation for extending concepts, or constructing new concepts and the meanings derived from them. Nevertheless, we would like to illustrate the extent and intensity of these ideas in order to portray the complexity of the problem we are up against here. To do so, we draw from a vignette involving the work of a teacher education student, Kevin.

Kevin

The excerpts below are taken from an interview between four Grade 8 pupils and Kevin during his 'extended', thirteen-week practicum. Much of the interview dealt with a unit test Kevin had given on heat and temperature, which included the following question:

> If you have a large ice cube and a small ice cube in water, the small ice cube will melt first.
> 1 Are both ice cubes at the same temperature? Yes/No
> 2 Why do you think the small ice cube melts first?
> 3 Do you think both ice cubes need the same amount of heat to melt them? Explain your answer.

The four pupils were selected for an interview with Kevin on the basis of their answers to this question. All four pupils circled 'Yes' for the first part — they all thought the ice cubes were at the same temperature. Their answers to the second part of the question were the following:

> **Kate** I think the small ice cube melts first because not as much heat is needed to melt it.
>
> **Mary** Because it has less mass and the latent heat of fusion says that water needs a certain amount of Joules of energy/kg to melt.

Lucy   Because there is less matter and therefore it will melt faster.
Sara   Probably because of its mass (in size). The bigger one is bigger and takes longer. The small one is smaller and will not.

The pupils' answers to the third part of the question concerning the amount of heat required to melt the ice cubes fell into two groups. Kate and Mary's answers were as follows:

Kate   No, I don't think they need the same amount of heat because the larger cube has more room for heat to be transferred into it.
Mary   The larger ice cube needs more heat because it has a greater mass and latent heat of fusion.

Here, Kate and Mary are using a conception of heat that is more-or-less consistent with the scientific one — 'heat' being the amount of thermal energy transferred from one body to another. Thus, the larger ice cube requires more heat to melt because it has a greater mass than the small ice cube. In contrast, the responses given by Lucy and Sara to the third part of the question engage a very different use of the term 'heat':

Lucy   Yes both ice cubes need the same amount of heat to melt them because they are both at the same temperature. The smaller cube will just melt faster because there is less mass.
Sara   Yes, but the big ice cube will take longer to melt because of its mass.

Lucy and Sara's responses invoke a concept associated with the word 'heat' that derives from 'ordinary language'. This concept of heat is roughly equivalent to the concept of temperature in that it refers to a 'level' of hotness. We say we can stand only so much heat on a sunny day before seeking out a shady area. The word heat, in this context, refers to a particular air temperature that is tolerable, or to the amount of time spent in the sun. Similarly, for Lucy and Sara, the two ice cubes require the same amount (level) of heat to melt, but one will require a longer time. Their answers to the third part of the question make sense in ordinary terms, yet they answered the question incorrectly because they failed to use the term 'heat' in its proper scientific sense.

On the basis of their answers to the 'ice cubes' question, these four girls were interviewed to investigate further their understanding of heat. Kate and Mary were chosen because they seemed to understand the scientific concept of heat, while Lucy and Sara were selected because their answers suggested they did not. Kevin and the first author interviewed the four pupils together so they could discuss their answers to the question about melting ice cubes:

Kevin   Okay, what about the second question? Why do you think the small ice cube melts first? Lucy, what did you put?
Lucy   Because there's less mass in the small one. Like there's less of it so it'll melt quicker.

Sara	And it's sort of like it has a head start because it's smaller.
Lucy	Yeah.
Sara	So it'll melt faster.
Kevin	(to Kate) What did you put?
Kate	I put the same.
Kevin	So what did you say?
Kate	I said the small one will melt first.
Kevin	Because . . .
Sara	This could be a trick question.
Mary	I put that the small one melted faster because the bigger one will need more heat because of the latent heat of fusion. And you need a certain amount of Joules of energy to melt each kilogram?
Kevin	Okay. I see where you're coming from there. Okay, what about the last question . . . do you think both ice cubes need the same amount of heat to melt? What did you put, Lucy?
Lucy	Yeah.
Kevin	Okay, and explain why.
Lucy	Well, because they're . . . they're the same. Uhm, they're the same temperatures, so this one will just melt before.
Kevin	Okay . . . what did you put, Sara?
Sara	Uhm, I put that it would . . . uhm, because the smaller one uhm, because its mass is already smaller and it would melt, like, faster?
Kevin	So, does it require the same amount of heat?
Sara	Uh, yeah.

This portion of the dialogue supports the idea that two different concepts associated with the word 'heat' are being used. Mary says that the ice cubes require different amounts of heat to melt likely because she is conceiving of heat as energy. It is feasible that Lucy and Sara say that the ice cubes require the same amount of heat to melt because they are conceiving of heat as the 'level of hotness'. Their discussion continues:

Mary	I put that the larger ice cube needs more because it has a greater mass.
Kate	That was the same as mine.
Kevin	Is that what you guys put? Could you rephrase that question for me? Lucy or Sara? Do you think both ice cubes need the same amount of heat to melt? And you said yes, but it just takes longer.
Lucy	Yeah, it just takes longer to melt the bigger one.
Kevin	Okay. (to Sara) And that's what you were thinking?
Sara	Yeah.
Lucy	Well, 'cause they're at the same temperature.
Kevin	I agree it probably takes longer. Well . . . we . . . why do you think the small ice cube melts first? Do you think both ice cubes need the same temperature to melt? Is that the same question, Lucy?
Lucy	Uh, yeah.
Kevin	(referring to Lucy's test paper) You said yes, they need the same amount. And then you went on to say that one would require longer to melt. What did you put, Mary?

Mary   I put the larger ice cube needs more heat because it has a greater mass . . . because of the latent heat of fusion.

Kevin   Okay . . . (to Kate) how does that . . . ?

Kate   That's about the same as I had.

Kevin   Okay, could you rephrase that . . . like how did you answer that one?

Kate   I just said that they don't need the same amount of heat because the larger ice cube has more mass that the heat can be transferred into.

Kevin   Okay, the answers are a bit different here. I'm just wondering why they're different . . . or what you think about the difference.

Lucy   What I think . . . oh, uhm . . .

Kevin   Do you see any hang ups?

Lucy   No.

Kevin   Okay, they [Mary and Kate] said no . . . and you said yes [the ice cubes need the same amount of heat to melt].

Lucy   Well, I mean if you wanted to, *you could do it both ways.*

Kevin   Why could you do it both ways?

Lucy   *'Cause I mean you can melt it at the same temperature, but you can also do it at different temperatures. If you want it done at the same time.*

As the dialogue continues Sara eventually seems to grasp the scientific concept of heat, allowing her to reinterpret the question, and reformulate her answer.

Mary   (looking at Lucy's test paper) I think that what she has there is . . . uh, the temperature. Like, like . . . they need the same temperature of heat going into them, but they need more heat going into them. Like the bigger one will need more heat to go into it to melt it than the little one.

Kevin   You mean *the same temperature for a longer time.*

Mary   Yeah, the same . . . yeah, yeah.

Kevin   What do you think, Kate, about that?

Kate   I don't know . . . uh . . .

Kevin   (to Lucy) What do you think?

Lucy   Well that's right, because it [the answer to the test question] is *yes and no.*

Kevin   Why is it yes and no?

Lucy   Well, I mean . . . you could do it either way, right? You could use the same amount of heat or you could use different amounts of heat.

Kevin   Could you?

Sara   Oh yeah.

Lucy   Yeah, because if you wanted them both melting at the same time then you just increase the temperature.

Sara   *Yeah, actually the larger one does need more heat though because it's bigger.*

Lucy   (to Sara) It could do the same heat for a longer time, though, because . . . couldn't it?

Sara   It's because the larger one's bigger, but the smaller one's already had a head start so it wouldn't need as much heat to melt it.

The impasse between Sara and Lucy in this last exchange is fascinating to us because it seems as though the two girls are really 'talking past' each other. We believe this minute example is not unlike many communication problems occurring in classrooms. In our judgment, much of being successful in school has to do with being able to *see* situations appropriately. In the dialogue above, Mary and Kate show that they are able do this — they seem to know what the intent of the question is. Sara, too, seems to come to accept the idea that the large ice cube requires more heat to melt than the small one because 'it's bigger'. Indeed, Sara seems to come to an understanding of both senses in which the word 'heat' is being used in the conversation. Her earlier comment, 'This could be a trick question', suggests that one of her strategies in school is looking out for alternate ways of thinking about questions. But not all students are so flexible in their thinking, and we are left wondering what Lucy was experiencing during this impasse.

The remainder of the interview dealt with another question about heat, in which the context of the situation was shifted considerably. Here, the first author took the principal role of interviewing the pupils while Kevin listened. Second, it could be argued that the context of the question shifted from 'school science' to 'everyday life' — the idea was that the girls were to help prepare a lunch by spreading butter on a filet of frozen fish. It was hoped they would be surprised by the stiffening butter, and then spontaneously discuss this event:

Allan　Actually, the way you're spreading, the butter almost looks hard.
Mary　It is.
Allan　It was nice, soft butter too.
Lucy　Is something going to happen? (laughs)
Allan　Kate, would you like to put a little bit more on?
Mary　That knife is bending, and it doesn't . . .
Allan　Is it easy to spread?
Kate　It's hardening.
Mary　No because it's having a heat transfer from this to that . . . it gets harder.
Allan　From what to what?
Mary　From the fish.
Sara　(touches fish and butter) Oh, it's so cold.
Mary　It's frozen and so it's transferring . . . to the . . .
Lucy　It makes the butter cold . . . the margarine a little bit colder.
Kate　Heat is being *released.*
Sara　(touches the butter dish) Hey, this is warm.
Kate　No, heat is being *taken.*

It is tempting to say that Mary's thinking about heat has shifted with the context of the question. She seems to be saying that *there is cold moving from the fish into the butter, and therefore the butter gets harder.* It is interesting that Mary seems to have shifted from using the scientific concept of heat, even though she was using it just minutes before in the context of the ice cube question. Kate, on the other hand, seems to have read the situation in a different way, having recognized that the the fish and butter problem can be represented in terms of *heat being 'taken' from the butter by the fish.*

Allan	Heat is being released? Did you say that the cold goes from the fish to the butter?
Mary	Yep.
Sara	I agree with that.
Mary	It's taking . . . no, it's taking heat away from the butter.
Allan	Oh, I see.
Mary	So it can use it for its phase change.

Mary, too, appears to shift her thinking here. It is plausible that she realized the possibility for dealing with the phenomenon in the context of 'school science', and resumed working with the scientific concept of heat:

Allan	When my daughter tried that she said that the cold was going from the fish into the butter. Does that make sense?
Sara	The cold going into the butter?
Mary	No . . . 'cause it's not cold transfer . . . it's heat transfer.
Sara	No, but it's cold.
Lucy	The cold's going into the butter.
Mary	The fish is taking away the heat from the butter.
Kevin	Why is the cold going into the butter?
Lucy	Because the butter's hard now . . . well, kind of.
Sara	That was warm . . . and then . . .
Mary	Yeah, but the fish takes it [the heat] away.
Sara	It was warm . . .
Lucy	It was that (points to soft butter) and then it went to that (hard butter on fish).

The girls' difficulty seems to stem from using two different ways of regarding the phenomenon of the butter getting harder. Mary and Kate seem to be using the scientific concept of heat to say that *heat is being transferred from the butter to the fish*; it is required for the fish to thaw. Lucy and Sara, on the other hand, seem to be using the ordinary concept of cold to say that *the cold is being transferred from the fish to the butter*. In order to move beyond this difficulty in communication, Allan attempts to point out the two different ways of thinking about the phenomenon:

Allan	I think my daughter was sort of thinking that. And that's sort of the way we think in the everyday world, isn't it? We think about cold being moved here and there as well as heat being moved here and there. But, Mary, what you were saying is that in science we don't think about cold moving.
Mary	We think about heat moving, yeah.
Kate	Heat transfer.

Allan What do you think about that, Lucy?

Lucy I don't know. Uhm, well I guess she's right. 'Cause well this [fish] is melting kind of.

Kate It's getting nice and soft.

Allan It might even be getting soft. You probably don't want to touch because your hands will smell fishy . . . but (puts wrap around the fish) you can feel it's getting a little soft on the bottom if you touch the wrap. Can you feel it?

Mary Yeah. That's from the desk.

Sara The desk's warm . . .

Mary Warmer anyways [than the fish].

Sara It's at room temperature, sort of.

Allan (touches the spot of the desk that the fish was resting on) Is it warm there?

Sara No . . . it's freezing.

Kate 'Cause the heat's been taken away from the desk by the fish.

Kevin Why is heat being taken away from the desk by the fish?

Kate 'Cause the fish is trying to melt.

Kevin Like it doesn't . . . I mean . . . how would you explain that in terms of energy . . . or whatever? Can you explain it?

Kate The fish is taking energy.

Lucy 'Cause it's warmer than the fish.

Sara The desk?

Lucy Yeah, the desk and the butter's warmer than the . . .

Kevin And so why would it go from the . . .

Kate 'Cause the fish needs heat . . .

Lucy *'Cause it's trying to melt . . .*

It is not clear in the dialogue that Lucy and Sara have *seen* the hardening butter phenomenon in terms of 'heat being removed by the thawing fish'. Even Kate's thinking is difficult to comment about when she used an anthropomorphic explanation (the fish is trying to melt) in response to Kevin's question about why the heat from the desk was being taken by the fish.

What is quite intriguing, though, is the clarity with which Mary's 'ah ha' experience appears when one is prepared to notice the shift in her use of language. The difference in perception enabled by the ordinary sense of the word 'heat' (a similar concept to temperature) and its scientific sense is striking in terms of the ways the hardening butter can be conceptualized. In ordinary terms, the butter hardens because it takes the cold from the fish. According to convention in science, the butter hardens because its heat is taken for the change of phase in the fish. Again, the impasse in the conversation is rather striking.

We present this dialogue not only to illustrate how individuals construct different understandings of events in science classrooms, but also to portray the intensity and complexity of the kind of impasse which we believe is typical of discourse in science teaching. This problem is not insignificant!

We would also like to comment about how our analysis so far stems from an 'individualistic' quality of thought. In this example of Kevin's work, we are concerned about how individuals construe and represent their experiences, how they come to assign meaning to events. We actually speak of concepts within a person's mind as though they were things to be found, examined, replaced, or extended. But, what could be done to ease the impasse in the discussion above? What could we do to improve the communication of participants? What would make their interaction more *educative*?

We believe there is value in helping student teachers and science pupils come to understand alternate ways of thinking about words and events in science. The kind of dialogue that Kevin sought with his students was highly educative, both for him in learning about problems of teaching, and for his pupils in learning science. We believe that constructivism helps us to see how sense is being made — particularly in problematic discourse such as the dialogue presented above. We concede, however, that there is a certain naiveté to the idea that we could somehow use a constructivist perspective to repair discourse in science classrooms, and we are reluctant to think of constructivism as a source of 'teaching methods' or a kind of 'quick fix' for such difficulties in cognition.

Trisha and Erin

Let us consider another scenario which highlights the sociocultural influences of cognition. First, it is worth commenting that we do not see the two approaches — individual and social — as incompatible. As Bereiter (1994) comments,

> . . . constructivism tells us to pay close attention to the mental activities of the learner, and socioculturalism tells us to pay close attention to cultural practices in the learner's milieu. Except for the practical difficulty of doing both at once, there is nothing incompatible in these proposals. Neither one implies rejection of the other. (Bereiter, 1994, p. 21)

In this section we attempt to illustrate the kind of analysis that emanates from what Bereiter refers to as 'socioculturalism'. Specifically, we hope to illustrate a 'sociocultural approach to mediated activity' (Wertsch, 1991). Again, the setting of the account is teacher education students' work with science pupils.

Here, Trisha and Erin work with elementary school children investigating the effects of static electricity on the behavior of balloons. Of interest here is a part of the lesson in which balloons were charged by rubbing them on hair or wool clothing. The charged balloons were then used for a variety of demonstrations, such as repelling each other, or picking up small bits of paper from a table.

At one station there was a 'fishing pond', made from a small swimming pool containing small fish shapes cut from plastic gift wrap and cellophane. The children were given a plastic fishing rod with a balloon dangling from a string attached to one end. The objective of the station was to collect fish from the pool by rubbing the balloon, dipping it in the pond, pulling up as many fish as the charged balloon would attract, and collecting the fish in a pile on the floor beside the pool. A 7-year-old oriental child named Vanessa tried unsuccessfully for one and a half minutes to pick up her first fish, before Trisha — a teacher education student — gave her a wool sock to rub over her balloon (Trisha had been helping three other students around the pool). After Vanessa rubbed the balloon, she was able to pick up fish and begin her own collection at the side of the pool — first one, then two at once, then a fourth, and a fifth. While she was catching her sixth fish, the following exchange took place between Trisha and another child, Denise, at the side of the pool:

Trisha   You have a silver one (fish).
Denise   A tin foil one.
Trisha   Right.
Denise   I don't have any more static on mine.
Trisha   Well, maybe you can rub it . . . maybe you can try rubbing it on your pants. See if that'll do it.

After her seventh catch, the charge on Vanessa's balloon had dissipated to the extent that it could not quite pick up another fish. She tried for about fifteen seconds, during which time there were two points at which she almost caught the eighth fish. Finally, she held the balloon and waited for her turn to use the wool sock again. Meanwhile, Denise had tried rubbing the balloon on her pants (cotton corduroy) with no result, and was now using the sock to recharge.

Seeing that the sock was in use, Vanessa tried rubbing her balloon on her pants and was then able to catch four fish with one dip into the pool. On the second trial with the recharged balloon she caught two fish; on the third, one. There were three unsuccessful dips before she recharged the balloon on her pants again. Trisha had been helping another child who had joined the group at the fishing pool. She noticed Vanessa rubbing the balloon on her pants.

Trisha   Good, you're using your pants. Try that. See if that works as well.

Vanessa caught three fish, then none during the next four trials.

Trisha   See how sometimes it wears out . . . it doesn't work after a while?

Vanessa rubbed again. Two fish were caught on the next dip, followed by only one unsuccessful trial. Thereafter, Vanessa rubbed the balloon on her pants between every trial.

After another minute of fishing, Vanessa moved along to the next station, where another teacher education student, Erin, was helping children charge balloons in order to pick up bits of sparkles from pie plates. Erin greeted Vanessa, and pointed to the corner of the room, where a few balloons had been stored. Vanessa picked out a pink balloon and was joined by another girl, Susan, who chose a blue one. Erin's balloon was orange.

Erin beamed when the two girls returned to the table with their balloons. She was exciting and excitable in her manner and enthusiasm for the children.

Erin	How do you charge your balloon?
Susan	By rubbing it on your hair.
Vanessa	(appears uncomfortable about messing up her hair)
Erin	Well, you can use my hair . . . 'cause look how charged my hair is.

Giggling, the girls rubbed their balloons on Erin's head together, Susan somewhat more vigorously than Vanessa. They walked a few steps from Erin to the table where the pie plates lay. But while Susan's balloon picked up many sparkles, Vanessa's didn't budge one. A slow motion viewing of the video tape revealed that Vanessa bumped her balloon into the table, which probably 'grounded' it. Vanessa tried, unsuccessfully, to pick up sparkles from three different plates, while Susan and Erin concentrated on what was happening with Susan's balloon:

Susan	Wow!
Erin	Look at that. What happened to it?

Vanessa walked back to Erin, apparently for another rubbing on her hair. She waited while Erin crouched to observe Susan's balloon.

Erin	What's happening?
Susan	(silence)
Erin	What's on your balloon?
Susan	Sparkles.
Erin	The sparkles are doing what?
Susan	They're sticking to the balloon 'cause of all the static.
Erin	That's right. Very good. My goodness.

At that point, Erin gestured to Vanessa — still, with an uncharged balloon — to move to the next table, where there were pie plates of various kinds of breakfast cereals. Once again, the challenge was to charge the balloon and try to pick up little bits (of cereal) from the plates. Several other children were working at this station, and, due to some commotion, it was another few minutes before Vanessa could rub her balloon on Erin's hair again. Still, she waited. When the time finally came, Vanessa and Susan rubbed their balloons on Erin's head, again in tandem. At that point, Vanessa's balloon caught and broke on a sharp corner of Erin's barrette. Off to the corner she went to find another, and, when she came back, she had an orange one.

Several features in this string of events are intriguing. Vanessa's engagement at the fishing pool reveals something of the dynamic interplay between the material, experiential, and social resources available in the activity. The length of time spent dipping an uncharged balloon at the beginning of the sequence suggests that she had no initial understanding of how to charge a balloon, or, simply what was required to pick up a fish, never mind the idea of charge. Although we have no direct access to her mind, the 'rubbing, dipping, collecting' succession provides a telling display of her learning. In this succession, we can readily see the effects of Trisha's mediation: first, by giving Vanessa the sock for rubbing; second, in a suggestion made to another child at the pool (*Well, maybe you can rub it . . . maybe you can try rubbing it on your pants. See if that'll do it.*); and, third, in a question to Vanessa (*See how sometimes it wears out . . . it doesn't work after a while?*). The result of the first mediation is seen as Vanessa's initial success at the pool, to the effect of catching one fish per dip, on average, for six dips.

The second mediation was somewhat more tangled in the situation in two senses. First, it was a suggestion made to another child around the pool several seconds previously. Second, it seemed to 'precipitate' only when the situation was conducive: Vanessa rubbed her pants only after she saw that the sock was being used by Denise. The size of the catch was certainly worthy: four fish on the first dip, as opposed to an average of one per dip when the sock was used to charge the balloon. Vanessa didn't use the sock again. Finally, the effect of the third mediation (*See how sometimes it wears out . . .*) is seen in the final technique Vanessa adopted in the fishing activity, which was to rub the balloon between each dip, and therefore maximize her catch.

Why Vanessa did not charge her balloon on her pants in the subsequent activity with the pie plates is something of a mystery. The social dynamic of the situation had likely changed, now that she had become partnered with her friend, Susan. Erin, too, with her enthusiasm and effervescence for the children, presented a different sort of social resource than Trisha had been in the fishing activity. Further, since Erin had introduced the morning's activities, the girls may have identified with her a little more to begin with. They certainly enjoyed her company, demonstrated by their gleeful expressions and giggling when rubbing their balloons on Erin's hair. It is interesting in itself that on both trials, the girls rubbed their balloons together in something of a duet. Erin's effervescent demeanour likely contributed to this kind of camaraderie with the children, together with her invitation for the physical contact of rubbing balloons on her hair. This line of thinking suggests that Vanessa was socially implicated in the events to the extent that it may have been more desirable to charge her balloon on Erin's head than proceed with the activity by using her pants to charge the balloon, even if she had to wait. After popping her pink balloon, the fact that she picked out an orange one — the same colour as Erin's — may be significant, given this interpretation.

Another interpretation emanates from the statement that Erin made about her own hair (*Well, you can use my hair . . . 'cause look how charged my hair is.*). This may have established a reason of a different sort — that by rubbing on Erin's hair, the charge would be greater and therefore pick up more bits. This interpretation doesn't hold up, however, if we consider Vanessa's learning in the fishing activity. There, she did not wait for the wool sock to charge her balloon when it was unavailable, but rather began charging on her pants instead. With a degree of success using this tactic, she did not return to use the wool sock again, even when it was available. Given this background, we might expect Vanessa to resort to another tactic in the pie plate activity. Once she found that her balloon didn't pick up anything on the first trial after rubbing with Erin's hair, why wouldn't she have used her pants? Perhaps Vanessa was merely responding to Erin's authority as a teacher.

There are no firm answers to the question of why Vanessa's understanding about charging a balloon did not appear to transfer from the first station to the second. It is plausible that the sociocultural dynamic may have shifted from one setting to the other. Perhaps the shift had something to do with Vanessa's peers. Perhaps Erin figured prominently as a role model. Perhaps there was a cultural influence at hand, or there was some combination of several influences. What is clear in the vignette, however, is the fact that Vanessa's ability to charge her balloon — what we can infer is a manifestation of her understanding of how to do so — is tangled in her interaction with the material resources available as well as the mediational influences of other children and adults. We see that what has been learned in the mediated activity of one situation is not transferred to another, even moments later.

So What *Is* Constructivism?

We have attempted to demonstrate that constructivism is a way of thinking about the formation of knowledge and understanding. It provides a lens with which we can examine the world — attend to and render events, and, in many cases but not all, explain them. Like its own tenets purport, constructivism provides a way of apprehending and representing the events of teaching and learning; it is not a literal representation. We worry that a constructivist perspective on the teaching and learning of science is often presented to student teachers, not as a way of examining teaching events, but as the only viable perspective. Perhaps we need to view constructivism as one kind of lens through which to view science teaching events — *a* way of examining events, not the only way. This would be much more consistent with a constructivist epistemology.

Teacher education students need opportunities for testing, discussing, and comparing various perspectives and approaches to teaching. We are strongly in favour of developing in teacher education students what Schwab (1973) would refer to as 'polyfocal conspectus', or what Roberts (1980) dubbed 'informed eclecticism' — a composite view of practice achieved by viewing events from a variety of theoretical vantage points. We believe that by striving for such a composite view, teachers become more responsible for their pedagogical choices.

Many writers recognize that students continually construct meaning of classroom events based on their prior understandings and experiences. Further, it follows that a constructivist science teacher will have a disposition for attempting to *see* science classroom phenomena from students' perspectives in order to accommodate these perspectives in the instructional program. The disposition and ability to *see* from students' points of view is fundamental to sorting out what is 'right' about their thinking as well as what is inconsistent or incoherent about it.

To see a phenomenon from a student's point of view requires 'reconstruction' on the part of the teacher. The phenomenon in question must be seen in a 'new light', much as Kevin was able to *see* how two ice cubes of different masses require the same 'heat' (temperature, in scientific language) to melt, or why students spoke about 'cold' moving from the frozen fish into the hardening butter. In our estimation, a critical aspect of the teaching of science is a teacher's ability to see how such perceptions arise from students' perspectives and uses of language — the capacity to appreciate the reasonableness of students' ideas and build these into the instructional plan. But how can such a capacity be nurtured in teacher education programs?

Teacher Education

We support the kinds of experiences Kevin, Trisha, and Erin had in their teacher education programs. Somehow, there should be a way of slowing down the pace of teacher education to allow professors and students to work closely together in practice, and so together observe and try to untangle the many mysteries of learning or failure to learn. In our experience as teacher educators we appreciate the difficulty of imparting a constructivist orientation to teacher education students. In practice, they often appear to us as 'discovery learning teachers', with hands-on activities related to the science idea of the day. For example, there might be an exploratory activity with different types and sizes of pendulums, or various kinds of floating objects. Pupils are typically encouraged to create tentative models of explanation out of these experiences, to share them with each other and the rest of the class. Often lessons stop at this point, however, and there is no serious effort made to carefully examine children's conceptions and understandings of science. Rather, the expectation seems to be that children will inductively arrive at an understanding of the phenomena for themselves, frequently with little or no critique or attempt to clarify or challenge ideas.

It is worth stating that we do not wish to portray a deficit view of teacher education students. Nor do we wish to blame them for anything. We do feel, however, that their concerns to 'get through teacher education and on to the real world' may not be consistent with the kinds of research and professional commitments of professors. As we listen to their talk in the hallways, we hear bizarre renditions of what we believe we have taught in methods courses. Some statements about constructivism are particularly troubling and lead us to believe teacher education students are formulating a truncated, or rudimentary version of constructivism. Consider the following writing of one of our elementary science methods students:

> I am very anxious to return to my classroom and teach science. Constructivism has taught me [that] I do not need to know any science in order to teach it. I will simply allow my students to figure things out for themselves, for I know there is no *right* answer.

Examples of the kind of 'teaching' practice that we believe emanates from such a view help to show what we are concerned about. The following mini-vignettes reveal ways in which pupils have 'figured things out for themselves', with the novice teacher apparently being satisfied with the final results. The important thing is that in each case the teacher left pupils with their own representations and explanations of science events — what Roberts and Silva (1968) refer to as the 'abandonment' style of teaching.

Example 1

Joyce opens a bottle of perfume and sets it aside throughout a science lesson. Near the lesson's end, with the perfume odor pervading the entire classroom, she asks pupils, 'Where does the perfume go?' Answers ranged from 'It changes into something else', to 'It disappears into nothing except for the smell'.

Example 2

Debra introduces a grade 5 class to the concept of food chain. At the end of the lesson she asks, 'Where does energy, which is transferred within the food chain, originate?' John says, 'All energy starts in the soil.' Debra repeats the answer, commends John for his thinking, and dismisses the class.

Example 3

Randi lights two candles of different lengths and holds an empty beaker above them. She asks, 'When I place this inverted beaker over the two burning candles, which one will go out first?' and later, 'Why does the tall candle always go out before the short one?'

In the staffroom after class, Randi expressed delight at Jason's answer to the candle question, which was, 'The tall candle goes out before the short one because it requires more air.' 'That answer is *close*, isn't it?' she asks a colleague.

Challenges

We believe that 'constructivist talk' seems to evoke in some teacher education students a distorted image, or a truncated version, of 'constructivist teaching'. In some representations by students, constructivism sounds like a recipe, a procedure for teaching. In many cases, 'constructivism' looks like discovery learning, when children put forward their science ideas as discoveries, and the cross-checking and testing of those ideas with other references (peers, teacher's scientific knowledge) is omitted.

We believe there are great challenges lying ahead for those of us wishing to portray and nurture a constructivist perspective in teacher education programs. Not only do we need to concern ourselves with the manner in which students 'hear' or 'read' constructivism, but also the ways in which we represent it to ourselves as researchers. We sometimes speak of 'constructivists' as though a person can either be one or not. In truth, constructivism is a way of thinking about the events of teaching and learning. It is neither a person nor a method, but a theory of knowledge. And it is not the only theory drawn upon in teaching by any of us, whether he or she is aware of it or not.

We have tried nevertheless in this chapter to portray our sense of the usefulness of a constructivist perspective in examining problems inherent in the teaching of science. We see the individualistic variety of constructivism and sociocultural approaches to the study of cognition as being compatible, and we have devoted the bulk of this chapter to demonstrating how we have drawn upon the two schools of thought in examining our own work in science teacher education.

Our broad goal in this chapter has been three-fold: to show how we believe constructivism has merit as a vantage point from which to view the practice of teaching, to clarify this vantage point by distinguishing its epistemology from discovery learning and emphasizing its status as a theory — not a representation of any sort of 'reality' in the world of teaching, and to use this distinction as a way of pointing out what we believe in some cases to be a disparity between teacher education students' understandings of constructivism and our own professional commitments.

Notes

1 Much of our analysis is drawn from the area of science education and science teacher education — an area in which numerous reform projects are taking place currently. In the Canadian provinces, ministries of education are undertaking revisions in their science curricula, following the lead of Project 2061 in the US, the National Curriculum in the UK, and similar projects in Australia and New Zealand. The discussion on teaching and learning found in the *Benchmarks* document, published by the American Association for the Advancement of Science, is exemplary of constructivist influences on science curricula.

2 The 'Private Universe Project' (PUP) teleconference on science education consisted of nine weekly satellite broadcasts produced by the Harvard Smithsonian Institute of Technology and the National Science Foundation in the fall of 1994. This teleconference engaged educators from over two hundred sites across North America and the UK in viewing the broadcast and dialoguing with the PUP team in Boston via telephone links, electronic mail, fax, and post. Despite efforts of the PUP team

to distinguish between a philosophical position on the nature of knowledge acquisition, participants repeatedly referred to 'the constructivist teaching method' as though it were something of a monolithic, technical procedure.

References

BEREITER, C. (1994) 'Constructivism, socioculturalism, and Popper's World 3,' *Educational Researcher*, **23**, 7, pp. 21–3.

DRIVER, R., GUESNE E. and TIBERGHIEN, A. (1985) *Children's Ideas in Science*, Open University Press.

GLASERSFELD VON, E. (1991) 'Cognition, construction of knowledge, and teaching,' in MATTHEWS, M.R. (Ed) *History, Philosophy and Science Teaching*, Toronto, OISE Press.

HACKING, I. (1972) *Representing and Intervening*, Cambridge, Cambridge University Press.

HANSON, N.R. (1958) *Patterns of Discovery: An Inquiry into the Conceptual Foundations of Science*, Cambridge, Cambridge University Press.

HANSON, N.R. (1971) *Observation and Explanation: A Guide to Philosophy of Science*, Harper and Row.

MARGENAU, H. (1973) 'The method of science and the meaning of reality', *Main Currents in Modern Thought*, **29**, 5, pp. 163–71.

MATTHEWS, M.R. (1992) 'Old wine in new bottles: A problem with constructivist epistemology', Paper presented at University of Auckland, Auckland, New Zealand.

MILLAR, R. (1989) 'Constructive criticisms', *International Journal of Science Education*, **11**, 5, pp. 587–96.

NERSESSIAN, N. (1991) 'Conceptual change in science and science education', in MATTHEWS, M.R. (Ed) *History, Philosophy, and Science Teaching: Selected Readings*, Toronto, OISE Press, pp. 133–48.

ORMELL, C. (1993) 'Is the uncertainty of mathematics the real source of its intellectual charm?', *Journal of Philosophy in Education*, **27**, 1, pp. 125–33.

ROBERTS, D.A. (1980) 'Theory, curriculum development, and unique events of practice', in MUNBY, H., ORPWOOD, G. and RUSSELL, T. (Eds) *Seeing Curriculum in a New Light: Essays from Science Education*, Toronto, OISE Press, pp. 65–87.

ROBERTS, D.A. (1988) 'What counts as science education?', in FENSHAM, P. (Ed) *Developments and Dilemmas in Science Education*, London, Falmer Press, pp. 27–55.

ROBERTS, D.A. and SILVA, D. (1968) 'Curriculum design, teaching styles and consequences for pupils,' *Samplings*, **1**, 4, pp. 16–28.

SCHWAB, J. (1973) 'The practical 3: Translation into curriculum,' *School Review*, **81**, pp. 501–22.

SOLOMON, J. (1994) 'The rise and fall of constructivism,' *Studies in Science Education*, **23**, pp. 1–19.

WERTSCH, J.V. (1991) 'Voices of the mind: A sociocultural approach to mediated action,' Cambridge, MA, Harvard University Press.

II *Research and Practice*

4 Constructivism in Teacher Education: Applying Cognitive Theory to Teacher Learning

Nancy Winitzky and Don Kauchak

Introduction

The central mission of this volume is to draw appropriate applications from constructivism to the practice of teacher education. The essence of constructivism is the learners' knowledge-building process (Derry, in press; Fosnot, 1996). Understanding knowledge acquisition therefore seems to be a central task for those attempting to define the role of constructivism in teacher education. As a result, key questions guiding our own research agenda for the past several years have been:

1 what does teacher candidate knowledge growth look like?
2 what is the relationship between this knowledge growth and program experiences?

This chapter describes our attempts to document how teachers construct knowledge, to understand this knowledge growth within a constructivist theoretical perspective, and to apply these findings in refining and redesigning teacher education programs.

The Place of Knowledge in Teacher Education

Despite the centrality of knowledge in both cognitive (Shuell, 1996) and constructivist (Derry, in press) views of learning, the importance of knowledge in teacher education is controversial. Under challenge is the applicability of theoretical knowledge to the complex and everyday practical concerns of teachers. Kessels and Korthagen (1996), for example, dispute the relevance to teacher education of abstract knowledge derived from systematic research on classrooms. They argue that the problem with such knowledge is that it is universal, and that the type of knowledge needed to be a good teacher is knowledge of particular situations and contexts. Kessels and Korthagen define universal knowledge as

> propositional; i.e., it consists of a set of assertions that can be explained, investigated, transmitted, and the like. These assertions are of a general nature; they apply to many different situations and problems . . . Consequently, they are formulated in abstract terms. (p. 18)

They claim that such knowledge is not particularly useful to teachers, and that practical knowledge, that is, '. . . understanding of specific concrete cases and complex or ambiguous situations' (p. 19) is preferable. In their view the problems with universal knowledge are threefold. First, it must be moderated by practical, contextual knowledge in order to be applied in any given specific situation. The implication is that universal knowledge is rendered superfluous by the need for practical knowledge of a particular context.

A second, related problem with universal knowledge according to Kessels and Korthagen is that in any given context, the particulars of the case rule over principles. 'All practical knowledge is context-related, allowing the contingent features of the case at hand to be, ultimately, authoritative over principle. This is, according to Aristotle, "why people who lack a grasp of general ideas are sometimes more effective in practice"' (p. 19). The argument is that because universal knowledge is at best secondary, it is therefore unimportant and even at times a hindrance. As the outsider at the Grateful Dead concert looking for the boss was told by a helpful Deadhead, 'the situation is the boss'.

The final problem is in the different ways decisions based on the two types of knowledge can be justified. With scientific knowledge, justification derives from principles and explanatory models. An action can be judged right or wrong based on an evaluation of the relevant evidence. In contrast, the

> ultimate appeal of . . . (practical knowledge) is not to principles, rules, theorems, or any conceptual knowledge . . . the appeal is to perceptions. For to be able to choose a form of behavior appropriate for the situation, one must above all be able to perceive and discriminate the relevant details. These cannot be transmitted in some general, abstract form. (p. 19)

While Kessels and Korthagen acknowledge that theoretical knowledge may be of some limited use, they argue that practical wisdom, i.e., detailed knowledge of the particulars of a situation, is vastly more important, and that '. . . practical choices cannot even in principle be completely captured in a system of universal rules' (p. 19).

We do not agree with this view of knowledge. The mere fact that principles must be adapted in order to apply to particular situations doesn't render them useless. One principle guiding our actions, for example, is to be honest, but honesty with a son or daughter would look very different from honesty with a professional acquaintance. It would be nonsense to abandon the principle just because we apply it differently from one context to another. By the same token, it would be nonsense to abandon principles of teaching and learning such as 'authoritarian learning environments suppress intrinsic motivation' just because the principle must be adapted in different ways in a first grade versus a college classroom or in a self-contained special education context versus an inclusive environment.

Further, even granting the proposition that principles come second to particulars (which we do not) does not mean principles have no place; secondary in no way implies irrelevant. For example, how could a teacher who had no knowledge of the relationship between motivation and learning environment create and maintain a democratic classroom learning community? Without such foundational knowledge, a beginning teacher has nothing but a wish and a prayer to guide her actions. Also, how might teacher candidates begin to understand which particular details of classroom situations were salient without some general guidance in what, where, and how to look?

Anderson, Reder, and Simon (1996) attacked the view that all learning is situational by illustrating the value and generalizability of well-learned abstract knowledge. For example, in one study of mathematics learning, abstract instruction enabled students to apply their knowledge to a novel problem while students taught the same information through a concrete method were unable to do so. The topic under study was algebra problems involving mixtures.

> Some subjects were trained with pictures of the mixtures while other subjects were trained with abstract tabular representations that highlighted the underlying mathematical relationships. The abstract training group was able to transfer better to other kinds of problems that involved analogous mathematical relations. (Anderson, Reder and Simon, 1996, p. 8)

In another study, Biederman and Shiffrar (1987) examined the difficult task of sexing day-old chicks. Under an apprenticeship instructional format, people spend years acquiring this skill. In the study, however, novices were able to reach the level of experts after a mere twenty minutes of abstract instruction. In yet another context, hitting an object under water, abstract instruction focusing on knowledge of principles promoted learning more effectively than concrete, trial-and-error learning (Judd, 1908). Children practiced hitting a target twelve inches underwater, but only some of them were also taught abstract information about the refraction of light. Children in both groups performed equally well at hitting a target twelve inches under water. But in a follow-up test involving a target only four inches under water, the abstract instruction group did much better. Anderson, Reder, and Simon concluded that instruction that combines both the abstract and the concrete is optimal, noting that: 'This method is especially important when learning must be applied to a wide variety of (frequently unpredictable) future tasks' (p. 9).

Other research in cognitive psychology also supports the value of abstract or propositional knowledge. In particular, how individuals organize this knowledge has special import. Individuals' knowledge structures differ, and these differences influence perception, understanding, and memory, processes central to learning. For example, experts have been compared to novices in many domains. It has been found that experts have more organized knowledge structures than novices and that, as a result, they perceive, organize, and remember more details of a situation than novices (Bruning, Schraw and Ronning, 1995). Importantly, experts use the deep structure of their domain (i.e., abstract knowledge about principles) rather than the superficial features of a situation to solve a problem. These findings apply to children as well as adults; in one study, children who knew a great deal about spiders were able to understand and learn more new information about spiders than children whose initial knowledge was low (Pearson, Hansen and Gordon, 1979). Similar results have been found for teachers; expert teachers see and remember more details about classroom events than novices, and the details they remember are more significant in terms of teacher actions that can promote student learning (Berliner, 1994).

Cumulatively, the research on knowledge suggests that understanding of general principles provides a knowledge foundation that transfers to a variety of situations. Such knowledge contributes in critical ways to the ability of learners to understand, frame, and solve problems and to adapt the application of knowledge in novel ways to changing circumstances. Applied to teacher education, we argue that abstract knowledge derived from systematic research and theory on teaching and learning plays an important role in helping teacher candidates make sense of, and effectively teach within, complex learning environments. As such, it deserves a central place in programs of teacher education. Because this type of knowledge is so essential for teacher growth, we focus in our research on the development of abstract, conceptual knowledge in teacher candidates as they progress through our program.

Constructivism in Teacher Education

An essential companion task to documenting knowledge changes in teacher candidates is to link those changes to program experiences. As teacher educators, we want our research to inform and improve our own practice. But the link between learning and instruction is not simple. As argued by Richardson (this volume) and by Gelman (1994), constructivist principles of learning do not automatically engender principles of teaching. Learners construct meaning on their own terms no matter what teachers do. Whether a teacher lectures about the different types of bacteria or has students culture bacteria and create their own key, students still construct their own individual and often idiosyncratic meanings about bacteria under each instructional format. In this sense, it is impossible for a teacher to be anything other than a constructivist.

Constructivist theorists would maintain, however, that learning is better or more effective when teachers use constructivist teaching methods, like culturing and keying bacteria as opposed to lecturing about bacteria. Constructivist teaching typically involves more student-centered, active learning experiences, more student–student and student–teacher interaction, and more work with concrete materials and in solving realistic problems (Shuell, 1996). Nevertheless, students still create their own meanings based on the interaction of their prior knowledge with instruction, and the meanings they make may not be the ones the teacher had in mind, no matter how constructivist the instruction. 'Learners can and do find interpretations that differ from those intended by experts' (Gelman, 1994, p. 55). Teachers create constructivist learning experiences for students based necessarily on what they, the teachers, find salient. But what is salient to the teacher is not necessarily so to the learner.

That this is so in teacher education has been convincingly demonstrated by Holt-Reynolds (1992; 1994). She observed preservice classes and then asked teacher candidates what they understood about those classes. The professor she observed emphasized the importance of using active teaching methods, stressing that the student passivity inherent in the lecture method was not conducive to learning. The candidates readily agreed that active teaching was important and that student passivity negatively impacted learning. Unfortunately, in reaching this conclusion they redefined passivity, maintaining that motivated students are actually actively listening during a lecture. Holt-Reynolds concluded:

> When preservice teachers believe that teaching well depends rather exclusively on making school work interesting, they reject as irrelevant parts of the course that focus on teaching students to use metacognitive strategies for reading to learn . . . When they believe that student effort is the salient factor contributing to success as a learner, they reject as irrelevent learning how to foster comprehension skills . . . When they believe all students will be like themselves — able learners a bit bored by school — they find little reason to learn how to analyze the demands inherent to subject matter texts . . . When they believe that teacher telling — lecturing — is a primary vehicle for communicating teacher's enthusiasm for subject matter, they react negatively to ideas for cooperative learning. (Holt-Reynolds, 1994, p. 5)

Within teacher education, as well as in other domains, then, the link between teacher-designed learning environments and student outcomes is uncertain and unclear.

Constructivism, while eliciting considerable energy and dialogue at the theoretical level, still has significant gaps. Connections between teaching and learning are undeveloped. Because learners can create any number of meanings, intended or otherwise, out of the same learning experience, it is critical at this juncture to develop a 'theory of supporting environments', to use Gelman's term. What isn't clear is what aspects of instruction learners attend to and how they use these in tandem with their prior knowledge to construct meaning. Needed are theories of instruction based upon constructivist learning principles that describe optimal learning environments. Such theory tailored to teacher education would offer ways to combine theoretical and practical knowledge in effective ways and would thus minimize the problems of misconstruction that Holt-Reynolds revealed. To advance the development of a theory of supporting we need information on candidates' prior knowledge, on their interpretations of program experiences, and on what they learn from these experiences. In the next section we present data gathered from candidates in our teacher education program that begin to address these issues. We then explore alternative theoretical orientations within the cognitive/constructivist paradigm that we've found useful in interpreting and understanding these data. Finally, we offer suggestions for further research and practice that grow out of this analysis.

Research Summary

Several themes have emerged from our research on teachers' knowledge growth in recent years. These have developed from studies using a variety of designs and measures. For example, an experimental design was used to determine whether knowledge structures were alterable by instruction (Winitzky, 1989). Correlational designs using a variety of measures of cognitive structure were employed to explore the concurrent validity of those measures and to examine the relationship of cognitive structure with other important variables (Henderson, Winitzky and Kauchak, 1996; Winitzky, Kauchak and Kelly, 1994; Winitzky, 1992). Longitudinal designs using both quantitative and qualitative measures have been used to describe the process of knowledge growth in teaching (Winitzky, 1992; Winitzky and Kauchak, 1992, 1995a, 1995b; Winitzky *et al.*, 1994).

Concept mapping has been our primary measurement tool. The collection of concept map data can be handled in two ways. Unstructured or free recall tasks provide subjects with a general topic, ask them to brainstorm terms, and to organize these into a concept map. In contrast, structured concept mapping provides subjects with a fixed list to draw upon and organize (McKeachie, 1987).

There are advantages and disadvantages to each approach. The unstructured method provides a picture of subjects' individual and idiosyncratic views of a domain, but lost is the capacity to focus specifically on course or target concepts of particular interest to the researcher. In addition, because each subject's map is unique, cross-subject comparisons are more difficult. On the other hand, the structured approach allows focused analysis and cross-subject comparisons, but is less useful for investigating individuals' developing conceptualizations of the domain. To counteract the deficiencies of each, we have used both approaches.

In scoring concept maps, we have assessed both conceptual accuracy, or coherence, and structural complexity. The coherence score is based on judgments about the logical relationship between each superordinate–subordinate pair and each chunk in the map. (A chunk is a group of concepts linked together.) Structural complexity includes scoring the number of concepts and the depth and breadth of the map. In practice we have relied most heavily on measuring structural complexity, because for beginners, structural complexity is highly correlated with coherence (Winitzky *et al.*, 1994). These scoring procedures have been validated by several researchers (Novak and Gowin, 1984; Roehler, Duffy, Conley, Herrmann and Johnson, 1988; Winitzky *et al.*, 1994). In addition, we have assessed turbulence, an indicator of conceptual stability, (Stoddart and Roehler, 1990) by measuring the degree of turnover of concepts from one point in time to the next. We have also evaluated maps qualitatively.

While concept mapping has anchored our methodology, we have complemented it with a variety of other measures. Structured interviews, for instance, provided insights into candidates' interpretations of their maps and thus their interpretations of their own knowledge growth. We've also asked candidates to analyze teaching cases to investigate how they applied abstract knowledge in particular situations, and how that changed over the course of the program (Winitzky and Kauchak, 1995a). Classroom observations and assessments of student learning have demonstrated connections between cognitive structure, classroom behavior, and student outcomes (Henderson *et al.*, 1996).

We review the major findings derived from this line of research below.

1   Initial knowledge is fragmentary and unstable

One of the most striking findings that surfaces again and again in our research is the fragmentary, incoherent, and unorganized nature of candidates' initial knowledge. Cognitive structure scores at the beginning of a program are consistently low. Candidates use few concepts in their maps, and the terms used do not represent professional or technical language. Inspection of early-program concept maps reveals little or no structure. Concepts are not linked to each other in organized hierarchies that would indicate that candidates relate terms logically to each other. Rather, terms are arranged haphazardly. In one first map on classroom management, for example, mini-maps on separate topics were spread out over the page and were not connected to each other. One of these mini-maps started with the term 'individual management' under which were subsumed 'good behavior' and 'bad behavior', indicating a very simple orientation to management.

Candidates often denote concepts in ways that suggest they think about them in functional or operational terms. Initial maps on classroom management frequently contained prescriptions like 'Don't sweat the small stuff', 'Be ready', and 'Love the kids into submission' as well as 'Procedures planned' and 'Rules need to be modelled and practiced especially at the beginning'. These rules-of-thumb suggest that candidates are struggling to make sense out of and integrate new professional learnings into plans of action for the classroom.

2   Structural knowledge increases over the course of preservice teacher education, and continues to increase with teaching experience

We have tracked teacher candidates' knowledge structures for different periods of time varying from a quarter to a year, and up to one year past graduation. In addition, we have examined expert teachers' knowledge structures in cross-section. In all but one case (Winitzky and Kauchak, 1992), structural knowledge increased with increased study and experience. Expert teachers' structures were the most highly organized and elaborated, followed by early-career teachers, then by teacher education students at program exit, and finally by candidates at the beginning of their professional studies.

Students at program exit used far more concepts and far more professional concepts than they did at program-start, often doubling the size of their maps with concomitant increases in complexity and coherence. In one study conducted one year after program completion, the structure scores of graduates who had taught continued the growth trend at an even steeper rate than they had during the program. These graduates also continued to use professional terminology to describe their teaching, suggesting that professional knowledge can lay the foundation for future professional growth (Winitzky *et al.*, 1994).

While teacher candidates tended to produce maps that contained twenty to forty concepts, experienced teachers produced coherent, elaborate maps that contained upwards of 100 concepts. In concept these findings suggest that concept maps are a valid indicator of knowledge growth, and that knowledge construction continues over the course of teachers' professional lives.

3   Knowledge growth is uneven and idiosyncratic

We have also been struck strongly by the variation and turbulence in knowledge growth displayed by beginning teachers. Concept maps revealed substantive differences between candidates and even in the same candidate over time. In one study focusing on instruction, for example, candidates used only about 4 per cent of the same concepts at program's end that they used at the outset (Winitzky and Kauchak, 1995b). At each measurement point, candidates seemed to be continuously trying on and discarding concepts. In one case, the candidate organized her initial map on instruction around the idea of teachers working either independently or cooperatively; at mid-program she structured her map around various teaching functions like management, assessment, and planning; near the end of the program, her map had increased in size sevenfold, had vastly improved in coherence, and she had expanded her simple classroom orientation to include cultural, community, and philosophical perspectives.

Another interesting trend across studies is the lack of between-student convergence in conceptualizations over time. In studies of our preservice candidates, even though they were progressing through the same program, taking classes from the same professors, and working in fairly similar field settings, our candidates still constructed idiosyncratic concept maps that converged only minimally over time. For one student, the concept of audience was a central feature in her final map on instruction; for another the notion of teaching as a career predominated; for yet another, management and curriculum duties were the focus. Similar patterns of idiosyncratic structural knowledge were also seen in experienced teachers (Henderson *et al.*, 1996). All four experienced teachers organized their maps for their subject area, history, in unique ways, some chronologically, some conceptually. Even though they were all elaborate, well-organized, and coherent maps, they were all very different from each other. These findings support the constructivist view that learners make meaning in unique ways, raising implications for a number of issues ranging from program design to evaluation.

4   Cognitive structure is influenced by a variety of factors, including instruction
While individual knowledge construction was predominately idiosyncratic, some patterns were still discernible. For example:

- Over the course of programs, candidates' use in their maps of a common professional language increased dramatically.
- Graduates who had taught for one year exhibited greater cognitive structure than those who hadn't (Winitzky *et al.*, 1994).
- Expert teachers' maps evidenced greater structure than novices' (Henderson *et al.*, 1996).
- Student teachers who were placed in field settings where the pedagogy closely matched that espoused in university coursework experienced greater structural growth than those in more conventional settings (Winitzky and Kauchak, 1992).
- In an experimental study, students taught cooperative learning in a traditional lecture format developed less organized knowledge structures than those taught with an approach grounded in schema theory (Winitzky, 1989).
- In one study of knowledge growth in classroom management, many candidates' maps at mid-program focused on classroom organization while at program's end, many centered on self-regulated learning; both conceptualizations reflected program emphases (Winitzky and Kauchak, 1992).

Taken together, these findings suggest that even though teachers construct knowledge in unique ways, program experiences in the form of both formal instruction and clinical experiences, as well as teaching experience itself, do influence what is learned.

Concept maps also appear sensitive to proximate contexts. In interviews candidates reported that they organized their maps the way they did because of last week's discussion in seminar, or a class they had just taken the quarter before, or a lesson and supervisory conference they'd just completed, or other recent events. This finding suggests that mapping may be an action representing emergent knowledge rather than a reflection of an intact knowledge structure, at least for beginners.

5   Cognitive structure is associated with other important variables
Several studies indicated that structural knowledge is linked to other desirable outcomes. For example, even though experienced teachers had larger, more

organized maps overall than novices, differences were still found between more versus less expert experienced teachers. Expert teachers, those with higher Advanced Placement pass rates, had more organized, elaborated knowledge structures than those teachers with lower pass rates, although both were equally highly coherent. Students of the high-structure teachers themselves displayed greater cognitive structure, and obtained higher scores on objective tests of the content than students of the less expert teachers (Henderson *et al.*, 1996).

In another study, cognitive structure was significantly correlated with the ability to reflect deeply about teaching (Winitzky, 1992). In another, the maps of students who were struggling in the program were much less elaborated and grew more slowly over time than those of more successful students (Winitzky and Kauchak, 1995b). Knowledge structure, it appears, correlates with a variety of indicators of teaching effectiveness.

6   Beginning teachers are often unaware of their own learning

Even though ideas represented on maps often changed in ways consistent with university methods classes and learning activities, candidates reported that they had not learned that much from methods classes or texts. For example, in a study on knowledge about instruction, candidates demonstrated no knowledge of direct instruction based on initial concept map and interview data. Later, after learning about direct instruction in methods classes, both map and interview data demonstrated that they had learned about it. But at the final interview, candidates reported that they had always known about direct instruction and had not learned about it in the program (Winitzky and Kauchak, 1995b). These findings lend themselves to differing interpretations. Perhaps candidates are unaware of the sources of their learning. Alternatively, certain types of knowledge, like procedural knowledge, may be automatized, rendering it unavailable to conscious thought or reflection. These results and interpretations are consistent with research on skill learning where tacit knowledge proves to be difficult for learners and researchers to access (Ford, nd).

Overall, our findings are consistent with the larger literature on beginning teachers' structural knowledge. Others have also documented the increase in knowledge structure over the course of teacher preparation programs (Roehler *et al.*, 1990; Stoddart and Roehler, 1990) and similar expert–novice differences (Strahan, 1989). Connections between structural knowledge and other variables of interest have also been established. Roehler *et al.* (1990), for example, showed that candidates with more sophisticated concept maps for reading instruction displayed more effective responsive elaborations during reading lessons. Michelson (1987) documented that student teachers with greater cognitive organization received higher ratings from supervisors. Artiles, Mostert, and Tankersley (1994) found that differences in candidates' concept maps were associated with differences in their patterns of classroom interaction and with student learning.

Making Sense of the Data

While this body of data provides a helpful starting point in elucidating beginning teacher learning, it is insufficient by itself. Needed are theoretical frameworks in which to embed these data, without which we are hampered in our
ability to interpret, understand, and apply our findings. To apply results in
refining constructivism and in creating an appropriate supporting environment
for teacher education students requires theory to make sense of data. We now
turn to exploring two alternate theoretical approaches: ACT-R and conceptual
change. We will briefly describe each perspective and then discuss how well
it helps us account for our data.

ACT-R

ACT-R (Adaptive Character of Thought-Rational) is a theory of skill learning
that has been referred to as 'the dominant cognitive architectural model' (Derry,
in press) and 'the most comprehensive model of memory and cognition'
(Bruning *et al.*, 1995). ACT-R appears to be a useful theory for understanding
knowledge growth in teaching for several reasons. First and foremost, it is a
theory of skill learning, and teaching ultimately involves doing. Also, ACT-R
grounds skill learning in problem solving, a view of teaching gaining currency
(Shulman, 1996; Sykes and Bird, 1992). In addition, two key findings from
our research pointed us in the direction of ACT-R. We found that candidates
often represented their knowledge on concept maps in the form of procedural guidelines or rules-of-thumb (eg., 'Love the kids into submission'). Such
heuristics suggest connections between declarative and procedural knowledge
consistent with ACT-R's representation of skill acquisition. Further, candidates
frequently seemed to be unaware of the sources of their learning. Such inability
to access skill knowledge at the conscious level is also consistent with ACT-R.
For these reasons, we explored ACT-R further.

ACT-R is a theory of skill learning developed by John Anderson (1993).
It posits two separate memory stores for declarative and procedural knowledge. Declarative knowledge involves facts and concepts, like understanding
the workings of the internal combustion engine, while procedural knowledge
involves skills, like knowing how to fix such an engine. Declarative is 'knowing that'; procedural is 'knowing how'. According to ACT-R, when confronted
with a novel problem, the learner integrates relevant declarative with procedural knowledge in working memory, executes some action with the goal
of solving the problem, and receives feedback on this effort. This feedback is
used to revise what is stored in memory. When next confronted with the same
type of problem, the learner begins the loop anew.

Over time, this process results in the creation of a production for executing
that specific skill, i.e., for solving that particular problem. A production is like

an action schema, and is defined in ACT-R as an 'if-then' statement: If a certain set of conditions are perceived, then a certain action is executed. A very simple example of a production one would use in driving a car might be: If you want to make a left turn, and if you are nearing the point at which the turn is to be made, then turn on the left blinker and move into the left lane now. In ACT-R, procedural knowledge is stored in the form of these if-then productions.

The learner acquires a skill, then, by actively engaging in problem solving in the new domain, bringing to bear any declarative knowledge that may be relevant, and receiving feedback on the outcome of his or her efforts. As the learner gains experience in solving problems within the domain, he or she 'compiles' that knowledge, that is, creates new, efficient, domain-specific productions.

Knowledge compilation accomplishes two things. One, it integrates and builds relevant declarative knowledge into a production; as this happens, it becomes unnecessary to hold that declarative knowledge any longer in working memory. Two, compilation collapses a series of smaller, fragmented productions into one production which now does the work of the whole sequence, allowing learners to string together a complex series of related skills into a smoothly coordinated process.

Let's use learning to drive a car to illustrate this process. Imagine you're 16 again and getting ready for driving lessons. You already know something about cars — you know what the steering wheel is for, you know you have to turn on the ignition with a key, and you have a vague idea about shifting gears. These and other pieces of information constitute your declarative knowledge about driving. Now you must convert that knowledge into actual skilled driving, or procedural knowledge. You sit in the driver's seat and turn the key over in the ignition. The car makes a terrible grinding sound. Your driving coach tells you that you've turned the key too long, that the engine has already started, and you can let up. This is feedback. In attempting to solve the problem of starting the car, you drew your declarative knowledge about ignition keys into working memory, applied that knowledge in turning the key over, received feedback from the car and your coach, and created your first set of productions: If I want to start the engine, then I must turn the key over; if I hear the engine turn over, then I let up on the key. You have proceduralized declarative knowledge, integrating it into a production for action. The next few times you start the car, you will need to stop and think about letting up on the ignition when the engine turns over. But with further practice, you will compile that knowledge, combining this and other starting-the-car productions into one smooth operation. Knowledge compilation frees you from having to stop and think as you execute each step. The same process is carried out with every aspect of learning to drive; step-by-step, through efforts to solve problems and through receiving feedback on those actions, jerky, error-ridden behaviour which has to be thought through at every point in the operation becomes a smooth, flowing, automatic, skilled performance.

What happens to declarative knowledge once it's compiled into productions? In answering this question, let's look at the process from the coach's perspective. Why doesn't the coach give a warning about not holding the ignition key over for too long? It is likely that the coach has so long ago compiled her knowledge about driving that this point has dropped out of conscious awareness, until reminded of it by the awkward error. This is often a characteristic of expert performance — the ability to verbalize procedural knowledge decreases with increasing skill. Most of us have had the experience of trying to tell a 5-year old how to tie his shoes, and know first-hand the frustrations for both parties. It's very hard to return to the step-by-step details once you have mastered them yourself, and unless you're reminded about these details, you've forgotten that you ever had to think about them. A by-product of increasing skill, then, appears to be the loss of awareness, and ability to describe the many subcomponents of skilled performance.

How does ACT-R help us understand our findings and the process of learning to teach? It does so in several ways. First, it highlights the reciprocal nature of the connection between declarative and procedural knowledge. The way our candidates mixed concept labels and rules-of-thumb in their maps is one piece of evidence of a connection between the two. It also suggests that they were actively seeking to integrate these two types of knowledge, as predicted in ACT-R. Also, our findings of a relationship between cognitive structure and a variety of indicators of teaching skill is further evidence of an important interaction between the two knowledge stores. These findings highlight the importance of developing declarative knowledge in teacher education programs.

Second, the fact that candidates were often unaware of the sources of their learning supports the ACT-R contention that as knowledge becomes proceduralized, it becomes less accessible to conscious awareness. If we really follow through on the implications of this, the impact on assessment of student learning and on program evaluation could be sizeable. For example, much more assessment would focus on performance and much less on self-reports.

Conceptual Change

ACT-R focuses on procedural learning. In contrast, the conceptual change literature focuses on declarative knowledge — on students' prior knowledge and on how their conceptions change in response to instruction. Since we argue that abstract, declarative knowledge has an important place in teacher education and since ACT-R suggests declarative and procedural knowledge interact, exploring the conceptual change literature was a natural choice.

The Conceptual Change Model (CCM) as originally formulated by Posner, Strike, Hewson, and Gertzog (1982) viewed the process of declarative knowledge growth as driven by the rational evaluation of opposing knowledge claims (Demastes, Good and Peebles, 1995). Conceptual change was considered a holistic, all-or-nothing process, similar to the way Thomas Kuhn (1970) described paradigm shifts, a battle between opposing views of the world, resulting in a victory of one conceptualization over another, one concept swapped for another.

These early dichotomous notions about conceptual change have gradually given way to a more complex picture. Chinn and Brewer (1993), for example, expanded the range of conceptual change response options available to learners. Based on their analysis of both the history of science and the conceptual change literature, they proposed that when confronted with a discrepant experience, learners respond in one of seven ways:

1   Ignore anomalous data, leaving original concept unchanged.
2   Reject anomalous data, invoking defence of the original concept.
3   Exclude anomalous data in such a way that the new experience is explained away as being outside the realm of the original concept.
4   Hold anomalous data in abeyance, leaving original intact.
5   Reinterpret anomalous data so that incompatible concepts are viewed as complementary and not antagonistic. (This was the response chosen by the teacher candidates Holt-Reynolds studied.)
6   Change conception peripherally, making minor modifications but leaving basic concepts intact.
7   Major conceptual change in which core concepts are rejected and replaced by new ones.

Conceptual change theory was further refined by including the notion of *conceptual ecology*, originally coined by Toulmin (1972). It is now argued that learners nest concepts within larger, interconnected networks termed conceptual ecologies. Within these ecologies are subsumed 'the learner's epistemological commitments, anomalies, metaphors, analogies, metaphysical beliefs, knowledge of competing conceptions, and knowledge from outside the field' (Demastes *et al.*, 1995). As the learner encounters new information, specific items within the ecology interact and influence how he will make sense of it (Strike and Posner, 1992). Depending on the interplay of his conceptual ecology with new material, the learner may reject the new conception, modify his ecology peripherally, or undergo one of the other possibilities listed above. No longer conceived as a battle between competing ideologies or unitary concepts, conceptual change is instead construed as a more interactive process in which prior concepts and beliefs influence and are influenced by new experiences. It is the interactive nature of the ecological perspective that makes it interesting to researchers attempting to understand learning within a constructivist perspective.

Implicit in these views of conceptual change, however, is the notion that learners bring with them to any learning experience a firm, coherent, existing knowledge structure that may be in opposition to the conception to be taught. The notion of resistance or at least inertia is assumed in most conceptual change models. Recently, though, that view has been challenged. DiSessa and his colleagues (diSessa, 1993; Smith, diSessa and Roschelle, 1993/94) argue that, rather than developed knowledge structures, learners more often bring instead 'knowledge-in-pieces' with them to the learning table. These small knowledge fragments, termed *p-prims* for phenomenological primitives, are isolated, disconnected bits of information floating about in memory that may be invoked by learners to help them make sense out of a new problem or situation. While a conceptual ecology might be analogous to a fully constructed house, p-prims are like the lumber lying around at a job site, ready to be used in a variety of ways as the situation warrants.

Hammer (1996) provides an illustration of the distinction. In one study grounded in the misconceptions tradition, students were asked why it is hotter in the summer than in the winter (Sadler, Schneps and Woll, 1989). Many replied incorrectly that it is hotter because the earth is closer to the sun. From a conceptual change perspective, this misconception must be an integral part of the students' knowledge systems, a faulty element in their conceptual ecologies, which was accessed by the question. But:

> Another interpretation would be that the students constructed that idea at the moment. This construction would be based on other knowledge, such as the (appropriate) knowledge that moving closer to the sun would make the earth hotter, but it is not necessary to assume that the idea itself existed in some form in the students' minds prior to the question . . .
>
> (Alternatively) . . . the question . . . may activate for them a p-prim connecting proximity and intensity: *closer means stronger*. This p-prim is an abstraction by which one may understand a range of phenomena: Candles are hotter the closer you get to them; music is louder the closer you get to the speaker; the smell of garlic is more intense the closer you bring it to your nose. It may be through the activation of *closer means stronger* that students generate the idea that the earth is closer to the sun in the summer. (Hammer, 1996, p. 102)

Conceptual ecologies and p-prims should not be considered mutually exclusive. A learner's prior knowledge could conceivably include both sturdy, well-organized knowledge structures as well as many disconnected p-prims. From an instructional perspective, however, it is important to distinguish learners' p-prims from their well-developed but erroneous knowledge structures. When encountering stable misconceptions, the teacher needs to confront these directly, providing discrepant experiences plus discussion and other activities to allow the learner to repair errors.

In contrast, however, when faced with p-prims, a different strategy is in order. P-prims are not misconceptions or erroneous beliefs; instead they represent unorganized, often accurate, abstractions that have not been subjected to instruction, analysis, and reflection and that are applied inappropriately in the absence of principled knowledge. Accordingly, teachers need to provide students instruction that helps them invoke p-prims appropriately, and integrate these with concrete experiences and concepts in the development of principled, structured knowledge. It is a matter of learning when the p-prim should and should not be applied and of organizing it into a coherent hierarchy, rather than rejecting the p-prim entirely. The student doesn't need to metaphorically tear down and rebuild the house, she just needs to use the right piece of lumber in the right place to construct the house in the first place.

In what ways are the conceptual change, conceptual ecology, and p-prim approaches consistent with our data? First, the anemic initial maps that candidates produce, in concert with the considerable turbulence they display from one map to the next, lead us to conclude that our students do not come to us with stable, well-organized knowledge structures about teaching that are resistant to change. Rather, they appear to bring with them many vague school-related notions that behave more like p-prims. In the absence of domain-specific, principled knowledge, both the ACT-R and p-prim views maintain that novice learners apply a 'next-best-thing' strategy in attempting to solve novel problems or interpret novel experiences. Lacking knowledge about instruction, for example, they may invoke their experience as a musician and emphasize the importance of audience, as one of our candidates did. The audience concept allowed her to organize a new situation in a way to make sense out of it. The task for the teacher educator in this situation, then, coming from a p-prim orientation, would be to guide the student in understanding in what ways teaching is like and unlike a musical performance. Of great theoretical and practical interest would be clarifying the p-prims that candidates bring with them and use to make sense of teaching and teacher education.

Another finding that suggests p-prims may be a productive way of thinking about candidates' prior knowledge is the fact that our candidates reported that recent events greatly influenced the way they constructed their maps. For example, one student said that a recent course in special education focused her on issues of student diversity and the ways that different professionals can work together to meet the needs of special populations. Whenever she observed in schools, she said, that is what she noticed, and that is how she organized her map. She emphasized that she would literally not have seen what was happening with special needs students without the preceding class (Winitzky and Kauchak, 1995b). We draw two conclusions from this. One, again we are struck by the importance of declarative knowledge and its inter-action with experience in focusing candidates' meaning making. University coursework helped this student attend to important aspects of teaching and schooling in the field. Two, this finding lends credence to the notion that mapping for beginners is a task of emergent knowledge, of knowledge construction, rather than a representation of an existing, solid knowledge structure. This student mapped what was on her mind, and what happened to be on her mind was the class she had just taken and the ideas she'd gleaned from it; she did not bring an elaborated structure with her to her teacher education program. If mapping does tap emergent knowledge, then thinking about beginners' knowledge in terms of p-prims makes even more sense.

Next Questions

In previous sections we discussed our research program on teachers' developing knowledge structures and explored alternate theoretical explanations of the findings. In this section we explore possible implications for constructivist teacher education research and instruction. We examine various theoretical principles derived from ACT-R and conceptual change, and speculate on how they might be applied in formulating a constructivist theory of supporting environments for teacher education.

For example, one precept from ACT-R is that it is through repeated efforts to solve a problem that learners acquire skill knowledge. This process takes time. One implication for teacher education might be to lengthen the period in which beginners participate in field experiences, since these are optimal settings for procedural learning to occur. If candidates have more time in the same setting, they will have more opportunities to solve teaching problems, more opportunities to experience feedback, and thus more opportunities to refine their productions for teaching. An inadequate amount of time in the field, or a field experience that is segmented into several different placements, could undermine this cumulative learning process.

This practice of extended field experience in a single setting is a key element in our elementary teacher education program. Candidates are placed with a cooperating teacher from their first week in the program. They spend two full days per week in that classroom for two quarters, and then spend the third quarter student teaching there full time. To compensate for this extreme focus on depth over breadth, in the fourth and final quarter of the professional preparation program we provide weekly observations in a variety of schools and classrooms to give candidates a sense of the diversity of school settings.

One problem with this arrangement is its rather haphazard, catch-as-catch-can nature. Different problems present themselves in no particular order, and candidates must do the best they can to make sense of and solve them. Of course, this is the essence of classroom life and unavoidable for practicing teachers. It may not, however, be an ideal learning environment for beginning teachers. Would it be possible, or even desirable, to incrementally stage the kinds of problems beginners face, perhaps through variations on microteaching or studying cases? What kinds of problems do beginners find easy to solve, and which ones are beyond their zone of proximal development? Research that systematically varies this aspect of the teacher education experience could prove fruitful in redesigning programs along constructivist lines.

There are further implications of this element of ACT-R. If skill learning relies so heavily on actual attempts to solve problems, what role does that leave for university-based teacher educators? We have basically only one kind of learning environment available to us, the university classroom. We may have access to public school classrooms where skill learning can actually take place, but we have little influence on that setting. Many lines of research, including our own, indicate that this can be problematic (Zeichner and Gore,

1990). If the concepts, beliefs, and skills dominant in the field are different from those advocated in the university, then ACT-R would predict that the view of the field will prevail. This is because skills are acquired in an environment of problem solving and feedback, in action, not in reading, discussing, or writing. Student teaching provides such an environment, university classes do not. Research and experience confirm this prediction. Many teacher educators and public school teachers are struggling to reduce this gap through Professional Development Schools and other collaborative reforms (Winitzky, Stoddart and O'Keefe, 1992). The instructional effectiveness of these efforts will ultimately be determined by the extent to which they construct productive problem solving environments for candidates.

In our own programs, we pursue several strategies for unifying field and university perspectives. For example, we meet regularly with cooperating teachers in a variety of formats to exchange information and perspectives. We maintain long-term relationships with a small number of schools to facilitate mutual understanding. We offer on-site cooperative master's programs to site-based teacher educators (Crow, Stokes, Kauchak, Hobbs and Bullough, 1996). We have created several district-university liaison positions to forge stronger connections between the two institutions. We also rely heavily on clinical faculty to advance coherence between the university and the field (Bullough, Kauchak, Crow, Hobbs and Stokes, in press). Public school faculty and administrators make frequent visits to our classrooms and conference rooms to provide input into programs. These all help, but further research and development is needed to create more powerful ways to link university and field and, in the meantime, to compensate for the disjuncture between our very different worlds.

Also helpful would be a more finely detailed understanding of how teacher candidates make sense out of their field experiences. If we had a better idea about what candidates find salient in the field, we might be able to create more effective ways to forge connections between the declarative and procedural knowledge learned in university and clinical settings. What aspects of field experiences do they attend to, and why? Concept maps may prove an economical tool to aid in this process. In the past, we have asked candidates to construct a map around a particular concept, like instruction or classroom management. Perhaps the prompt could be modified to capture significant insights or ideas gleaned from daily experience. Candidates could be directed to 'map what happened in your classroom today' or 'map the lesson you just completed'. Measures like these could provide valuable information about how candidates interpret field experiences.

Another principle from ACT-R involves feedback. Feedback is a key step in the loop creating the more and more efficient productions which guide skilled performance. Every teacher education program provides feedback to candidates through supervision from the university and the cooperating teacher. In our program, we provide additional avenues through our cohort structure in which candidates develop strong peer relationships over an extended period of time. The cohort structure, its concomitant seminar, coupled with multiple opportunities to observe and critique each others' teaching, provide additional ways for beginners to assess the success of their teaching. Another way, one probably underexplored, is through feedback from K-12 students themselves. The crux of successful teaching is its impact on students, so students should represent the most powerful feedback source for candidates from which they can refine their productions for teaching. Morine-Dershimer and her colleagues (see Artiles *et al.*, 1994) have found that candidates who think about their students are better teachers. Morine-Dershimer has also developed strategies for encouraging candidates to attend more to their students. We need to develop better ways for candidates to seek out and receive feedback from their own students on the success or failure of their teaching. An important theoretical question from an ACT-R perspective is how candidates interpret feedback from different sources. What counts to them as significant feedback? Whose feedback is most significant, and why? How do they determine when they've done well and when they haven't? How do these judgments influence their subsequent teaching?

ACT-R also specifies that in the initial phases of skill learning, relevant declarative knowledge is pulled into working memory and used to develop strategies for solving the new problem at hand. This suggests that declarative knowledge is important for acquiring procedural knowledge. We and others have found evidence of a relationship between declarative and procedural knowledge. This leads us to wonder how enhanced declarative knowledge could be used to improve beginners' initial efforts at learning the myriad of teaching tasks involving procedural knowledge. Most teacher education programs front-load declarative information and place field work later. From an ACT-R perspective, this is sensible when applied to the very earliest phases of skill learning. How much impact could be gained by strengthening this component of our programs?

To strengthen the declarative knowledge aspects of our programs requires us to look in turn at relevant theoretical constructs like conceptual change, conceptual ecology, and p-prims. DiSessa and his colleagues, for example, suggest that how beginners make sense of learning experience depends on which p-prims these experiences evoke. What p-prims do beginning teachers use to make sense of teacher education experiences? Do different experiences lead them to invoke different p-prims? How can we guide them to develop p-prims into more coherent, professional schemas? How can we productively use p-prims as a resource rather than an impediment to learning to teach? Current practices in teacher education like journalling and case study analysis may afford windows into candidate thinking that provide clues to these questions. Concept mapping used as an instructional as well as a research device may also be helpful in providing teacher educators with an efficient way of accessing candidates' thinking. Longitudinal research tracking program experiences in parallel with candidates' developing knowledge, as well as experimental studies systematically varying instruction and looking at variations in how candidates then make sense of it, would both advance our understanding of and our ability to provide an optimum learning environment for candidates.

Many teacher educators (e.g., Borko and Putnam, 1996) advocate openly challenging candidates' misconceptions about teaching and learning. This suggestion is in keeping with conceptual change perspectives on learning and the development of declarative knowledge. Certain program experiences may activate organized, firm conceptions that differ from those espoused in programs. In this case, it would be important to directly challenge these misconceptions. Challenge can come in a number of forms, ranging from field work that provides discrepant experiences, to analysis of complex case studies, to interaction with others whose views differ. These strategies are presently employed in many teacher education programs. For example, field sites are often located in low-income areas where students don't respond in ways that candidates anticipate. Also, seminars are usually conducted in which candidates can discuss differing perspectives on teaching. Both strategies are pursued in our program. Our extended cohort experience, because it allows candidates to develop the safety of close relationships over a long period of time, gives candidates the chance to feel comfortable enough to disagree with each other. However, the conceptual change literature, the teacher education literature, and our own experience as teacher educators all lead us to conclude that these strategies are less than effective in reshaping candidates' declarative knowledge. What is the problem? Is it that these experiences are not challenging enough? Or is it a faulty assumption that candidates invoke highly structured and resistant schemata to make sense of program experiences? If we're wrong about the knowledge candidates use to make sense of instruction, then our instructional strategies for modifying this knowledge may be misguided. We need to look more closely at how candidates interpret and respond to different learning experiences in order to design learning experiences matched to learning needs. This is central to constructivism. We need to sort out when p-prims versus complex knowledge structures are activated. And we need to create a more detailed understanding of what these p-prims and knowledge structures consist of. For this kind of in-depth understanding, case study research on individual teachers' knowledge construction appears promising (see Heaton and Lampert, 1993, for a prototype).

These are all essentially issues of prior knowledge. There is virtual consensus among teacher educators that understanding candidates' prior knowledge is key to improving teacher education (Borko and Putnam, 1996). Prior knowledge is central to constructivism, to ACT-R, and to all variations on conceptual change theory. Prior knowledge is pivotal in developing a constructivist theory of supporting environments. To provide learning experiences which appropriately challenge misconceptions, which appropriately build upon and develop p-prims, which help candidates appropriately apply declarative knowledge in the service of procedural knowledge development, and which most enhance procedural learning requires a more thorough understanding of the knowledge that teacher candidates bring with them to our programs. We need a better understanding of candidate knowledge in general, and we need better tools within programs to gather specific formative information on candidates' developing knowledge structures in our classes. Existing methods like concept mapping, journalling, and biography need to be refined and strengthened for both research and instructional purposes.

We also need to learn how to use various measures to complement each other. Rather than pit a narrative, say, versus a p-prim approach to understanding prior knowledge, we should ask, instead, what can we learn from each? For example, we have given thought to how findings from the narrative tradition inform our own work. Several scholars (e.g., Carter, 1993; Doyle, 1996) argue that it is through narrative that teachers organize their knowledge about teaching, and it is through narrative, as a consequence, that beginning teachers should be taught. In our studies, however, we find little evidence of narrative thinking. In interviews, candidates neither responded to questions in terms of narrative nor did narrative prompts evoke much from them (Winitzky and Kauchak, 1995a). How can these divergent findings be reconciled? We speculate that narratives, like concept maps, may represent emergent rather than crystallized knowledge, at least for beginners. Depending on task demands and recency effects imposed by the researcher, candidates represent their knowledge in a variety of forms. Combining data from different traditions, then, may provide additional insights into the workings of candidates' minds; our understanding is enhanced by drawing on multiple lines of evidence.

There may be other kinds of connections that can be made between these various ways of depicting and studying candidates' knowledge. For example, narrative may be one way to represent procedural knowledge. Recall that a production, the form in which procedural knowledge is stored in memory according to ACT-R, is an if-then statement giving the conditions under which an action is to be taken. Memory for skills in ACT-R consists of tying a particular action to a particular set of circumstances. Similarly, when knowledge is stored in narrative form, a context is given and the characters take certain actions in response to that context. Again, specific actions are tied to specific circumstances. Clearly there is a parallel structure in productions and narratives that link particular contexts with particular actions.

Alternatively, narrative may be more closely connected to declarative knowledge. For example, perhaps narrative represents the vehicle by which p-prims are invoked in particular situations. Since p-prims are abstract knowledge fragments, they require some contextualization in order to be sensibly applied to a given situation. Narrative may provide that sense-making structure. Or narrative may constitute an intermediate stage of knowledge development joining the fragmented p-prims with more elaborate, coherent propositional knowledge structures. This is a rich area meriting much further research.

Let's sum up. We stated at the outset that to accomplish our central task of developing a constructivist theory of supporting environments, of generating powerful applications of constructivism to the practice of teacher education, we needed to know several things. We need to have a much clearer picture of the prior knowledge candidates bring with them to our programs. We need to understand how they use this knowledge to interpret program experiences and what they then learn from these experiences. Our data and analyses have shed some light on these issues. For example, we have found that candidates' prior knowledge is quite idiosyncratic and fragmentary, more likely involving p-prims than elaborate, resistant misconceptions. We know they actively engage with program experiences to make sense out of them, that to a certain extent the sense they make is idiosyncratic, but that they do learn much of what we hope they will. We also know that they very often are not aware of how they came to learn this material.

We've also found that our research raises more questions than it answers. What is the relationship between declarative and procedural knowledge? How can we more accurately assess candidate knowledge for both research and formative instructional purposes? In what ways do candidates represent their knowledge? What are the implications for instruction of these various representations? Understanding the relationships between alternate knowledge forms — procedural and declarative, p-prims and conceptual ecologies, narrative and propositional — may be at the center of understanding how teacher candidates grow and develop. These questions should guide constructivist teacher education research over the next few years.

Devising a robust theory of supporting environments, in which developing abstract knowledge constitutes a central goal, is a critical next step in building constructivist teacher education. Borrowing principles from related theories of teaching and learning, like ACT-R, conceptual change, and p-prims, can help advance this process. Our own thinking has been enriched by cognitive learning theory, and we encourage others to explore the potential contribution that such theories can make to understanding teacher learning.

References

ANDERSON, J.R., REDER, L.M. and SIMON, H.A. (1996) 'Situated learning and education', *Educational Researcher*, **25**, 4, pp. 5–11.

ANDERSON, J.R. (1987) 'Skill acquisition: Compilation of weak-method problem solutions', *Psychological Review*, **94**, pp. 192–210.

ANDERSON, J.R. (1993) *Rules of the Mind*, Hillsdale, NJ, Lawrence Erlbaum Associates, Publishers.

ARTILES, A.J., MOSTERT, M.P. and TANKERSLEY, M. (1994) 'Assessing the link between teacher cognitions, teacher behaviors, and pupil responses to lessons', *Teaching and Teacher Education*, **10**, pp. 465–81.

BERLINER, D. (1994) 'Expertise: The wonder of exemplary performances', in MANGIERI, J. and COLLINS, C. (Eds) *Creating Powerful Thinking in Teachers and Students*, Fort Worth, TX, Harcourt Brace, pp. 161–86.

BIEDERMAN, I. and SHIFFRAR, M. (1987) 'Sexing day-old chicks: A case study and expert systems analysis of a difficult perceptual learning task', *Journal of Experimental Psychology: Learning, Memory, and Cognition*, **13**, pp. 640–5.

BORKO, H. and PUTNAM, R.T. (1996) 'Learning to teach', in BERLINER, D.C. and CALFEE, R.C. (Eds) *Handbook of Educational Psychology*, New York, Macmillan, pp. 673–708.

BULLOUGH, R., KAUCHAK, D., CROW, N., HOBBS, S. and STOKES, D. (in press) 'Professional development schools: Case studies of teacher and school change', *Teaching and Teacher Education.*

BRUNING, R., SCHRAW, G. and RONNING, R. (1995) *Cognitive Psychology and Instruction,* 2nd Ed, Englewood Cliffs, NJ, Merrill Prentice Hall.

CARTER, K. (1993) 'The place of story in teaching and teacher education', *Educational Researcher,* **22**, 1, pp. 5–12.

CHINN, C. and BREWER, W. (1993) 'The role of anomalous data in knowledge acquisition: A theoretical framework and implications for science instruction', *Review of Educational Research,* **63**, 1, pp. 1–49.

CROW, N., STOKES, D., KAUCHAK, D., HOBBS, S. and BULLOUGH, R. (1996) 'Masters cooperative programs: An alternate model of teacher development in PDS sites', Paper presented at the annual meeting of the American Educational Research Association, New York.

DEMASTES, S., GOOD, R. and PEEBLES, P. (1995) 'Students' conceptual ecologies and the process of conceptual change in evolution', *Science Education,* **79**, 6, pp. 637–66.

DERRY, S.J. (in press) 'Cognitive schema theory in the constructivist debate', *Educational Psychologist.*

diSESSA, A. (1993) 'Toward an epistemology of physics', *Cognition and Instruction,* **10**, 2 and 3, pp. 105–225.

DOYLE, W. (1996, April) 'Heard any really good stories lately? A critique of the critics of narrative in educational research', Paper presented at the annual meeting of the American Educational Research Association, New York (Also in press *Teaching and Teacher Education*).

FORD, J. (nd) 'Distinguishing tacit knowledge: Lessons learned from knowledge acquistion', Unpublished manuscript, Provo, UT, Brigham Young University.

FOSNOT, C. (Ed) (1996) *Constructivism: Theory, perspectives, and practice,* New York, Teachers College Press.

GELMAN, R. (1994) 'Constructivism and supporting environments', in TIROSH, D. (Ed) *Implicit and Explicit Knowledge: An Educational Approach,* Norwood, NJ, Ablex Publishing Corporation, pp. 55–82.

HAMMER, D. (1996) 'Misconceptions or p-prims: How may alternative perspectives of cognitive structure influence instructional perceptions and intentions?', *The Journal of the Learning Sciences,* **5**, 2, pp. 97–127.

HEATON, R. and LAMPERT, M. (1993) 'Learning to hear voices: Inventing a new pedagogy of teacher education', in COHEN, D.K., MCLAUGHLIN, M.W. and TALBERT, J.E. (Eds) *Teaching for Understanding: Challenges for Policy and Practice,* San Francisco, Jossey Bass.

HENDERSON, J., WINITZKY, N. and KAUCHAK, D. (1996) 'Effective teaching in advanced placement classrooms', *Journal of Classroom Interaction,* **31**, 1, pp. 29–35.

HOLT-REYNOLDS, D. (1992) 'Personal history-based beliefs as relevant prior knowledge in course work', *American Educational Research Journal,* **29**, 2, pp. 325–49.

HOLT-REYNOLDS, D. (1994, April) 'Learning teaching, teaching teachers', Paper presented at the annual meeting of the American Educational Research Association, New Orleans.

JUDD, C. (1908) 'The relation of special training to general intelligence', *Educational Review,* **36**, pp. 28–42.

KESSELS, J.P.A.M. and KORTHAGEN, F.A.J. (1996) 'The relationship between theory and practice: Back to the classics', *Educational Researcher,* **25**, 3, pp. 17–22.

KUHN, T.S. (1970) *The Structure of Scientific Revolutions* (2nd Ed), Chicago, University of Chicago Press.

McKEACHIE, W. (1987) *Teaching and Learning in the College Classroom: A Review of the Research Literature*, Ann Arbor, MI, National Center for Research to Improve Post-Secondary Teaching and Learning (ERIC Document No. ED 314–999).

MICHELSEN, S.S. (1987) 'Knowledge structure change of preservice teachers during field experiences and instruction', Paper presented at the annual meeting of the American Education Research Association, New Orleans.

NOVAK, J. and GOWIN, D. (1984) *Learning How to Learn*, New York, Cambridge University Press.

PEARSON, P.D., HANSEN, J. and GORDON, C. (1979) 'The effect of background knowledge on young children's comprehension of explicit and implicit information', *Journal of Reading Behavior*, **11**, pp. 201–9.

POSNER, G., STRIKE, K., HEWSON, P. and GERTZOG, W. (1982) 'Accommodation of a scientific conception: Toward a theory of conceptual change', *Science Education*, **66**, pp. 211–27.

ROEHLER, L.R., DUFFY, G.G., CONLEY, M., HERMANN, B. and JOHNSON, J. (1988) 'Knowledge structures as evidence of the "personal": Bridging the gap from thought to practice', *Curriculum Studies*, **20**, pp. 159–65.

ROEHLER, L., DUFFY, G.G., CONLEY, M., HERRMANN, B., JOHNSON, J. and MICHELSEN, S. (1990) *Teachers' Knowledge Structures: Documenting their Development and their Relationship to Instruction*, East Lansing, MI, Institute for Research on Teaching, Michigan State University.

SADLER, P.M., SCHNEPS, M.H. and WOLL, S. (1989) *A Private Universe*, Santa Monica, CA, Pyramid Film and Video.

SHUELL, T. (1996) 'Teaching and learning in a classroom context', in BERLINER, D. and CALFEE, R. (Eds) *Handbook of Educational Psychology*, New York, Macmillan, pp. 726–64.

SHULMAN, L. (1996) 'Just in case: Reflections on learning from experience', in COLBERT, J., DESBERG, P. and TRIMBLE, K. (Eds) *The Case for Education: Contemporary Approaches for Using Case Methods*, Boston, Allyn and Bacon, pp. 197–217.

SMITH, J., diSESSA, A. and ROSCHELLE, J. (1993/94) 'Misconceptions reconceived: A constructivist analysis of knowledge in transition', *The Journal of the Learning Sciences*, **3**, pp. 115–63.

STODDART, T. and ROEHLER, L. (1990, April) 'The development of preservice teachers' knowledge structures for reading', Paper presented at the annual meeting of the American Educational Research Association, Boston.

STRAHAN, D.B. (1989) 'How experienced and novice teachers frame their views of instruction', *Teaching and Teacher Education*, **5**, pp. 53–67.

STRIKE, K.A. and POSNER, G.J. (1992) 'A revisionist theory of conceptual change', in DUSCHL, R.A. and HAMILTON, R.J. (Eds) *Philosophy of Science, Cognitive Psychology, and Educational Theory and Practice*, New York, State University of New York Press, pp. 147–76.

SYKES, G. and BIRD, T. (1992) 'Teacher education and the case idea', in GRANT, G. (Ed) *Review of Research in Education* vol. 18, Washington, DC, American Educational Research Association, pp. 457–521.

TOULMIN, S. (1972) *Human Understanding*, Princeton, NJ, Princeton University Press.

WINITZKY, N. (1989, March) 'Inducing expert-like knowledge structures about co-operative learning in novice teachers', Paper presented at the annual meeting of the American Education Research Association, San Francisco.

WINITZKY, N. (1992) 'Structure and process in thinking about classroom management: . An exploratory study of prospective teachers', *Teaching and Teacher Education*, **8**, 1, pp. 1–14.

WINITZKY, N. and KAUCHAK, D. (1992) 'Cognitive structures for classroom management: Conceptual change in preservice teachers', Unpublished manuscript.

WINITZKY, N. and KAUCHAK, D. (1995a) 'Learning to teach: Knowledge development in classroom management', *Teaching and Teacher Education*, **11**, 3, pp. 215–27.

WINITZKY, N. and KAUCHAK, D. (1995b) 'Teacher candidates' knowledge acquisition: Tacit and explicit growth', Paper presented at the annual meeting of the American Education Research Association, San Francisco.

WINITZKY, N., KAUCHAK, D. and KELLY, M. (1994) 'Measuring teachers' structural knowledge', *Teaching and Teacher Education*, **10**, 2, pp. 125–39.

WINITZKY, N., STODDART, T. and O'KEEFE, P. (1992) 'Great expectations: Emergent professional development schools', *Journal of Teacher Education*, **43**, 1, pp. 3–18.

ZEICHNER, K. and GORE, J. (1990) 'Teacher socialization', in HOUSTON, W.R. (Ed) *Handbook of Research on Teacher Education*, New York, Macmillan.

5   Teaching about Thinking and Thinking about Teaching, Revisited

Magdalene Lampert

From 1978 until 1980, I was a participant observer in a professional develop-ment project for teachers in the Division for Study and Research in Education at the Massachusetts Institute of Technology.[1] Although we did not refer to it then by this term, the project would certainly qualify as 'constructivist'. In fact, it was constructivist in at least four different senses. First, it was intended to result in a change in classroom instructional practices toward teachers paying attention to students' ways of thinking about subjects like science, mathematics, and music. Teachers were to become 'researchers' in that they would do local inquiries into their students' ways of thinking about these domains. The project was designed such that the staff of the program did not 'tell' teachers either about the theory of constructivism or about how to apply it in their classrooms. So a second way in which the project was constructivist was that the teachers were to construct their own learning theories by reflecting on how they used and generated knowledge while doing tasks in the domains of music, mathematics, and science. A third constructivist thrust was that the teachers were expected to design methods for applying these theories to their classrooms. The teachers worked on these constructivist activities as a group in weekly meetings over a two year period. They talked about their teaching and about their observations of children, so the project was also a site for the social construction of ped-agogical knowledge,[2] even though it drew directly on the work of Piaget.[3] Finally, the project was constructivist in that the teachers were expected to construct their actions as teachers in face to face encounters with students while con-ducting research on students' thinking. We now refer to this way of thinking about knowledge as 'situative' or situated cognition.[4]

In 1978, the promotion of such practices was rare both in teaching children and in teaching teachers. In the past twenty years, however, many similar projects have been carried out. Teaching that is responsive to students' ways of thinking is supported in all subject matter areas by new curricula and assessment tools. We believe we should pay attention to how teachers and prospective teachers think about teaching and about subject matter, and to take their thinking into account in the design of preservice and inservice teacher education. The notion that teachers design instruction interactively with students is still uncommon, but not unheard of.

In 1984, I published the essay, 'Teaching about Thinking and Thinking about Teaching'.[5] *One purpose of this essay was to describe the teacher development project that I refer to here. That was the 'teaching about thinking' part. A second purpose was to 'think about teaching' — to examine the characteristics of teaching practice that might make it difficult to do the kind of teaching the project was designed to foster. Because the teachers who participated in this project were encouraged to make sense of the connection between learners' ideas and the formal knowledge traditionally taught in school, their talk about teaching included many references to the difficulties involved in integrating these ideas. They were treated as 'collaborators' by the members of the group whose profession was research, and their special contribution was interpreting the realities of the classroom in the context of the project.*

An analysis of the talk among project participants revealed the inherent tensions for teachers and teacher educators that result from adopting what we now generally call 'constructivist pedagogy'. The essay ends with the conclusion that the tension between individual construction and formal standards is endemic to knowledge building and cannot be resolved analytically by teachers, researchers, or teacher researchers. Teachers do teach, however, and they also do pay attention to students' ways of thinking. In the essay reprinted here, I explore the notion of the teacher as a person who can manage conflicting goals, even when those goals are analytically contradictory. I argue that the 'stories' teachers tell about their practice can represent these conflicts and how teachers cope with them, whereas paradigmatically expressed theories require resolution or choice.[6]

The kind of teaching and teacher education I wrote about in 1984 has become more common, but we still have few tools for examining how teachers cope with practical dilemmas and we know little about how to teach teachers to cope.[7] *The recognition that even traditional instruction is constructed interactively with students permeates the literature on teacher planning and classroom discourse that has mushroomed since 1984. There is continued controversy about how much of their knowledge teachers need to invent for themselves and how much they can learn from 'experts'.*[8] *The relationship between what scholars 'know' about teaching and the knowledge teachers use to do their jobs is a matter of continuing concern. There are many different conceptions of the 'teacher researcher' and arguments about the role of inquiry and reflection in competent practice.*[9] *It is for these reasons that we revisit this 'constructivist teacher education project' and the essay I wrote about it now, almost twenty years after the project occurred.*

A 10-year-old boy asked his fourth-grade teacher: 'Does Dataman have eyes?' He was wondering about his hand-held computer game that looks like a robot. 'If not, how does he know if my answers are right?'

There are several different ways a classroom teacher might interpret and respond to these questions, depending on how she understands children's thinking and her role in their learning. If she sees herself as the source of students' knowledge and the judge of their 'wrong answers', her response might be a short lecture about how 'computers know the answers because they are programmed by people'. The boy's question would be taken as evidence that he is not very intelligent: and his teacher would relate to him in the future on the basis of this judgment. From another perspective, the teacher might think of the boy's question as a distraction from the task she has assigned to the class. She might see herself as responsible for planning appropriate lessons and activities for all of her students, throughout the day, to meet particular goals. She would thus respond by refocusing the boy's attention and behavior on the lessons the class is supposed to be learning. In both of these views, the teacher is the source of knowledge and the organizer of its acquisition.

Another way to interpret the boy's question about Dataman's 'eyes', however, is to see it as his attempt to understand a new experience. He could be using an idea that makes sense to him as a way to figure out how computers process information. From this perspective, the teacher's response might be to explore the implications of *his* way of thinking about the mechanical toy, perhaps asking him, 'How do you think Dataman can tell what your answers are?'[10] It would be crucial for the teacher to understand what the boy already knows about how 'Dataman' works, so that she could direct his learning process in a way that would make connections with this knowledge. Even though his idea about Dataman's 'eyes' is at odds with the conventional way we explain how computers process information, it is intuitively meaningful to him, and therefore suggests an appropriate place for the teacher to begin her lessons.

This third — personal and active — view of the learning process redefines the teacher's work to include on-the-spot clinical research into the way a learner thinks about something.[11] During the past four years, this concept of teacher-as-researcher has been the subject of a study at the Division for Study and Research in Education at Massachusetts Institute of Technology. The study was built around a series of weekly seminars attended by both researchers and public elementary school teachers. The seminars had several aims, and both their form and their content have raised some interesting questions about the relationship between scholarly inquiry and classroom practice.

The first goal of the project was to train the teacher-participants to recognize what its designer, Jeanne Bamberger, called 'intuitive knowledge'. In her view, each individual builds a store of this commonsense sort of information from personal experimentation on the physical environment. Such knowledge is not usually made explicit, but is often useful and powerful. It contrasts, therefore, with the 'formal knowledge' one is taught in school: a commonly accepted set of well-articulated 'descriptions' of experience, which may have little connection with the knowledge individuals regularly apply in their everyday lives.[12] The project staff devised activities which would help the teachers to distinguish between their own intuitive ways of making sense of various phenomena and the formal knowledge they had been taught in school.

Given this background, the teachers and researchers together were to pursue the second goal, and major purpose of the project: to explore how this appreciation of intuitive knowledge could be useful in educational practice. The hope was that this work would result in practical strategies to help individual children connect their intuitive ways of understanding experience with the conventional formulas everyone needs to know to succeed in school and society. Developing and implementing these strategies was to be the work of 'teacher-researchers':

> center[ing] on the image of teacher as teacher-researcher as opposed to the prevalent image of teacher as link in a knowledge-delivery system . . . extends the teacher's self-image and her intellectual engagement by providing a richer intellectual definition of her task.[13]

By this redefinition of the teacher's work, the project sought to bring teaching practice closer to the work of researchers trying to understand how children learn.

The staff of the project included two cognitive psychologists: Bamberger, who has done considerable research relating intuitive knowledge of music to learning formal music theory, and Eleanor Duckworth, who has endeavored to make Piaget's theories and research accessible to teachers. Bamberger and Duckworth constructed musical, mathematical, and physical tasks for the teachers which were meant to make them more conscious of the usefulness of their own intuitive knowledge. They demonstrated clinical research methods with children, and they led discussions with teachers of the use of these methods in the classroom.

The teacher-participants volunteered in response to an advertisement for the project which was circulated in their school district. It briefly described the idea of a 'teacher-researcher' and explained the proposed format of the project. The seven teachers who became involved represented a wide variation in grades taught, kinds of schools and classrooms in which they worked, age and years of experience, ethnic and educational background, and personal life styles. All of them participated actively in the project during the 1978–1979 and 1979–1980 school years. The teachers continued their daily work in classrooms while they met once a week with the staff of the project, and members of the staff observed periodically in each teacher's classroom to develop a shared context for discussion.

As an experienced school teacher and teacher-educator, my role in the project was to help the teachers articulate their perspective on classroom practice. I also documented the activities and discussions that occurred in the weekly seminars. It is the perspective of practice, therefore, which I bring to this case study of the project, informed by a careful analysis of what the teachers said about teaching in their conversations with one another during the seminars. From my perspective, as participant-observer, the identification of the teachers as both practitioners *and* researchers and the multiple aims of the seminar put them in a somewhat ambiguous and often frustrating position. I will address this problem in my analysis of the project. In training the teachers to do clinical investigations of children's thinking, the project looked like many other attempts at staff development or in-service training, with the teachers being 'students' of academic researchers who had ideas about how practitioners could do their job better. The notion that the teachers thus trained would then become collaborators in addressing a research problem defined by psychologists complicated their role considerably. The teachers who participated in this project were also paid and treated as 'consultants', and they were encouraged to articulate their own ideas about the problems of teaching. These varied definitions of the relationship between the teachers and the researchers often left everyone confused about who was 'in charge' of the weekly meetings. Yet the structure did allow the teachers to question the researchers' definitions of pedagogical problems and their assumptions about how to 'fix' the practice of teaching.[14]

Whatever else it accomplished, the project raised fundamental questions inherent in the relationship between academic research and classroom practice. It is these questions that I wish to examine in this paper. In the first part of the paper I describe how the project operated; in the second I consider the conflicts that teachers faced as a consequence of participation. The teachers' conflicts arose out of their attempts to translate theory into practice. Ideas about children's thinking which had been useful to researchers in a loosely defined form led to impossible practical dilemmas as these practitioners tried to make sense of them in terms of concrete classroom procedures. However, when the same teachers diverged from the researchers' agenda and told informal stories about their work, the conflicts that they had conceived seemed to be managed within their sense of themselves as teachers. The teachers' stories reveal ways in which the practitioner uses her 'self' to manage the potential contradictions in her work, thus challenging the traditional notion that conflicts are resolved through research and then research 'implemented' by practitioners.[15]

Teaching Teachers about Thinking

The work of the teacher-researcher, as conceived by Bamberger, is 'helping the child to coordinate his own intuitive knowledge (what and how he knows already) with the more formal knowledge contained in the privileged descriptions taught in school and shared by the community of users'.[16] The belief that such coordination is necessary is built on the assumption that the *intuitive* knowledge of the individual child can be understood separately from the *formal* knowledge of school and society. Therefore, in order to build connections between these theoretically disparate elements, the teachers first needed to learn to be able to distinguish between them. They needed to acquire both the psychologists' way of thinking about knowledge, and the clinical research skills that would enable them to put aside conventional assumptions about what is worth knowing so as to examine a child's way of making sense of something.[17] Bamberger framed the following questions to guide the teacher-researchers' inquiry:

> How are the child's descriptions different from those formal descriptions accepted as norms in the school setting; what is the nature of the mismatch; and finally, how can [the teacher] help him to integrate his own useful, even powerful, ways of knowing with the expectations of school and community?[18]

The view of knowledge underlying the project's design places a high value on the child's intuitive understanding. Intuitive knowledge is considered to be powerful and useful to the individual person. In contrast, formal knowledge is thought of as separate from the persons who are learners. It is considered 'privileged', and thereby presumably alien to the child. At the same time, it is the kind of knowledge 'taught in school' and 'shared by the community of users'. Thus the design of the project echoed a familiar theoretical dichotomy between the individual and society.

As the teachers were trained to become teacher-researchers, they were expected to use this dichotomous perspective to understand classroom practice. As they did this, the *distinction* between intuitive and formal knowledge was translated into a set of practical *dilemmas*. The job of making connections between these two kinds of knowledge, i.e., between the child, and school and society, thus became much more difficult than the project's designer had anticipated. While the teachers agreed that doing research on their students' ways of understanding something seemed essential, they perceived a conflict between that sort of attention to individual differences and implementing the school curriculum. The teachers' new appreciation of the psychology of individual learning seemed to be at odds with their understanding of the responsibilities of their job, yet a clear choice between these two alternatives was also out of the question if they were to take both the project and their jobs in schools seriously.

This dilemma did not surface immediately. At the beginning of the project, the teachers were involved primarily in examining their own thinking processes in areas unrelated to the subject matter they were teaching. They participated in a variety of activities designed to help them recognize the usefulness of their own, informal strategies for solving problems. Bamberger chose to have the teachers do musical tasks in the early weeks of the project precisely because it was a subject in which they would not have had much formal training. She assumed that, although music was a domain in which nearly everyone has experience, it was not as encumbered with learned formal descriptions and societal expectations as the more central school subjects like mathematics and reading.

One of the first tasks the teachers were given, for example, was to compose a tune that would 'sound good', using a set of five individual metal bells.

The bells would make sounds of different pitches when struck with a wooden mallet. Bamberger encouraged each teacher to articulate the various qualities which she thought made *her* tune sound good. The teachers thus practiced doing clinical investigations of individual understanding by reflecting on their own ways of making sense of music. They also analyzed videotapes of the researchers interacting with children who did similar tasks.

After doing these activities for several weeks, the teachers were asked to bring the group instances from their own classrooms in which a child talked about something in a way that seemed 'puzzling'. The research staff helped the teachers to speculate on the structure of the intuitive knowledge that the child was bringing to the situation. Suzanne, a fourth-grade teacher, told about Lenny, who had asked her, 'Does Dataman [a small computer] have eyes?' She reported her first reaction to his question as follows:

> My immediate thought was that he thought it was a living thing, had eyes, was connected with a living thing. At first, my aide and I were both so flattened by the idea that a fourth grader would think that Dataman could have eyes or could hear or speak that we just left it and said, 'No. It doesn't'. He said he thought it could see because it — 'he' — told you whether your answer was right and if 'he' wasn't able to see, 'he wouldn't be able to do that'.[19]

Suzanne explained that she and her aide were 'flattened' because they just couldn't believe that this 10-year-old boy did not know that machines could not have eyes, and she expressed her distress at the thought that Lenny might actually think computers are alive. She assumed, at first, that he did not *know* something he should know, and that explaining to him how computers work was *her* job. It was in such discussions of their own students that teacher views about the importance of formal knowledge in classrooms began to surface.

In presenting this problem to the group, Suzanne called Lenny's question 'silly' and wondered about the boy's 'intelligence'. She said that he 'was not very smart in math, either', she worried about whether he would learn all that she was supposed to teach him during that year, and she said she told him that Dataman recognized his answers because it is 'programmed'. However, she admitted that she did not really know exactly how the machine works. But what she did know, and what she said she really wanted Lenny to know, was 'that there was definitely not a person or a brain in there working'. Suzanne favoured transmitting formal knowledge rather than examining how she or the child might make sense of the machine's workings.

The staff asked the teachers: 'what might Lenny have been thinking that prompted him to ask his question in the first place?' Although whether Lenny was right or wrong in his thinking, or whether he needed to be taught something about how computers work, were issues of some interest to the teachers, the group was directed to try and imagine how someone might think that a computer might have 'eyes'. The teachers began to wonder whether the boy may have been asking a question that was somewhat more complicated than the literal ones: 'Does it have eyes?' or 'Is it alive?' and they found themselves questioning just how Dataman could, in fact, tell you whether your answer was right or wrong if it didn't somehow 'see' your answer. One member of the group compared Lenny's reasoning process with the way she, and other adults, might think about computers:

> We talk about a computer as a 'brain' with a 'memory' and we also talk about memory being a human being's memory. The eyes are the pathway, the input to the brain. This is getting very theoretical about what this child was up to, if any of these things. But how *could* this thing know whether the answer was right or wrong?

This teacher was using her own way of thinking about computers to assess the legitimacy of the student's way of thinking. These considerations of how Dataman 'knows' led to the idea that it was not necessarily 'stupid' or 'silly' to refer to the computer as having 'eyes'.

What Suzanne had first presented as a 'silly question', which had distracted her and her student from what he was *supposed* to be learning, thus came to be understood as a question of considerable significance: 'He got a machine and he wondered about the essential differences between machine and man; but it's just that he wasn't sure . . .'. At the end of this session of analyzing the child's question, Suzanne had quite a different view of Lenny's 'intelligence':

> I had not thought of this child as being very intelligent, but you're right, in that he *should* be thought of in that way since he did ask that kind of question. It's a higher level of thinking, if he's thinking about trying to make that distinction between robot and computer and man and whatever.

By working on this and similar 'puzzles', we hoped that teachers would gain a new perspective for looking at their interaction with students — the possibility of responding to a student's question, not with an answer, but with more questions constructed to help the teacher better understand the *student's* way of thinking.

An example presented by Helen, another fourth-grade teacher in the group, illustrates the development of the teacher's experiments with sustained inquiry into their students' ways of understanding what they learn. It represents the other side of the work of the project: an application of that research in classroom practice.

Mario had come into school one day asking his teacher, Helen, for an explanation of something he had been told by his father. Helen told the group:

> Mario, in his usual (somewhat belligerent and challenging) way said: 'My father said we didn't have whatever that thing was yesterday'. Then I said, 'The *eclipse*. What did your father tell you about it?' Mario answered (with doubled assurance) 'He said we didn't have it because it was snowing'.

Helen recognized Mario's confusion, and at first, she believed it would be relatively simple to clear up. She thought that he had misunderstood his father. What he needed to know was that the eclipse was happening behind the clouds even though he didn't see it because it was snowing. But the lesson turned out to be not so simple: 'I told Mario we had it; even though it was snowing, you look behind the clouds. He walked back to his seat and about half an hour later, he said to me, "My father doesn't lie to me, we didn't have it"'.

Initially, Helen perceived a difference between the boy's understanding of the eclipse and her own. But rather than simply telling him *her* understanding, she also tried to explore *his* construction of what happened to the eclipse. She explained her initial attempts to get the matter cleared up:

> That next day was also a very cloudy day, and so I asked, 'Where do you think the sun is today?' and he just shrugged his shoulders. I took a book and put it in front of the shade cord and asked him if he could see the cord. He said 'no', and I explained to him that is how it is with the sun when it is behind the clouds. And he said, 'But my father —'. I concluded that he still couldn't understand that it [the eclipse] happened behind the clouds. So anyway, I didn't know what to do.

When Helen presented this problem for discussion, the staff encouraged the group of teachers to try to figure out what Mario might have been thinking.

At the next seminar session the following week, Helen said that what she thought about was 'how I could phrase my question [about the sun] to him so he would say, "It's in the sky", which is what I want to know if he understands'. Her approach to Mario became a combination of figuring out how *he* was thinking about the problem and finding out whether he knew what *she* considered to be some essential basic information about how the solar system works.

She reported her subsequent interaction with him as follows:

> So when it was a cloudy day on Friday, I said to him, 'What happened to the sun today?' and he looked at me like I was from Mars, and said, 'It's in the sky'. He must have seen the look of relief on my face because he said 'What's the matter?'

Having ascertained that he understood that the sun was there, behind the clouds, on a cloudy day, Helen then came back to the question of the eclipse:

> Then I said to him 'you know that eclipse we had? Did we have it here?' He said 'Well, no. Well, I guess. Well, I'm not sure'. I said, 'I guess what I'm asking you is did it happen in the sky over us?' He said, 'Yah'.

Still testing her understanding of Mario's understanding, Helen said she had asked him some more questions and found that he was aware that the eclipse did happen behind the clouds, even though we couldn't see it. By 'not having it', he had meant 'not seeing it'. She presented her conclusions to the group: 'I have been on such a wrong track with him. The "where" meant: he wanted to point to "there, there it is". But I was thinking he didn't know it was there at all. So I was happy to find out he did'. Helen's probes demonstrated to her that Mario thought she had initially been asking him to point to the exact spot in the sky where the sun was behind the clouds. He did not think he could do that when he made his first comments, and so she had tentatively concluded that he didn't know that the sun was there behind the clouds. Yet after the second interaction, she thought that *she* was the one who had not understood what he was thinking.

Helen had decided that Mario did not need a lecture about where the sun is on a cloudy day. In fact, such a lecture may have only served to confuse his sense of the relationship between the sun, the clouds, and the Earth. Through discussion of Mario with the group Helen had developed a different sense of the *purpose* of teachers asking students questions. She had not simply judged Mario's answers to be right or wrong, but had considered them as indicating how *he* perceived the position of the sun on a cloudy day.

Based on my analysis of examples like these and teachers' reflections on their own intuitive ways of making sense of various phenomena, it became clear that the teacher-participants had changed their thinking in at least three significant ways: they had expanded their sense of what it means to know something so as to include what the knower figures out for himself or herself, thus complicating the meaning of a 'right' answer and their sense of what makes a student 'intelligent'; they had become more confident in their own ability to figure things out, ranging from problems in music and physics and mathematics to problems of how and what to teach in schools; they had begun to think that clinical-style research investigations, with individual children in classrooms, *might* be a part of their classroom work.

The teachers seemed equipped to examine and appreciate students' intuitive ways of making sense and to see, by reference to their own experience, how such individual ways of making sense were different from the formal descriptions accepted as norms in the school setting. However, having learned the *researchers'* distinctions between intuitive and formal knowledge, these teachers had a difficult time with the idea that the two different ways of knowing could be *integrated* in the classrooms where they worked. As they thought concretely about how their teaching was organized and their own position as knowledgeable authorities, they raised several problems which had not been among the researchers' concerns:

> If students construct their own understanding of something, like how machines work, or relationships in the solar system — what is the connection between what they understand and what a teacher knows to be 'the right answers?'
>
> And these right answers, which are printed in the textbooks we use, and measured on the tests we give — where did they come from? And aren't they important? And what does it mean for teachers and students to know something if they don't really understand it?

What Bamberger had called 'formal knowledge', the teachers called 'right answers'. This distinction suggests some of the reasons why what had been an interesting difference for the researchers became a *practical* problem for the teachers. The formal knowledge that is 'taught in schools' is, in fact, taught by *teachers*. It is the source of their power and authority in the social institutions where teaching and learning occur and where norms are established. These norms include what is to be defined as useful knowledge in the classroom. It is not surprising, then, that formal knowledge would have a different *functional* meaning for teachers than it has for researchers.

In school, formal knowledge is not one among many ways of knowing; it is the 'right' way. When the teachers worked as teacher-researchers, however, they were expected to be detached from this formal standard. They were supposed to accept intuitive knowledge as useful and powerful, and to refrain from judging the child in terms of what they or other authorities thought he should know. At this stage of the project the teachers began to sense some of the contradictions involved in adopting the project's view of their role *vis-à-vis* knowledge. Here, the case of Lee is instructive.

Lee, a sixth-grade teacher, wondered whether accepting the reality of differences in individual understanding meant that she would have to give up assigning the *same* textbook work to her whole class. If her students came to an assignment with different ideas about what they were supposed to do, she concluded that she would not be able just to look at their answers as a way of judging what they did or did not understand. Her dilemma was a choice between acknowledging individual differences and measuring students' knowledge by textbook standards. She knew she had to do both, but in the context of the project, she was worried: 'I have the terrible feeling that if this process [the research] goes too far, I'm *never* going to be able to assign page 98 again'.

Here, Lee uses 'assigning page 98' to represent an essential aspect of the way teaching and learning are organized in schools. In a given classroom, one teacher is responsible for instructing a large group of children, all of whom have roughly the same level of knowledge of the subjects taught in school. Textbooks are a standard measure of the class's and the teacher's assignment and their *progress*.

In giving an assignment in a textbook to a whole class, Lee assumes that these twenty or thirty different students are supposed to be able to do something — long-division, let's say — and she has a clear responsibility to ensure that her students can do long division correctly. It is not surprising, therefore, that being asked to give up the functions served by the knowledge needed to complete 'page 98' correctly might give this teacher a 'terrible feeling'.

This use of knowledge is different from exploring a child's knowledge about 'Dataman' or 'the eclipse'. In these cases it was not too difficult for the teachers to imagine themselves as *researchers*, exploring and appreciating *one* student's particular way of thinking and indeed, their sense of a student's 'intelligence' was enriched by such exploration. There were no curricular guidelines on these particular subjects to provide a sense of school norms or expectations. No long division was there to be mastered by all of the students.

In the seminar, Bamberger responded to Lee's worry about giving up the standards reflected in the textbooks with the comment: 'It would be interesting to see how all these different mixes of things would interlace with page 98', i.e., what different children, with different prior knowledge and different abilities, would do with the same assignment. As a researcher, for whom the 'mismatches' between individual understanding and the school curriculum are *valuable* data, she has no responsibility for what children have or have not learned. However, the teachers had a different view of the situation. Jessica, for example, responded to the nature of the *researcher's* interest in children's thinking with the assumption that Lee probably *'already knows . . .* how many different things can be done on page 98!' — implying, by her tone of voice, that for a teacher to have such information would be, not interesting, but troublesome. If it is the teacher's job to get students to learn what is in the textbook, different answers indicate that her job has *not* yet been accomplished. There may be little feeling of accomplishment for a teacher in recognizing that a *variety* of answers may result from each student's unique interpretation of an assignment. But more importantly, Lee thought that she must decide *either* to continue to assign 'page 98' and disregard individual interpretations *or* to give up making uniform assignments based on the textbook which she considered to be a necessary tool of her trade. Her sense of the demands of the theory she was learning seemed to make the first inappropriate, and the nature of her practice as a sixth-grade teacher to make the second impossible. She felt immobilized by the contrary ways in which her responsibilities seemed to be defined. Lee saw herself faced with a choice between understanding individuals and succeeding as a teacher in terms defined by the institutions within which she was working. As one of the other teachers put it, her 'thoughts' about theories of individual learning seemed to be contrary to the 'facts' of practice in a public school classroom. Such ambiguous interpretations of what they were supposed to be doing left the teachers frustrated, and sometimes even angry about their participation in this project. We turn now to an analysis of these contrary tendencies which flowed from assumptions of the project.

Thinking about Teaching

The way these teachers analyzed their work into contradictory responsibilities is not unique. Although their thinking could be attributed to the dichotomous way in which the project defined the work of the teacher-researcher, the conflicts they felt parallel those identified by several scholars who have attempted to understand the work teachers do. Philip Jackson, for example, describes the institutional standards of classroom life as 'threatening to the student's sense of uniqueness and personal worth'; he sees the teacher's role, therefore, as 'fundamentally ambiguous': '[The teacher] is working for the school and against it at the same time. He has a dual allegiance — to the preservation of both the institution and the individuals who inhabit it'[20]. In these terms, if a teacher distinguishes among the individual learners in her classroom, according to the differences in how they understand something, her allegiance to school stand-ards like textbooks and tests is called into question. Gertrude McPherson, who did an intensive study of teaching in a small-town school, found similar con-tradictions in the job. She analyzed the differences in expectations placed on teachers in their various professional relationships: by students, other teachers, administrators, parents, the larger community. These relationships define the teacher's 'role set'. McPherson concluded:

> It should be clear from this study that much of the teacher's internal conflict
> is built into the role set; that the conflicting expectations of different interested
> parties are not easily changed or made congruent either through organizational
> changes or improved communication.[21]

One endemic conflict in the teacher's 'role set' is between the needs of students and the standards of the institution. McPherson found that what the teacher has come to believe is appropriate practice in relations with *individual* learners is contrary to what is expected by others outside the classroom, who have the power to decide whether she is doing a good job. Teachers cannot easily resolve their dilemmas by allying themselves with one set of expecta-tions or another. The nature of the relationships among the people who can influence what they do — parents and children, for example, or the principal and the other teachers in the school — makes that solution impossible.

When Dan Lortie asked teachers how they manage the conflicting expecta-tions that result from the way schools are organized, he found them to be 'ambivalent' and conflicted about how their job should be defined. He summed up their sentiments as follows:

> There is a certain ambivalence, then, in the teacher's sentiments. He yearns
> for more independence . . . but he accepts the hegemony of the school system
> on which he is economically and functionally dependent. He cannot ensure
> that the imperatives of teaching, as he defines them, will be honoured, but he
> chafes when they are not . . . In any event, the feelings I have discerned among
> Five Towns teachers are internally contradictory and reflect dilemmas in the
> role.[22]

Lortie interpreted teachers' general feelings about their work as expressing a contradiction between their own ideas about how to relate to students as individuals, and the constraints and rewards of the organization in which their teaching occurred.[23]

The teachers who participated in the MIT project seem to have arrived at the same conflicted conclusions. Bamberger had hoped that the teachers could find pedagogical strategies for making *connections* between individual under-standing and institutional expectations. But as the teachers examined the purposes of their work in terms of the distinctions between individual and formal knowledge, and as they continued their work in classrooms, these connections seemed to them something of a *practical* impossibility. The more they accepted the theorists' view of learning and teaching, the more they were frustrated — alternately wanting to understand individual children better, and feeling that such understanding might actually *get in the way* of the job they have to do in the classroom. These teachers' sense of contradiction between a researcher's concerns and their own practical concerns in the classroom (such as class size, behavior problems, and external interference) parallels that described by John Elliott in his analysis of a program in Great Britain designed to train teachers to plan activities to match an individual child's developmental level. In Elliott's view, teachers could not assume a researcher's perspective on their students because it did not take account of the complexity of their responsibilities; they saw the program's expectations as 'isolating certain events for special attention to the neglect of others'.[24] Even though the teachers may have concurred that the researcher's concerns for individual children were important, they could not give them the absolute attention that seemed to be expected.

The tension between individual and social standards seems to be at the very heart of teachers' work.[25] Students have had different experiences and have different ways of making sense of those experiences, and therefore bring a wide range of interpretive frameworks to the lessons they are learning in school. It is also the case that there are certain things taught in school that are useful for *everyone* to know, and that a student's success in learning them may affect his or her whole life. From the perspective of an individual's system of ideas, however, this standard knowledge is only one among many ways of understanding and describing experience. From the project's point of view, an individual's way of understanding his or her own experience was considered to be a more useful and powerful way of knowing, and, in the long run, a more powerful base on which to erect teaching strategies.[26]

As these teachers sought to move from being teachers to being teacher-researchers, it is not surprising that they felt some contradictions in their work. While learning to recognize children's ways of constructing their own knowledge from experience had informed their teaching and the way they thought about children, the dichotomous ways of thinking about practice which they derived from the project's psychological theory did not appear useful. Trying to figure out whether it would be better to pursue a child's intuitive knowledge *or* to teach the formal curriculum seems to have been counter-productive. While arguing for the superiority of one purpose or another might have been an appropriate *academic* activity, it did not seem to the teachers particularly connected to the problems they worked on every day in their classrooms. These problems surfaced when teachers told 'stories' to each other at informal moments during our meetings about what they actually did in their classrooms.

The contrast between the contradictions the teachers expressed in their speculative *seminar* discussions and thus the ideas about teaching that can be found in 'stories' they tell about their practice is significant. It raises two questions that seem useful in examining the relationship between theory and practice. First, what is it about this *project* that led these teachers to feel that they needed to make impossible choices between children and curriculum, between inquiry into individual understanding and upholding school standards, between their own intellectual interests and their classroom responsibilities? And, secondly, what is it about *teaching* that made these choices seem essentially unrelated to their practice? The teachers' 'stories' about themselves at work suggest some answers to these questions and point to a possible framework for furthering our understanding of what teachers do.[27]

In one such story, a kindergarten-first grade teacher told the group about how she had used the occasion of a new child joining the class in the middle of the year as the subject of a lesson in counting, addition and subtraction. One girl in her class, Penny, counted the new boy twice, adding him both to the number of children who were 'present' *and* to the number of children who were absent. When Jessica finished her story, the other teachers in the group eagerly took up the puzzle, exploring what the girl might have been thinking. This was the problem from the perspective of a group of teacher-researchers. But as she spoke about her classroom, Jessica considered several other issues. First of all, she said she wanted everyone to be clear about the fact that there was a total of twenty-four children in the class, i.e., that twenty-two here, and two absent, added up to twenty-four altogether. She could not give equal legitimacy to Penny's conclusion that there were twenty-five without confusing the other children. The girl's understanding of the situation was not something she wanted anyone else to share. She needed to teach all of the children, including Penny, that each member of the group should only be counted once.

A teacher has a special position as the person in the class who knows formal mathematics. Her students look to *her* as the authority on addition. She personally represents the order of arithmetic in contrast to their own shaky sense of how it works. Particularly because Jessica was interacting with Penny in front of all the other children in the class, she thought it was important for her, as the teacher, to stand behind the formal knowledge represented by the correct sum and the correct procedure for arriving at the total number in the group.

Of course, there are many different ways of understanding this mathematics problem, and that might be what Jessica ought to have tried to understand about Penny's thinking. But examining how Penny constructed the problem was not possible; in addition to the mathematics lesson, Jessica said she also needed to give her attention to managing the transition of a large group of young children from one sort of activity to another. Penny's irritation, which may have caused some problems among the other children in the group, needed to be dissipated. These aspects of classroom teaching made it difficult for Jessica to engage in or even think much about an exploration of Penny's intuitive understanding of addition. From the distance of the seminar, however, Jessica reflected on what a good researcher might have done in the same circumstances, in contrast to her own, teacherly, response. She said to Duckworth, one of the researchers in the group:

> I wanted you there, because I knew you would ask her the right question. I kept saying, 'this is perfect, Jessica get it out'. But I couldn't think of a question to ask. Of course, I was worried about a few other items . . . I couldn't defuse her anger because I couldn't understand what she was talking about. And I didn't have the time — I tried — I gave it three sentences.

A researcher could have gone off on Penny's tangent with the confidence that someone else was responsible for managing the whole class's behavior and teaching this girl (and the rest of the class) how to add.

Although Jessica felt that she had not acted as a researcher would have in these circumstances, it was obvious that her participation in the project influenced her response to the child's way of thinking about arithmetic. She said she was aware of the child's intuitive understanding and how it differed from the formal knowledge first-graders are supposed to learn about addition. She assumed that there was some 'sense' to Penny's way of thinking and she tried to get her to articulate it. Even though there was clearly a tension between individual thinking and conventional social standards in this instance of practice, Jessica did not need to make a choice between them in the way she spoke about her work. Like Helen, who wanted Mario to know about the eclipse, she was able to manage both the child's understanding and the formal knowledge she wanted to convey.

In contrast to their stories, the teachers' discussions of the dichotomy between intuitive and formal knowledge communicated the belief that if they were going to value their own or any other individual's way of thinking about something, then they would have to disassociate themselves from the formal standards that are used to measure learning and teaching in schools. What was a distinction of interest to theorists (intuitive versus formal knowledge) had become a set of contradictory categories for defining their task: *teacher-researchers versus school and society*. If the teachers had fully identified with the researchers in the project, they might have settled on that self-definition. However, the structure of the project also encouraged them to see themselves as school practitioners. The researchers valued the teacher's perspective on their classroom practice, and recognized them as authorities in matters of classroom life; the teachers were told that they knew things about work in schools that the researchers did not know. Thus the teachers' authority as collaborators in the project was based on their work in schools. In order to perform this function they defended the importance of the formal knowledge that is taught to children in schools. From this perspective, they reasoned that aligning themselves with schools meant they could not also be researchers, and so they divided things up differently. The dichotomy became: *researchers versus teachers and schools and society*. They had been asked to collaborate on the project's research *because* they were public school teachers. Yet their association with all of the aspects of that role made it difficult for them to pursue the kind of inquiry which the researchers had hoped for.

Given these two quite opposite ways of thinking about themselves, it is not surprising that the teachers were frustrated by trying to play the role of both teacher and 'teacher-researcher'. The way they understood the project's assumptions led them to a choice: should they align themselves with children by focusing on the individual's intuitive knowledge? Or should they align themselves with the school as teachers of society's formal knowledge? They faced a dilemma; it seemed to them that they could not do both.[28]

What is most striking about the thinking of the MIT project teachers is that although they *analysed* their work into a set of forced choices, they did not seem to have to make such choices in their *practice*. Their 'stories' about themselves imply a variety of alternative strategies for coping with conflicts that enabled them to work *without* choosing. This is the significant point we should consider. The teachers' management, in practice, of concerns that they talked about as contradictory in their analysis of practice raises some very interesting questions about the relationship between *thinking* about teaching and doing it. They did not have an analytic language for reflecting on their practice to counter the contradictory themes that developed in their thinking about intuitive and formal knowledge. But what they did have was a way of working and a concrete way of talking about their work, and there is much to be learned from listening to their 'stories' about particular interactions with students.

How did they manage the tensions and contradictions inherent in their work? And why did their ability to manage them surface in their stories when it was absent from their more abstract analysis? In the stories the teachers told about specific instances of practice, they were talking about *themselves*. All of the various expectations that are a part of learning in schools seemed to be filtered through the person of the teacher in the act of teaching. She used her 'self' as a tool to manage the contradictions of her trade. Jessica portrayed herself as *more* than simply a conduit through which formal knowledge passes to students. When she talked about herself as a teacher of mathematics, it seemed important to her that children learn what *she is* teaching them. In talking with a child to find out what he or she thinks about something, her *personal* attitude towards the child and towards the skills being assessed make a significant difference in how she understands what the child 'knows'. Yet what Jessica's students learn from her is also part of the shared knowledge that is important to their success in school and society. The way this knowledge is structured by teachers themselves in relation to their students makes it difficult to say whether it is 'intuitive' or 'formal'.

The way the teacher uses her self in her practice suggests that the dichotomy between these two kinds of knowledge is a false one. In the person of the teacher, knowledge is conveyed to students in a way which is both socially useful and meaningful to the teacher herself. In the course of instruction the teacher attempts to make knowledge meaningful to students through her formal authority and the relationship she has established with them as individual persons. On the part of the student, there is a certain degree of trust that if something 'makes sense' to the teacher, it will eventually 'make sense' to the learner; both are part of a society in which the knowledge taught and learned in school has some usefulness. The 'mismatches' between intuitive and formal knowledge, posited by Bamberger, may thus be managed by the teacher without deliberate research into their incongruence.

The tensions in a teacher's work are the same kinds of tensions everyone feels as an individual growing up in society, writ large because of the teacher's official role in the growing-up process. We all feel enduring contradictions, for example, between what it seems other people, in various positions of power, want us to do and what *we* think we should do. But teachers have a special responsibility for managing these kinds of tensions in themselves and in their students. Given what these teachers have said, it seems appropriate, therefore, to consider the notion that teaching involves *inventing personal strategies for working with universal contradictions that cannot be finally resolved.* Coping with these conflicts in one's self seems related to how they are managed in practice, and we need to persist in trying to find out how teachers do cope, in practice, with these enduring and unresolvable tensions.

Theories of self like those of George Herbert Mead, which I have drawn on here in thinking about the teacher's self, may be useful in examining this aspect of the teacher's work.[29] In Mead's view, a person is both a spontaneous actor on the environment and an interpreter of the ways in which actions are received by others. The 'self' develops in the course of managing the tensions between one's own actions and the expectations of others. The perspective from which a person acts is thus different from a 'theory' of action, developed at some distance from the problems to be managed. At the same time, a person is understood to direct his or her own actions rather than involuntarily reacting to social expectations. A teacher's 'story' about *herself* at work might be understood, therefore, as something different from either a reflected-upon theory about why she did what she did or a list of impulsive behaviors.

Analyzing such stories may lead to a reflective language for talking about practice that is more congruent with what teachers do in classrooms. This language could be used by both researchers and teachers for teaching about thinking as well as thinking about teaching. Finding such a language is of critical importance for curriculum change.[30] With such a language teachers may be able to contrast the *personal* aspect of their work with the more abstract contradictory themes that emerged when they were asked by theorists to speculate about becoming teacher-researchers.

Clearly the project influenced the teachers' sense of the internal contradictions in their work, and the researchers on the project did not offer any way out. The problem stems from more universal characteristics of relationships between theories about teaching and practice, however. Our experience in the project points to a gap in the way researchers understand practitioner thinking: the gap emerges because teachers' particular 'stories' about what they do in classrooms have been given little attention in research and writing about practice. Teachers who participate in university seminars are often criticized for the 'stories' they offer about themselves and their students. Their contributions are considered irrelevant to focused discussions of educational theory and research. Judged by academic standards, the 'stories' seem like evidence for inadequate problem-solving ability; what teachers say they do seems uninformed by all the careful theoretical analysis of teaching and learning that goes on outside of the classroom.[31] Even though the designers of the MIT project did not take this perspective, the emergent differences between 'thinking like a teacher' and 'thinking like a researcher' had similar implications.

The way teaching has been thought about and written about by academics certainly has had an influence on how teachers themselves think about it. The conventional relationship between theory and practice has assumed that practitioners should be *consumers* of theory which is created by someone else. When researchers have tried to separate how teachers themselves think about their work from academic descriptions of practice, they have concluded that the language practitioners use is too concrete, too context-bound, and too inconsistent to inform good teaching.[32] Teachers who want to improve their practice, therefore, are expected to use the language of *researchers* both to define problems and to understand their solutions.

Researchers conceive of their own job as actively searching for *solutions* that can be applied to the problems of practice. A recent review by Richard Shavelson and Paula Stern of a wide range of research that has been done on teacher decision-making is illustrative; the authors admit, however, that the fundamental formulation of the research problem that has been examined in this work 'ignores multiple, potentially conflicting goals which teachers have to balance daily'.[33] Yet a teacher who tells 'stories' about *managing* problems rather than *solving* them is considered intellectually passive, if not helpless. Coping with conflict, rather than getting rid of its source, goes against our society's deep-seated hopes for progress. Enduringly unsolved problems remain something of an embarrassment, and thus while research is valued, it is a struggle to see a teacher's everyday acts of teaching, in spite of the essential contradictions in her work, as productive and creative. When compared with the problem-solving researchers, she appears to be naive or indifferent.

Much research has been built on the model of the sciences, in which the validity and reliability of a solution are defined by the qualities that a number of events have in common. We have, therefore, been drawn away from the 'anecdotal' ways teachers talk about themselves at work (and what that can tell us about what is problematic in that work) towards solutions for problems that are defined to be useful for improving 'teaching' in general. The specific ways in which a teacher manages her classroom are not as interesting, from this perspective, as are general principles derived from research that can be developed into a universal theory of practice.[34]

Our thinking about how the teacher affects what she does in the classroom by using her 'self' to manage conflict has also been limited by the psychological concept of 'personality'. Instead of thinking of each teacher as an intentional agent in the moment-by-moment management of contradictory ways of thinking as Mead suggests we do, we have placed teachers in theoretically derived trait categories like 'warm and friendly' or 'authoritarian', based on a statistical average of classroom behaviors. This led to attempts to 'solve' educational problems by identifying which sort of teacher produces the most learning and figuring how to get those kinds of teachers in classrooms. Such solutions could not take account of the *dynamic* nature of the teacher's identity. As Mead points out, who a person is and what she does is expressed in and shaped by the environment in which she works, and yet she may appropriately *decide* that it is useful to be warm and friendly in one instance and authoritarian in another. The teacher, while affected by the environment, is not driven by it.

No matter what kind of teacher is placed in a classroom, the essential contradictions in teaching persist. Jessica, for example, cannot choose between accepting the fact that students come to school with different ideas about the structure of counting *or* teaching them to add and subtract according to conventional mathematical rules. Lee does not have a choice between expecting students to correctly answer the questions on 'page 98' of the textbooks which the school district assigns to her or trying to make sense of the individual variations in students' answers on a class assignment. Theoretical arguments might lead to apparent resolutions of these dilemmas, but such arguments seem remote from what teachers do in their classrooms. Although a resolution may be accomplished in each particular incident of teaching, the underlying tensions do not go away. It is this difference — between the specific momentary, creative acts of management on the part of teachers, and the more general picture of their work as contradictory — that makes the MIT teachers' stories about their own practices so important.

Our project might have gone much farther if we had taken account of the richness of these teachers' language for talking about their work. Instead, we provided them with a researcher's language in the cause of teaching them about thinking. We did not concurrently examine *their* ways of thinking about teaching. If we could better understand the special qualities of the thinking revealed in the way teachers talk about their own work, researchers might be able to participate in a different sort of conversation with teachers about improving practice. Taking teachers' stories as evidence for their thinking about why they do what they do means developing both new ideas about what 'thinking' is and a different attitude towards teachers. If teachers are to be considered as 'intentional' practitioners whose own thoughts and feelings serve as the rationale for their actions, what researchers have to offer in the improvement of practice needs to be reexamined.[35]

The MIT teachers' stories suggest a conceptualization of the practitioner's teaching self — an actor in a situation who brings her personal history, knowledge, and concerns into a relationship with her working environment. Her own ideas about what should be happening in that environment (informed by educational research and theory or not) must be adjusted, by her, to the concrete reality which she faces in each situation. Because the teacher must thus use her 'self' in the Meadian sense, in her teaching, and because the materials on which she works are the 'selves' of her students, the relationship between thinking and doing, between research and practice, is created by her in moment-by-moment classroom interaction. She does not put aside the formal aspect of her own or a student's knowledge while she examines the intuitive, nor can she simply impose the formal without making some kind of sense of it for her self and for her class. It is the essence of the teacher's job to be a person who can manage both conventional social expectations and individual understanding, even though the two may often be in conflict.

Acknowledgment

The research reported in this paper was partially supported by a grant from the National Institute of Education (Grant No. G78–0219) awarded to the Division for Study and Research in Education at Massachusetts Institute of Technology, Cambridge, Mass.

References and Notes

1 *Many of the teacher-members of this project continued to meet well into the 1980's. See Eleanor Duckworth 'Understanding children's understanding' in* The Having of Wonderful Ideas and Other Essays on Teaching and Learning, *NY, Teachers College Press, 1987, pp. 83–97.*

2 *For an elaboration of this interpretation of constructivism, see Paul Cobb 'Where is the Mind? Constructivist and Sociocultural Perspectives on Mathematical Development',* Educational Researcher, ***23**, 7, October, 1984, pp. 13–20 and Carl Bereiter, 'Constructivism, Socioculturalism, and Popper's World 3',* Educational Researcher, ***23**, 7, October, 1984, pp. 21–3.*

3 *Eleanor Duckworth, who had studied with Piaget and popularized his ways of interacting with children in this country, was one of the teacher developers on the project.*

4 *See James Greeno 'On claims that answer the wrong questions,* Educational Researcher *(in press) for the origins of this term and the differentiation between situativity and constructivism.*

5 Journal of Curriculum Studies, *16*, 1, 1984, pp. 1–18. *The essay is reproduced here in its original form. An introduction and additional footnotes have been added and are distinguished from the original text by italics.*

6 *See Jerome Bruner,* Actual Minds, Possible Worlds, *Cambridge, MA, Harvard University Press, 1986, for an analysis of the distinction between narrative and paradigmatic ways of knowing.*

7 *See, for example: Philip W. Jackson,* The Practice of Teaching, *NY, Teachers College Press, 1986, and these first hand accounts and analyses by teacher researchers:*

Deborah L. Ball 'With an eye on the mathematical horizon: Dilemmas of teaching elementary school mathematics', Elementary School Journal, *93, 4, 1993, pp. 373–97; Lisa D. Delpit 'Skills and other dilemmas of a progressive black educator'*, Harvard Educational Review, *56, 4, November 1986, pp. 379–85; Ruth Heaton, 'Creating and studying a practice of teaching elementary mathematics for understanding', Unpublished Doctoral dissertation, East Lansing, MI, Michigan State University, 1994; Tim Lensmeir,* When Children Write: Critical Re-Visions Of The Writing Workshop, *NY, Teachers College Press, 1994; Suzanne Wilson 'Mastadons, maps, and Michigan',* Elementary School Journal *(in press).*

8   *See Magdalene Lampert and Christopher Clark 'Expert knowledge and expert thinking in teaching: A reply to Floden And Klinzig'*, Educational Researcher, *19, 4, 1990, pp. 21–3, 42.*

9   *For a review of these arguments and conceptions, see Magdalene Lampert 'Studying teaching as a thinking practice', in James Greeno and Shelly G. Goldman (Eds)* Thinking Practices, *Hillsdale, NJ, Lawrence Erlbaum and Associates, in press.*

10 *In terms of current theories of cognition, we might say that the teacher would be 'tuning to the affordances' In her attempt to integrate structuralism with situated cognition into a theory of knowledge use, Lauren Resnick asserts:*

> *In each new situation, learning is a matter of beginning to act in the environment on the basis of particular affordances of that environment. One's initial actions are either successful or not. If they are dramatically unsuccessful, that is, if there is no match at all between one's prepared structures and the affordances of the environment, the most likely response is to leave the environment, either physically, if possible, or by 'tuning out' when actual physical departure is not possible. If the match is complete, no learning takes place. One just acts. But if the match is partial — enough to keep one engaged, but not enough to provide a ready-made set of actions — a process of tuning to the affordances sets in. This tuning is what I mean by learning. It produces an ability to act 'perfectly' in the environment. But because it is a tuning process, it results in a specifically situated competence. The competence developed will not be perfect for any other specific environment.*

'Situated rationalism: Biological and social preparation for learning', in Mapping the Mind: Domain Specificity in Cognition and Culture, *LA, Hirschfield and S. Gelman, Eds, New York, Cambridge University Press, 1994, p. 480.*

11 *From the perspective of current thinking about systemic reform, we might also argue that it redefines the purpose of schooling to include respecting students' thinking.*

12 *For a more complete description of the distinction between intuitive and formal knowledge, see Bamberger, J. 'An experiment in teacher development' (A proposal submitted to the National Institute of Education, Basic Skills Group, June 1978a); and Bamberger, J. 'Intuitive and formal musical knowing: Parables of cognitive dissonance', in* The Arts, Cognition, and Basic Skills, Second Annual Yearbook on Research in the Arts and Aesthetics Education (CEMREL, Inc. 1978).

13 BAMBERGER, J. op. cit. (1978a), p. 1 (see Note 12).

14 *Of course, the frustration and ambiguity of this scenario has been repeated over and over again and experienced by many as we embark on more and more*

teacher-researcher collaboration. See for example, Marsha Levine, Ed Professional Practice Schools: Linking Teacher Education and School Reform, *NY, Teachers College Press, 1992. The jury may still be out on whether or not it is 'worth it' to blur the boundaries in this way. See Magdalene Lampert 'Looking at Restructuring from Within a Restructured Role', Phi Delta Kappan, **72**, 9 (May, 1991), pp. 670–74, David Wong, 'Challenges confronting the researcher-teacher: Conflicts of purpose and conduct', Educational Researcher, **24**, 3 (May 1995), pp. 22–8; and Suzanne Wilson, 'Not tension but intention: A response to Wong's analysis of the researcher/teacher', Educational Researcher, **24**, 8 (November 1995), pp. 19–21.*

15 *Narrative is developed as a teacherly way of knowing in Miriam Ben-Peretz,* The Teacher-Curriculum Encounter: Freeing Teachers from the Tyranny of Texts, *Albany, State University of New York Press, 1990; Michael Connelly and Jean Clandinin, 'Stories of experience and narrative inquiry', Educational Researcher, **19**, 5 (1990), pp. 2–14; Freema Elbaz 'Research on teachers' knowledge: The evolution of a discourse', Journal of Curriculum Studies, **23** (1995), pp. 1–19.*

16 *Ibid., p. 3.*

17 *A great deal has been written about the relationship between what one 'knows' and what one is able to 'see' and/or talk about. One current line of work worth noting here is the work on 'practices' and their 'discourses', for example, Edward Hutchins' 'The technology of team navigation', in J. Galegher, R.E. Kraut, and C. Egido, Eds, Intellectual Teamwork: Social and Technological Foundations of Cooperative Work, Hillsdale, NJ, Lawrence Erlbaum Associates, 1990, pp. 191–220, Jean Lave and Etiene Wegner, Situated Learning: Legitimate Peripheral Participation, New York, Cambridge University Press, 1991. Teachers are members of one community of practice, researchers of another. Each has a situated understanding of the nature of knowledge and of how it is acquired. This notion could also be extended to say that children and teachers are members of different discourse communities (by virtue of age and activity, or by virtue of culture) and in order to communicate they need a kind of cross cultural interpretation. Shirley Bryce Heath makes this argument in* Ways with Words, *NY Cambridge University Press, 1983.*

18 *Ibid., p. 9.*

19 *The quotations in this essay are all taken from transcriptions of tapes that were made during the teachers' weekly discussions. First names are used to identify the teachers in an attempt to convey the personal quality of their exchanges with one another and the staff. The quotations have been edited only insofar as was necessary to make them readable.*

20 JACKSON, P. (1978) *Life in Classrooms,* New York, Holt, Rinehart and Winston.

21 McPHERSON, C. (1972) *Small Town Teacher,* Cambridge, Harvard University Press.

22 LORTIE, D. (1975) *Schoolteacher: A Sociological Study,* Chicago, University of Chicago Press.

23 *More current related analyses of conflicts in teachers' work is being carried on in the field of critical theory, etc. and analysis related to issues of multiculturalism.*

24 ELLIOT, J. *Some key concepts underlying teachers' evaluation of innovation* (Paper presented at the British Educational Research Association Conference, London, 1977), p. 8.

25 *Recently, scholars have been examining an intermediate realm between the 'social' in informal, standardizing institutional terms and the individual: A local form of 'social' knowledge is thought to be developed in classrooms which enables*

the members of class groups to communicate with one another abut their work. See Paul Cobb and Erna Yackel 'Constructivist, emergent, and sociocultural perspectives in the context of development research', Educational Psychologist (in press), Elice Forman 'Forms of participation in classroom practice: Implications for learning mathematics', in Perla Nesher, Les Steffe, Paul Cobb, G. Goldin and B. Greer, Eds Theories of Mathematical Learning, Hillsdale, NJ, Lawrence Erlbaum Associates; Rogers Hall and Andee Rubin, '. . . there's five little notches in here: Communication and mathematics learning', in James Greeno and Shelly G. Goldman (Eds) Thinking Practices, Hillsdale, NJ, Lawrence Erlbaum and Associates, in press.

26 DUCKWORTH, E. (1979) 'Learning with breadth and depth' (The Catherine Molony Memorial Lecture, City College School of Education Workshop Center for Open Education, June.

27 These 'stories' are treated in greater detail in LAMPERT, M. 'Teaching about thinking and thinking about teaching', Mimeo (1982).

28 Olson also applies the term 'dilemma' to the situation in which teachers find themselves as implementors of curriculum innovation. See OLSON, J. 'Teacher influence in the classroom: A context for understanding curriculum translation', *Instructional Science*, **10**, 1981, pp. 259–75.

29 MEAD, G.H. *On Social Psychology*, University of Chicago Press, Chicago, 1956. See also BLUMER, H. 'Sociological implications of the thought of George Herbert Mead', in B.R. Cosin et al. (Eds) *School and Society: A Sociological Reader*, Routledge and Kegan Paul, London, 1971, and BERLAK, H. and BERLAK, A. 'Towards a political and social psychological theory of schooling: An analysis of English informal primary schools', *Interchange*, **6** (1975), pp. 11–22, for applications of Mead's theory to teaching.

30 See also OLSON, J. 'Teacher constructs and curriculum change', *Journal of Curriculum Studies*, **12** (1980), pp. 1–11.

31 JACKSON, P. (1971) 'The way teachers think', in Lesser, G.S. (Ed) *Psychology and Educational Practice*, Glenview, Illinois, Scott, Foresman, and Co.

32 A similar critique of this perspective on teachers thinking can be found in HAMMERSLY, M., 'Towards a model of teacher activity', in John Eggleston (Ed) *Teacher Decision Making in the Classroom*, Routledge and Kegan Paul, London, 1979, and FLODEN, R. and FEIMAN, S. 'Should teachers be taught to be rational?' (Paper presented at the annual meeting of the American Educational Research Association, Boston, April 1980).

33 SHAVELSON, R. and STERN, P. (1981) 'Research on teachers' pedagogical thoughts, judgements, decisions and behavior', *Review of Educational Research*, **51**.

34 For a similar criticism of generalized approaches to curriculum problems see REID, W.A. *Thinking about the Curriculum*, Routledge and Kegan Paul, London, 1978.

35 The implications of this view for improving practice have been examined by FENSTERMACHER, G.D. 'A philosophical consideration of recent research on teacher effectiveness', *Review of Research in Education*, **6**, 1978.

6 Mentoring as Assisted Performance: A Case of Co-planning[1]

Sharon Feiman-Nemser and Kathrene Beasley

For teachers to learn new ways of teaching, we must construct settings that assist teachers to perform the new skills before they are fully competent . . . Teachers, like their students, have zones of proximal development; they too require *assisted performance*. (Tharp and Gallimore, 1988, p. 190)

To change the way teachers teach, we must embed in the structure of their everyday lives continuing opportunities for *assisted performance*. (Tharp and Gallimore, 1988, p. 43)

For the past four years we (a university teacher educator/researcher and a second/third grade teacher/researcher) have been exploring new ways for experienced teachers to guide and support the learning of novices. We call this professional activity 'mentoring' which we define as face-to-face, close-to-the-classroom work on teaching undertaken by a more experienced and a less experienced teacher in order to help the latter develop his or her practice. More specifically we are interested in how experienced teachers can induct novices into the intellectual and practical challenges of reform-minded teaching. Our investigations have been carried out in a professional development school (PDS) affiliated with a new, five-year teacher education program that features a year-long internship.[2]

In trying to conceptualize a stance toward mentored learning to teach, we have been drawn to sociocultural theories which emphasize the social and situated nature of learning through joint activity. Building largely on the work of Vygotsky, researchers in this tradition describe how children and apprentices learn all kinds of skills by participating in authentic activities with more capable others who tailor assistance to fit the developmental level of the learner (e.g., Rogoff and Lave, 1984; Lave and Wenger, 1991; Collins, Brown and Newman, 1989; Tharp and Gallimore, 1988). By extension a mentor can promote a novice's learning by participating with the novice in the core tasks of teaching, helping the novice perform at a more complex level than he or she could on his or her own. Through their joint participation in activities authentic to teaching, the mentor and novice develop shared understandings about the meaning and purposes of these activities, and the novice gradually internalizes ways of thinking, problem solving and acting needed to carry them out.

Intrigued by this conception of mentoring as 'assisted performance', we have been experimenting with forms of mentoring which we call co-planning and co-teaching. Through close study of how Kathy enacts these forms, including the analysis of videotapes which document her work with novices over time, we are clarifying what these forms of mentoring entail and how they contribute to novices' learning. We have shared this work-in-progress with mentor teachers in a new, field-based teacher education program in order to stimulate thoughtful discussions about what experienced teachers can help interns learn, and how they can guide and support interns' learning through joint work on teaching.

In this chapter we illustrate our stance toward mentoring by looking closely at one extended mentoring episode — a two-hour, co-planning session between Kathy and her intern, Elaine. In this session, which took place mid-year, Kathy and Elaine plan a language arts unit around the works of Leonard Everett Fisher, an award-winning children's writer/illustrator, who visited the school later in the year. Analysing this session (one of ten mentoring episodes that we videotaped during the year Kathy and Elaine worked together) helped us develop a conception of mentoring as assisted performance and clarify the components of co-planning.

Mentoring as Assisted Performance

Learning to teach is generally construed as an independent process of trial and error. Certainly most beginning teachers learn to teach on their own, although the spread of mentoring legislation across the country may alter this pattern (Feiman-Nemser, 1995). For student teachers, the situation is less clear-cut. Since student teachers learn to teach in someone else's classroom, the opportunity to learn with and from a more experienced practitioner exists in principle. In fact, many preservice programs, especially those with a reform agenda, often try to distance their student teachers from the field by fostering a critical stance toward the practices they encounter or by maintaining control of student teachers' assignments and assessment (Cochran-Smith, 1991).

The emphasis on independent performance and the belief that each teacher must develop his or her own style leave mentors feeling uncertain about whether and how to participate in the novice's teaching. There seems to be an unwritten rule that mentors should not intervene (interfere) when novices are teaching unless things are going really badly. Some mentors prefer to leave the classroom rather than live with the tension of wanting to help, but feeling they should not get directly involved.

The idea of mentoring as assisted performance challenges these widespread assumptions. It provides a justification for mentors to participate with novices in the everyday activities of teaching in order to scaffold their learning. It offers a theoretical account of how novices' learning occurs through social interaction and cooperative activity. It implies that the practices being learned are not the sole invention of a single practitioner, but the products of a professional community which the novice is joining.

Actions by mentors that might otherwise be considered 'interference' may now be cast as assistance. By participating with the novice in the work of teaching, the mentor enables the novice to do with help what the novice is not yet ready to do alone. Of course the assistance must be responsive to the novice — atuned to what Vygotsky (1978) calls the 'zone of proximal development' or ZPD. The ZPD is the region of activity between what a novice can do alone and what he or she can do with the help of a knowledgeable other. Vygotsky uses this idea to explain how learners can, with the support of others, engage in, and learn, increasingly complex activities. The more knowledgeable other (e.g., parent, teacher, master) models and guides the joint activity, modifying the type and amount of support. The novice (e.g., child, student, apprentice) learns through observation and interaction, gradually internalizing ways of thinking and acting that make up the activity.

The idea of mentoring as joint participation in authentic activity differs from more conventional views of mentoring as providing emotional support or passing on local knowledge and practical advice. It also differs from models of clinical supervision with their cycles of observation and conferencing and their emphasis on drawing out the novice's thinking through questioning. When mentoring takes the form of joint participation in authentic activity, the primary purpose is to accomplish the task. The novice's learning results from his or her participation with the mentor in this activity.

Although these ideas were not developed to illuminate teacher learning, some researchers have begun to apply them to mentoring contexts, arguing that similar processes operate (see Tharp and Gallimore, 1988). This work has encouraged us to experiment with new approaches to mentoring which challenge more familiar ways of working. For instance, it persuaded Kathy to participate with her student teachers and interns in the work of teaching, rather than standing on the sidelines and giving them feedback on their performance after the fact. The idea of co-planning emerged from this new orientation. Once Kathy stopped expecting her novices to know how to plan, once she realized that planning was something novices need to learn which she was in a good position to teach, co-planning seemed like a reasonable way to go about it.

Co-planning as a Form of Mentoring

We came to think of co-planning as a form of assisted performance, a way for mentors to induct novices into the intellectual work of teaching. Through joint planning, a mentor can model an approach to planning, make explicit her thinking and decisionmaking, and share practical knowledge about students, subject matter and teaching. By participating with the mentor in the activity of planning, a novice can gradually construct a framework for planning, a way to approach the task and a sense of what it involves. Having such a framework is part of the knowledge base for beginning teachers (Zumwalt, 1990).

Most teachers do not think about how they plan, let alone how they might teach planning to a novice. For one thing, planning is usually a private, mental process which teachers carry out on their own. Moreover, the kind of planning that works for experienced teachers may not be adequate for novices. Experienced teachers have more developed frameworks for understanding and organizing content and learning activities, more knowledge of students as learners, a clearer picture of the overall curriculum. Consequently, their actual plans may lack specification because they have a lot of tacit knowledge about teaching (Borko and Niles, 1987; Clark and Yinger, 1977; Leinhardt and Greeno, 1986).

At the same time, university-based teacher educators generally assume responsibility for teaching planning. They introduce prospective teachers to rational planning models and require them to write up lesson plans and units. They encourage prospective teachers to think of themselves as developers of curriculum, not simply implementors of someone else's designs. Still, novices often have difficulty mastering the complexities of planning even when faced with a specific group of students to plan for.

When mentor teachers have an opportunity to investigate their own planning, to think about what novices need to learn about planning, and to consider how their own planning needs and practices differ from those of a novice, they begin to imagine a role for themselves in helping novices learn to plan. When mentor teachers have a chance to study cases of co-planning in writing or on videotape and to consider what and how novices can learn from the process, they begin to appreciate that planning draws on local knowledge and ways of thinking which they value. These understandings can motivate mentor teachers to take up the challenge of learning to teach planning through co-planning.

We did not bring a well developed theory to our work in mentoring and mentor teacher development. Rather the relevance of sociocultural theories became apparent over time as we discussed them in light of our practice and the data we were gathering.[3] Ideas informed our experiments and our experiments shaped our emerging conceptualizations. This dialogue between theory and practice helped us explore the potential of sociocultural views to shape mentoring practices and underscored the need to develop grounded theories of mentored learning that take into account the contexts and practice of teaching and the challenges of learning it.

A Case of Co-planning

To illustrate our thinking we examine one extended mentoring episode — a two-hour co-planning session between Kathy and her intern, Elaine. In this session, which we videotaped on a Monday afternoon in early February, 1994, Kathy and Elaine plan a literacy unit about the books of Leonard Everett

Table 6.1:   Components of a Co-planning Episode

Segment	Focus	Kind of Talk
1	Sharing 1st impressions	C
2	How to begin the unit	D
3	Studying *Up in the Air*	C
4	Summarizing key ideas	D
5	Reading *Storm on the Jetty*	C/D
6	Gathering up ideas	D
7	Studying *Boxes*; how to use it	C/D
8	Studying *Number Art*	C
9	Designing culminating activity	D
10	Clarifying roles	R
11	Planning 1st lesson	D/T
12	Blocking out unit/anthol. project	D/T

Notes: C = Exploring content   D = Designing learning activities   T = Coaching for teaching
R = Clarifying roles

Fisher.[4] Fisher was to visit the school in April and the two teachers were trying to figure out how to introduce students to his work and prepare them for the visit. From the moment we watched the tape, we recognized that this episode could push our thinking. Over a period of time, we subjected the tape and transcript to various analyses, probing the content, structure and dynamics of the interactions, and asking ourselves what we could learn here about the theory and practice of teacher mentoring and the teaching and learning of planning.

We begin with an overview of the conversation, focusing on its structure and component parts. Next we illustrate and discuss the three broad categories of work/talk that Kathy and Elaine engage in as they go about their planning. The illustrations provide a picture of what the work entailed and how Kathy and Elaine participated in it. Based on this portrait we argue that Kathy is teaching planning by doing the work of planning with Elaine at her side, and that this joint work is helping Elaine form an image of what the complex process of planning entails.

Components of co-planning

Our first analytic strategy was to divide the session into segments based on changes in the substantive focus or purpose of the interactions. Working with a videotape and transcript, we marked off places where the conversation seemed to change direction or focus, then summarized and labeled each segment. Studying the results (see Table 6.1), we noted a general pattern in the structure of the co-planning activity. We also identified three different kinds of talk/work (see Table 6.2).

In the opening minutes of their conversation, Kathy and Elaine share their first impressions of Leonard Everett Fisher's illustrations which they initially do not like very much (Segment 1). Then Kathy suggests a 'dramatic' way to introduce Fisher to the children by showing a lot of his books and telling them

Table 6.2: Amount of Time Devoted to Different Kinds of Talk

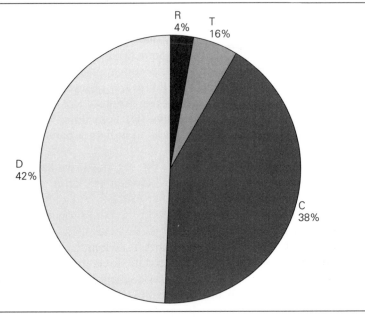

Notes: C = Exploring content   D = Designing learning activites   T = Coaching for teaching
R = Clarifying roles

some interesting anecdotes from his life (Segment 2). Elaine suggests that they start the unit with *Up in the Air,* a poem by Myra Cohn Livingston about riding in an airplane which Fisher illustrated. Kathy starts looking through the book and gradually draws Elaine into her exploration. Together they make some discoveries about Fisher's illustrations (Segment 3). Kathy and Elaine list aspects of the illustrations which they want students to notice such as light and dark contrasts, shadows, texture and perspective (Segment 4). They turn to another book with clouds *Storm at the Jetty* and discuss Fisher's fondness for painting clouds and storms (Segment 5). Elaine proposes an activity they can do with the book and the talk turns back to planning. Kathy suggests that they write down all the different ideas and activities they have come up with (Segment 6). She picks up the book *Boxes! Boxes!* which they read and discuss (Segment 7). Then Kathy starts looking through *Number Art,* a book about thirteen different notation systems. Because the class is studying Egyptian numbers in mathematics, this book holds special interest and Kathy and Elaine spend fifteen minutes reading and talking about it before setting it aside (Segment 8). Now they focus on the final activity for the unit. Initially they thought the unit would culminate in Fisher's visit, but Kathy has been mulling over a different idea — having the children make their own anthology of poems (Segment 9). Elaine initiates a brief exchange about who is going to launch the unit and how they will work together (Segment 10). They go back to the first day which they had begun to sketch out at the beginning of the session and finetune plans for the lesson that Elaine will be teaching the next day (Segment 11). Finally, they decide on a sequence and schedule for the unit and work out details for launching the anthology project (Segment 12).

As we studied this analysis, we saw that the talk and the intellectual work seem to fall into three main categories. Sometimes Kathy and Elaine are reading Fisher's books together as learners and studying his illustrations. We called this 'exploring content' (C). Sometimes Kathy and Elaine are developing ideas for learning activities and clarifying what they want students to get out of them. We called this 'designing learning activities' (D). Sometimes, Kathy gives Elaine specific information and advice about how to pull off a particular activity. We called this 'coaching for teaching' (T).

Using the three categories to code the segments, we saw that the conversation mainly flows back and forth between exploring content (C) and designing learning activities (D). Kathy and Elaine spend a little over a third of the time studying Fisher's work, poring over the books together, reading texts out loud, sharing their interpretations of the drawings. This activity leads into pedagogically oriented conversation (D and T). When the teachers move back and forth between looking at the book and thinking about what to do with it, we indicated a blended segment (C/D). Coaching for teaching (T) appears toward the end of the session after Kathy and Elaine have sketched out different possibilities and are ready to decide on a sequence and prepare for teaching.

The predominant C-D-C-D pattern has a certain logic. Teachers cannot decide what they want their students to learn or imagine appropriate learning activities if they are unfamiliar with the materials they are teaching. If they do not bring such knowledge to their planning, they must develop it as part of the planning process.

Educators do not usually conceptualize planning in this way. The rational-linear model of planning taught in many methods courses focuses on decisions about goals, activities, outcomes in that order. Cyclical models based on studies of teacher planning reverse the order, starting with decisions about activities from which outcomes and goals may be derived. Neither model explicitly acknowledges the exploration of content as part of the planning process.

Exploring content

While Kathy has done many author and illustrator studies with second and third graders, she has never taught Fisher's work before. So she needs to get inside the materials in order to discover what there is to learn and imagine how to teach it. This explains her moves in Segments 3, 5, 7 and 8 to read through particular books and study their illustrations, and the ease with which she moves back and forth between analysing the books herself and considering what students should notice or learn and what activities to do with the students.

Kathy's initial move to study *Up in the Air* surprises Elaine. She and Kathy have both attended a workshop on Leonard Everett Fisher and she has already taken some of the books home to read. Expecting to plan the unit, Elaine sits poised with pen and notebook, ready to write down all the specific things they are going to say and do in the actual teaching. She does not seem to share Kathy's picture of what the planning process entails, especially the step of exploring content with the eyes of both learner and teacher.

When Elaine proposes that they begin with *Up in the Air*, Kathy agrees and immediately spins out a general plan for the lesson. Then she reaches for the book which Elaine has been holding and starts looking through it. Extending the open book to Elaine, she invites her to look, too. Kathy models what she has in mind by saying out loud what she notices about the illustrations: 'One thing I'm noticing is that the two pages go together. They form a continuous picture, but they've been set in a frame.' She also sees that the pictures are drawn 'from a bird's eye view.' Elaine builds on Kathy's point: 'It starts you on the ground. It's a plane trip.' This insight triggers a series of joint discoveries about the illustrations which are accompanied by excitement and laughter:[5]

Kathy   So it . . . the perspective changes [slowly turning the pages].
Elaine It gets higher and higher.
Kathy   Like this is . . . like looking out of a window of an airplane.
Elaine [interrupting Kathy] They all are! That's what these frames are. [Laughing]
Kathy   You're right. That's exactly right! Ohhh! That's why it's like that.
Elaine They're going to love this one!

Kathy and Elaine have figured out that the frames around each page represent airplane windows — a clever device to enhance the reader's perception of riding in an airplane. They talk at the same time, smile and nod, their gestures, words and tone of voice registering the pleasure of their discovery. This is the first time the teachers are excited about Fisher and his work. As they have experienced 'the having of wonderful ideas' (Duckworth, 1987) while looking at the book, they recognize that the children are going to love it, too.

After studying *Up in the Air* with Kathy, Elaine seems more willing to set aside her pen and notebook — tools in her teacher identity kit — and become a student of Fisher's work. We hypothesize two possible reasons. Perhaps Elaine sees how Kathy uses what she notices as a learner to think about learning opportunities for students. Perhaps her substantive contributions at this early stage in the conversation help her feel like a real partner in the planning process.

Kathy and Elaine explore other works. Besides looking at several more poetry books written by Myra Cohn Livingston and illustrated by Leonard Everett Fisher, they spend time reading and discussing two books that Fisher wrote and illustrated himself, *Boxes! Boxes!* and *Number Art*.

Despite their complete absorption in *Number Art*, Kathy and Elaine set it aside. Later, during our analysis work, Kathy explained that the content posed too big a learning challenge at a time when she and Elaine were also trying to learn about Leonard Everett Fisher. In the exploration of *Boxes*, a playful book with less complex content, Kathy moves back and forth between reading the book and imagining different learning activities, while Elaine presses for a decision about how it will be used in teaching. Kathy seems more comfortable than Elaine with the open-ended quality of this exploration.

Kathy	What is this called?
Elaine	*Boxes.*
Kathy	We read something about this, where he had all these boxes in a studio and then his publisher or editor came and then he just wrote this book . . .
Elaine	This would be a good one for shapes.
Kathy	OK.
Elaine	It's not doing a lot for me, Kathy.
Kathy	. . . [Starts reading.] 'Took more than two years to create from idea to finished book. My editor and art director spent an afternoon in my studio in Westport, Connecticut. The walls were covered with very large paintings of boxes and shadows seen from various perspectives. These paintings, intended for gallery exhibition, started us thinking about what a box can be . . .'
Elaine	. . . And what do you want to do with this one?
Kathy	I can't decide. I mean, the striking thing about this is the colour. And there's all these boxes. So something about colour or boxes or shapes or . . . [She sits and thinks.] We could bring in some boxes and stack them up . . . You know how kids at this age start learning how to do that thing (perspective)? . . . So maybe it could be more an art skill lesson.

Exploring content blends easily into design work. Kathy and Elaine need to learn enough about Fisher — his writing and illustrations — so that they can figure out what will be important for students to learn and how they can guide students in their own study of Fisher, his art and writing. In the exploration of content, Kathy and Elaine are co-learners, studying new material for the first time. In the design of a literacy/art unit, Kathy takes the lead.

Designing learning activities

Kathy comes to the planning session with ideas about the 'pieces' that are needed to create a unit and the work involved in creating them. Her knowledge of design is implicit in her actions. Surrounded by stacks of books, with Elaine at her side, she goes about the intellectual work of designing a literacy/art unit that will span several weeks and involve students in reading and writing poetry, studying illustrations, experimenting with colour, brushstrokes and other artistic techniques, and creating their own poetry anthologies. At the beginning there are only vague possibilities. Two hours later, Kathy and Elaine have a shared vision of what and how they and their students will learn about Leonard Everett Fisher.

During our work on the videotape, Kathy said that planning a unit is like 'laying out a journey'. This image seems to guide her actions in the co-planning session. A unit, like a journey, has a beginning, a middle, and an end or culminating activity. Kathy comes to the session with an idea for an introduction which she further develops with Elaine. She spends most of the time gathering ideas from the books and hooking them up with ideas from her teaching. Once Kathy and Elaine have come up with a culminating activity, Kathy announces, 'OK, now we're ready to plan next week.' With a plan for the beginning, a list of possible activities, and a decision about where the unit will end, Kathy is now ready to pin down the itinerary. Elaine's suggestion that they begin with a poetry book provides a substantive focus for the unit and may further explain why non-fiction books such as *Boxes! Boxes!* and *Number Art* do not get incorporated into the developing plans.

Ideas for learning activities mostly come from Kathy's past experience teaching the works of other authors and illustrators. She easily maps this 'event-structured' knowledge (Carter, 1990) onto the new materials. For example, when Elaine suggests that they start the unit with *Up in the Air*, Kathy responds immediately with the outline of a lesson.

> **Kathy** We'll read it to them . . . We'll ask them to pay attention to his illustrations and then afterwards, we'll talk about what did they notice about his illustrations.
>
> **Elaine** I think that's a softer way to do it than just dig in (to one poem).
>
> **Kathy** And then after we have this discussion, we'll have them write about two things. We'll have them write about what did they notice about Leonard Everett Fisher as an artist and which illustration do they like best and why.
>
> **Elaine** Mmm.

Later Kathy explains: 'I've done this kind of lesson before, not with this book, but with other books, and other illustrators. I know in my bones how long it will take, how the children will respond, how to manage the transitions. I can feel how the lesson will flow.'

Beginning the journey

In the opening minutes of the conversation, Kathy proposes a way to introduce Leonard Everett Fisher to the children. Her idea reflects her knowledge of second graders, her flair for the dramatic, and her ability to imagine what a lesson will look and sound like:

> **Kathy** First we set out all the books we could get our hands on. And we show them each title and we say, 'It's by Leonard Everett Fisher or illustrated by him.' And we set it down. So when we're done, we have all these books sitting around us. And they're saying, 'Wow, two hundred books!' And we tell them just a little bit about this man — how old he is, that he's coming to our school, he fought in World

War II, he's an artist and some interesting anecdote about his life that we think will be interesting, that they'll listen to, because they're not going to be really interested in him until they start studying his works. And then they're going to want to know every single little fact that they can get their hands on. But they won't at first.

Knowing students and having a storehouse of ideas to draw on are vital, especially in planning a unit 'from scratch'. This is one place where the differences between Kathy, the experienced practitioner, and Elaine, the novice, stand out. An advocate of whole language learning, Kathy has a rich literacy program in her classroom with varied opportunities for writing, reading and discussion. Respectful of children and their thinking, she teaches in ways that builds on students' ideas and develops their understanding. Kathy brings all this knowledge and experience to the planning task. While Elaine shares Kathy's learner-centered stance, she has limited practical knowledge about how to enact it at this stage in her learning to teach.

Sketching out possibilities

Kathy distinguishes two levels of planning — 'sketching out different possibilities' and 'filling in the details'. She recognizes that Elaine is more concerned about the latter, while she, Kathy, is more interested in the former. Still, she holds off filling in the details until they sketch out the whole unit. (The work of filling in the details takes the form of coaching for teaching which we discuss in the next section.)

After Kathy and Elaine figure out what they want students to notice about *Up in the Air*, make connections with other poetry books and illustrations of clouds, and come up with some good learning activities, Kathy suggests that they start writing things down. Until now Elaine has been recording what *she* wants to remember from what Kathy has been saying. Now Kathy is ready to pull together their ideas.

Kathy   So at some point we should compare all these cloud pictures. That appeals to me. Maybe the thing that kids can understand from that is that an artist practices something and gets good at it and uses it in a lot of different ways.

Elaine   They experiment and play with ideas.

Kathy   Yeah, because he kind of does that with clouds.

Elaine   Yes.

Kathy   OK, so one is *The Storm on the Jetty*, that's one sort of lesson. Then another one is going to be comparing cloud illustrations. Then we have this introduction to *Up in the Air*. Lets write that down. And then another one, I don't know where, we're going to have to figure out how to sequence this to sort of build on each other, but the one where they hear a poem, they illustrate it, instead of his illustrations, they write a poem, they get someone else to illustrate it and they write a letter back about why they illustrated it the way they did. That's a lot. That's a couple of days.

Elaine   They write a poem, exchange it with a partner for illustrating, write the letter back. That's one. The other one is read a poem, they illustrate it, and then we divide into our groups, we talk about our illustrations and then we show his and we go around in a circle and each person says one thing about it. Why do you think he did it this way?

Kathy   That's the sequence.

Elaine   OK that's five which we could probably turn into six.

Kathy   Well, you know they'll get more involved as they go along. What do you think about doing another lesson, sort of like the first one, only use another book?

We can see from this exchange how Elaine's suggestion about starting with *Up in the Air* has provided a thematic focus for the unit. Besides the comparative work on cloud pictures, the activities that Kathy and Elaine have generated so far give the children a chance to experience the roles and explore the relationship of poet and illustrator. Even though they stop at this point in the conversation to look at other books, Kathy keeps the poetry focus in the back of her mind. It surfaces in the discussion of a culminating activity.

The culminating activity

Designing a culminating activity generates the same kind of excitement that we saw in the segment where Kathy and Elaine make some discoveries about the picture frames in *Up in the Air*. Although Kathy works out the idea with little substantive help from Elaine, the same quality of jointness and partnership pervades the effort. Elaine listens, encourages and, in the end, shares Kathy's pleasure at having developed another wonderful idea.

Initially Kathy assumed that Fisher's visit would be the culminating activity of the unit, but she has been mulling over a different possibility. 'I don't know exactly what our, I guess our culminating activity is meeting him [pause], unless we do that whole poetry idea.' Unclear about what Kathy has in mind, Elaine draws her out: 'Tell me again.' Kathy presents her idea — that the children would keep an anthology of poems which they illustrate in Fisher's style. Kathy continues to 'knead' the idea, a term she uses, until it has a satisfying shape and texture, while Elaine plays a supporting role in what feels like the most dramatic moment in the conversation.

Kathy   They have to see that she (Myra Livingston) has written these poetry anthologies based on a theme and he (Leonard Everett Fisher) has illustrated them carrying out that theme.

Elaine   And they never even met. That's one of the anecdotes that we should talk about.

Kathy   He gets her words and he interprets them.

Elaine   Over and over again.

Kathy   So maybe the whole idea of them having an anthology with a theme. [long pause] I don't know if that gets us too far off.

Elaine   If we spend time thinking like illustrators of poetry and we do it several times . . .

Kathy   [She gets up and moves to a different chair.] The thing I'm wondering about, I mean, if you look at all the poetry books each one has a theme. [She pulls the books toward her as she talks.]
Elaine   Right.
Kathy   I mean, if you look at this book, it flows because it's got the same color of grey and this aquamarine. The colors of every single page. So he has this art theme, color theme that ties the book together and she has a subject theme that ties the book together. If we could help them see that and then they could create their own anthology based on a subject and then using color, I think, style, too.
Elaine   And we are focusing on theme.
Kathy   And if we told them as soon as we got into this poetry stuff, now we want each of you to choose a subject and start looking for poems. If they want it to be whales, it can be whales. Dawn might do shells and I can see Daryl doing basketball or who knows what they'll choose, it might be something totally different. And then when they go to the library, they go to the poetry section. They find poems and they keep them in a special notebook or something. And then towards the end of the year, we say we want you to choose five that you want to put together in your special anthology. And they put them together and they illustrate them and they use all the stuff they have learned.
Elaine   And it can be their poetry or someone else's, a classmate or something they wrote.
Kathy   Yes, yes! Oh God! This is so good!
Elaine   It's going to be really good!
Kathy   I like this! Finally! I'm glad you're writing this down . . . Now I think we're ready to plan next week. Where do we start?

The culminating activity unites the children with the emerging curriculum. Building on what they have learned about how Fisher interprets Livingston's poetry and on their own individual interests, the children will collect and illustrate a set of poems to create their own anthologies. Exactly how Kathy formed this idea remains a mystery, part of the invisible creative side of planning. But Elaine has witnessed the process and feels some ownership of the results.

With a clear idea of how the unit will end, Kathy is ready to go back to the beginning and fill in the details. Many planning decisions still remain, such as the sequence and schedule of lessons and how to introduce specific activities. Elaine asks for a clarification about who is going to teach what. When Kathy suggests that she take the lead in teaching the unit, Elaine agrees, adding, 'I'm excited.'

Coaching for teaching

'Coaching for teaching' occurs in the last two segments of the conversation and has a very different form and feel from the other categories of work/talk.

Unlike 'exploring content' where Kathy and Elaine are co-learners, and 'design work' where they work as partners despite the unequal distribution of expertise, in 'coaching for teaching', Kathy is the master practitioner, and Elaine, the apprentice.

Kathy and Elaine already have an outline for the first lesson, but Elaine is still unsure about how to introduce Fisher. After working on that, Kathy models how to carry out the reading and discussion phases of the lesson. Through demonstration, coaching and direct instruction, Kathy helps Elaine get a clearer picture of what she should say and do at specific points in the lesson.

When Kathy suggested that they introduce Fisher by showing a lot of his books and saying a little bit about him, she gave Elaine some fairly specific advice along with a reason: 'Tell them just a little bit about this man . . . and some interesting anecdote about his life . . . because they're not really going to be interested in him until they start studying his works.' Elaine is still unsure about what to say even though Kathy has repeated her suggestions a second time. She wants to talk about the relationship between Fisher and Livingston and she asks Kathy if this is a good idea. Kathy gives more direct advice, then has Elaine practice on the spot.

> **Elaine** So back to the beginning. We're going to do *Up in the Air*, introduce Fisher the person, an anecdote, hopefully a naughty childhood story. I think we should talk about Livingston, too, and their relationship.
> **Kathy** Yes, that's good.
> **Elaine** Is that a good time to open it up, do you think? Or when we really start to go into the poetry?
> **Kathy** Well, what are you going to say? If you say two or three sentences.
> **Elaine** Two or three sentences only. They work a lot together. She's a poet. He's an illustrator and they do a lot together.
> **Kathy** And let them ask. Does she tell him what to draw?
> **Elaine** Yeah, that's right. And they will, too.

Next Kathy shows and tells Elaine how to introduce *Up in the Air*. Holding the book, she says: 'I think the way to start the book is, read them the title, read them the author and read them the illustrator so they see the names in writing on the cover. And then say, "What do you think this book is about? . . . How do you know that?"' She urges Elaine to push that since 'the illustrator tells us a lot more than the title.'

Kathy continues explaining and modelling for Elaine, telling her exactly what she should say: As an experienced teacher, Kathy feels the lesson in her bones. She knows how to talk to children so that they will listen and she knows what will interest them. Through her actions and words, Kathy provides an image that can guide Elaine's teaching.

> **Kathy** I think you should just say, 'I'm going to read this book. I want you to pay attention to Fisher's illustrations and enjoy the story.' . . . And then, when you're done [pause], sort of, imagine reading this to them and saying, 'What did you notice?' And they'll tell you a lot of stuff.

Anticipating what the children will say, Kathy realizes that some of their comments will not pertain to the illustrations. She suggests that Elaine take notes so that, at the end of the discussion, she can say: 'You probably noticed that I am taking notes. This is what I heard you say about Fisher as an artist . . . What I want you to do now is go back to your seats and write about what you learned about Fisher as an artist and which of these illustrations you like best and why. That's your lesson.'

As Kathy helps Elaine get inside the pedagogy of the lesson, Elaine spots a potential problem — how will different children be able to show what they noticed and talk about it when there is only one copy of the book? Kathy has a clear answer: 'Stay in control of the book.' Her detailed explanation shows that she has confronted similar situations before and has figured out a smooth procedure to assist second graders in sharing their ideas without getting distracted.

> **Kathy**   I find that it works better, they can come up and (you) say to them, 'Which picture do you want me to turn to?' And you turn to the picture and then they can point to it or talk to you. If you give them the book, they start looking at it and then they get distracted. We're all sitting there watching them look through this book. And then you have a problem.

This may seem like a small detail, but for a novice like Elaine, such procedural knowledge could mean the difference between an engaging discussion and a tedious or messy one. It is a good example of how teacher control enables or assists young children in expressing their ideas. Knowing how to manage this situation, Elaine can concentrate on what the children are saying rather than on traffic control. Kathy's advice assists her future teaching performance.

Teaching planning by co-planning

If we think of mentoring as helping someone learn to teach in the context of teaching, then we can say that Kathy helps Elaine learn to plan by engaging with her in the work of planning. With Elaine at her side, Kathy tackles the complex and creative task of designing a unit around the works of Leonard Everett Fisher. The planning involves studying Fisher's books and illustrations for information and ideas to focus the unit, coming up with engaging activities that connect children to those ideas, creating a culminating activity which allows children to use what they have learned, mapping out a teaching schedule, figuring out what it takes to pull off specific lessons and activities.

As the knowledgeable other, Kathy clearly plays the leading role. She draws extensively on her knowledge of children, teaching and planning as she guides Elaine on this journey and helps her prepare to teach the lessons and activities they have planned. Elaine participates as scribe and sounding board, partner and *protégé*. Despite the uneven distribution of expertise, the harmony of purpose and authenticity of the work contribute to a feeling of jointness and partnership.

Modelling, the main form of assistance, occurs in each category of planning work. In exploring content, Kathy models how to look at Fisher's work with the eye of a learner and a teacher. She also invites Elaine to notice what she notices for clues about what children will find interesting. In designing learning activities, Kathy models how to move from ideas about content and purposes to activities for learning. She thinks aloud as she does this planning work and occasionally offers a structure to organize the cognitive activity. In coaching for teaching, Kathy uses a combination of talk and action to help Elaine visualize what to do and say at specific points in the lesson. Here modelling is linked with direct instruction that provides a rationale for the recommended actions.

Why does Kathy adopt this approach to mentoring Elaine? Why does she take on the 'burden of planning' instead of helping Elaine do more of the work? Why does she choose to guide from the front rather than the side? We get important insights into how Kathy thinks about her actions from a journal entry that she wrote in response to the final coaching segment:

> As we begin talking about how to launch the anthologies the children will each create, there are clearly some things I know that Elaine couldn't know but that are critical in this decision . . . Given more scaffolding from me, Elaine could have figured out some of this for herself. That is not how we work in this session. I wonder why? I am doing a lot of thinking aloud. I am not sure I have such a firm grip on these ideas that I am able to think about how to scaffold Elaine's thinking. Also there are time constraints, and there is Elaine as a learner. Forcing her to figure all this out with me as a guide in the background instead of front and center as I actually am would be frustrating. The way we are working seems more honest. I am teaching Elaine, but we are also working as colleagues, planning a unit. It is true that the burden of planning falls on me, but why not? Elaine is, after all, a novice and I am not. We are both comfortable with our roles. It is important for me to listen to Elaine, to pick up on her clues, to support her ideas and contributions as they warrant and it is important for her to understand that she is involved in a process that she can learn from. (Beasley, 10/17/94)

Kathy identifies several factors that enter into her thinking about mentoring in general and her work with Elaine here. As always, the factor of time enters in — the time it takes to plan a unit from scratch compared with the time it would take to help Elaine figure things out on her own. Moreover, Kathy sees how this planning task consumes her own thinking and she wonders whether she could attend simultaneously to Elaine's learning needs. Measured against Kathy's extensive practical knowledge and experience and Elaine's status as novice and learner, it seems more honest for Kathy to take the lead.

Learning to plan with a knowledgeable other

Working alongside her mentor, Elaine has an opportunity to learn about planning and teaching from the inside. As she observes and participates in the design process, Elaine forms ideas about what planning entails while contributing what she can to the developing curriculum. As she attends to Kathy's demonstrations and advice, Elaine learns what to say and do in the lesson, while acquiring contextualized knowledge of students and pedagogy.

There is evidence in the session that Elaine is a student of the planning process. At one point, she says, 'This way of thinking is still baffling to me and I feel like I'm just learning how to do it.' In the midst of planning the Fisher unit, Elaine recalls a time when Kathy helped her plan lessons around a book about Frederick Douglas. She remembers specific questions Kathy asked her and all the decisions they had to make, and she acknowledges the importance of knowing your learners so you can build on what they already know. This is one of the few places in the co-planning session where Kathy explicitly talks about planning.

Elaine You asked me, what did we want these kids to get? In this chapter, what's important? What are we connecting to that they already know? All those decisions. You have to keep making decisions about what you're going to focus on.

Kathy That's what planning is about . . . it is making decisions about what to focus on and what to pursue.

Elaine And I read the book over and over, deciding what words to use, cause I don't really know what they understand and what they don't understand. There's a zillion things to think about.

Kathy It's interesting all the decisions you make.

Elaine And we talked about how we would respond to the questions. We thought a lot about what questions we would ask, how and why, what purpose those questions would serve.

Kathy So you learned a strategy — if I am going to ask questions, I need to think through what am I expecting and why am I asking it?

Elaine What's the big purpose anyway?

Kathy That's good.

Elaine But the big part is being able to get a real feel for kids.

The fact that Elaine recalls this experience while planning the Fisher unit suggests that she is forming a picture of what planning involves, including the questions a teacher has to ask herself and the knowledge she needs to acquire. As Elaine internalizes these questions and develops more knowledge, she will be able to take more independent responsibility for planning. Her needs for assistance will also vary depending on the nature of the planning task.

We can tell from the interchange that Kathy does not always take the lead in co-planning with Elaine. In helping Elaine prepare to teach a book about Frederick Douglas, she apparently adopted a different approach, assisting Elaine in figuring things out rather than doing so much of the thinking herself. Elaine learned a valuable strategy whose relevance she now sees in a new planning context.

This co-planning episode strengthens our belief that joint work on authentic tasks is a powerful form of mentoring. Through co-planning (and co-teaching), mentors can assist novices in learning the intellectual and practical work of teaching. One of the challenges they face is determining where novices are in their learning and what kinds of assistance will help them learn to plan. Elaine, like all novice teachers, faces what Schon (1987) calls 'the paradox of learning to design' — having to learn how to do something without knowing clearly what that something involves. Fortunately she has a mentor teacher who can show her how to plan by planning with her and by enabling her to teach a unit that she could not produce on her own.

Notes

1   This paper was prepared for V. Richardson (Ed) *Constructivist Teacher Education: Theory and Practice* to be published by Falmer Press.
2   In 1993, Michigan State instituted a new, field-based, five-year teacher education program. Four teams of faculty and graduate students offer a version of the program to a cohort of students. Each team has formal relationships with a set of elementary and secondary schools, including some professional development schools. Groups of teachers in these schools work closely with university faculty and graduate students to provide coordinated field experiences for juniors, seniors and interns.
3   In 1992 at a PDS Summer Institute, Kathy approached Sharon and asked for help in working with student teachers. That request launched an ongoing collaboration about how experienced teachers can support and guide novices' learning. For a discussion of their first year of work together which laid the groundwork for mentoring as joint work and co-planning as a form of mentoring, see Feiman-Nemser and Beasley, 1993.
4   In this professional development school, teachers could request a two hour block of 're-allocated' time each week to use for writing, planning and conferring with university colleagues on various PDS projects. A co-teacher, hired with PDS funds, rotated through the classrooms, providing each teacher with his or her re-allocated time.
5   All quotes and exerpts of dialogue are taken from a transcript of the co-planning session, unless otherwise indicated. Occasionally we quote from taped or written commentaries that Kathy produced as we worked on the analysis of the session.

References

Borko, H. and Niles, J. (1987) 'Descriptions of teacher planning: Ideas for teachers and researchers,' in Richardson-Koehler, V. (Ed) *Educators' Handbook*, White Plains, NY, Longman, pp. 167–87.
Carter, K. (1990) 'Teachers' knowledge and learning to teach,' in Houston, W.H. (Ed) *Handbook of Research on Teacher Education*, New York, Macmillan, pp. 291–310.
Clark, C. and Yinger, R. (1977) 'Research on teacher thinking,' *Curriculum Inquiry*, **7**, 2, pp. 279–304.
Cochran-Smith, M. (1991) 'Reinventing student teaching,' *Journal of Teacher Education*, **42**, 2, pp. 104–18.

Constructivist Teacher Education

Collins, A., Brown, A. and Newman, S.E. (1989) 'Cognitive apprenticeship: Teaching the craft of reading, writing and math,' in Resnick, L.B. (Ed) *Knowing, Learning and Instruction: Essays in Honor of Robert Glaser*, Hillsdale, NJ, Erlbaum, pp. 453–94.

Duckworth, E. (1987) *The Having of Wonderful Ideas and Other Essays on Teaching and Learning*, New York, Teachers College Press.

Feiman-Nemer, S. (1995) *Mentoring: A Critical Review*, ERIC Clearinghouse on Teacher Education, Washington, DC, American Association of Colleges for Teacher Education.

Feiman-Nemser, S. and Beasley, K. (1993) 'Discovering and sharing knowledge: Constructing a new role for cooperating teachers,' Paper presented at the Workshop on Teachers' Cognition, Tel Aviv University, Israel.

Fisher, L.E. (1980) *Storm at the Jetty*, Viking Press.

Fisher, L.E. (1982) *Number Art: Thirteen 1, 2, 3's from around the World*, Four Winds Press.

Fisher, L.E. (1984) *Boxes! Boxes!* Viking Press.

Lave, J. and Wegner, E. (1991) *Situated Learning: Legitimate Peripheral Participation*, Cambridge, England, Cambridge University Press.

Leinhardt, G. (1983) 'Novice and expert knowledge in individual students' achievement,' *Educational Psychologist*, **18**, pp. 165–79.

Leinhardt, G. and Greeno, J.G. (1986) 'The cognitive skill of teaching,' *Journal of Educational Psychology*, **78**, pp. 75–79.

Livingston, M.C. (1989) *Up in the Air*, Viking Press.

Rogoff, B. and Lave, J. (Eds) (1984) *Everyday Cognition: Its Development in Social Context*, Cambridge, England, Cambridge University Press.

Schon, D. (1987) *Educating the Reflective Practitioner*, San Francisco, Jossey Bass.

Tharp, R. and Gallimore, R. (1988) *Rousing Minds to Life*, Cambridge, England, Cambridge University Press.

Vygotsky, L. (1978) *Mind and Society*, Cambridge, Mass, Harvard University Press.

Zumwalt, K. (1990) 'Beginning professional teachers: The need for a curricular vision of teaching,' in Reynolds, M. (Ed) *Knowledge Base for the Beginning Teacher*, Elmsford, NY, Pergamon Press, pp. 173–84.

III   *Practice, Research and Theory*

7   Teaching about Constructivism: Using Approaches Informed by Constructivism[1]

Jolie A. Mayer-Smith and Ian J. Mitchell

Introduction

Research into the conceptions and understandings that students hold following instruction (e.g., Gilbert, Osborne and Fensham, 1982; Osborne and Wittrock, 1985; White, 1988) has generated a demand for teaching that is informed by a constructivist perspective on learning. Many preservice teacher education programs have been described that include such a perspective (Wideen, Mayer-Smith and Moon, 1994). But, adopting such an approach involves considerable conceptual change for most preservice teachers, and achieving this is not necessarily easy (Kagan, 1992; Northfield, Gunstone and Erickson, 1996; Wubbels, Korthagen and Dolk, 1992). Research studies indicate mixed results in promoting changes in preservice teachers' beliefs and practices. Hollingsworth (1989) found that preservice students enrolled in a constructivist teacher education program did undergo conceptual change and acquired new beliefs, but that entering beliefs were influential in mediating this process. She indicates that more significant change took place for those individuals who were involved in situations requiring them to confront their beliefs. Feiman-Nemser, *et al.* (1989) reported that an introductory teacher education course designed to assist preservice students in examining beliefs about teaching and learning, was successful in changing the students' conceptions concerning the complexities of teaching, the nature of teacher knowledge, and the relationship between teaching and learning. Fosnot (1992) cites a success story of how an 'immersion program' in which beliefs are discussed and challenged in university and field experiences, promoted preservice teachers to change their practices from traditional to constructivist.

While some scholars report success in promoting preservice students to examine, reconsider, and modify their pedagogical perspectives and practices, many others write about less successful attempts, or the complete failure of programs to impact on the typically traditional views that preservice candidates bring to teacher education programs. McDiarmid (1990) reported that when elementary preservice teachers were confronted with mathematics instruction that challenged their assumptions about teaching, some reflected on and re-evaluated their beliefs, while others resisted and retained their prior conceptions. Gore and Zeichner (1991) found that critically reflective teaching practice was not a predominant element in preservice teachers' reports of their action research projects, despite a strong emphasis on this in their teacher education program. An ongoing theme emerging from these less successful attempts to implement change is the enduring quality of the preservice teachers' entering beliefs. It is evident that even robust efforts of those involved in carefully crafted teacher education programs aimed to promote conceptual change may have minimal effect. This persistence of preservice candidates, entering views of teaching and learning is reminiscent of the resilient nature of pupils' alternative conceptions of science content.

The number of studies reporting similar disappointments (see e.g., Ball, 1990; Olson, 1993) has led some researchers to question the feasibility of changing entering teachers' conceptions through course or program interventions. Still, the research itself has been fruitful. While the results of efforts aimed at promoting conceptual change and an understanding of constructivist perspectives are generally discouraging, they do provide an opportunity for reflection on what isn't working. Scholars involved in this research area have proposed a number of possible explanations for the less than sterling track record. Reasons cited include the short duration of course and program interventions, the critical timing of field and university based experiences (Hollingsworth, 1989), conflicting pedagogical perspectives of universities and schools (Feiman-Nemser and Buchman, 1989), disciplinary backgrounds of the preservice candidates (Mayer-Smith, Moon and Wideen, 1994), mismatches in the theories and strategies espoused in teacher education programs (Eisenhart, Behm and Romagnano, 1991), and the powerful socializing influence of the school culture.

Both authors of this chapter had previously tested the choppy waters of promoting conceptual change in preservice teachers, and like other researchers had experienced mixed results for their efforts. An opportunity to examine this problem in depth emerged in 1990 when we came together to collaborate on the design and instruction of the science methods courses for preservice teachers enrolled in the secondary teacher education program at the University of British Columbia. Informed by our individual experiences we set out to explore whether we could promote a deep understanding of constructivist perspectives on learning, in our preservice students. In planning our course of action we struggled with one of the dilemmas Virginia Richardson introduces in the first chapter of this volume, namely, how could we introduce a constructivist paradigm and focus on teaching practices consistent with that perspective, without 'lecturing' to our students about it? Our thinking on how to manage this dilemma was influenced significantly by several writers (Gunstone and Northfield, 1992; Hewson, *et al.*, 1992; Shymansky, 1992) who had pointed to the need to teach *about* constructivism *using* constructivist-based, rather than didactic approaches. We agreed with this advice and were interested in exploring the extent to which it could overcome the barriers to promoting conceptual change in preservice teachers.

In the remainder of this chapter we describe the authors' perspectives on learning about learning and teaching within the constructivist paradigm, the secondary science methods course we ultimately designed to promote an understanding of these perspectives, and we share some of the outcomes and implications of our attempts to promote conceptual change among our preservice students. We will examine whether teaching about constructivism using approaches informed by constructivism in science methods courses can be used to promote conceptual change in preservice science teachers' views of teaching and learning. We also explore the interplay between conceptual change and the development of teaching practice within the practicum setting, and consider whether it is desirable and feasible for beginning teachers to adopt a constructivist perspective in their classrooms.

Objectives

The specific objectives of our preservice methods course and this study included the following:

1 to encourage reflection on previously held views of science teaching and learning;
2 to promote an understanding of a constructivist perspective on learning and its implication for teaching;
3 to examine the prospects and problems of implementing constructivist-based approaches for promoting conceptual change among preservice teachers; and
4 to examine whether it is feasible for preservice teachers to implement constructivist-based approaches in the practicum setting.

Conceptual Issues and Background Leading to Course Design

Before describing our course we will briefly set out our perspectives on learning and teaching and explain how these influenced the design of our course. We strongly embrace the constructivist view that learning is a process of building knowledge structures (Novak, 1987), and that sensory input such as spoken or written words about formal knowledge will only have meaning to the learner when they are linked to existing elements of memory (Osborne and Wittrock, 1983; Osborne and Wittrock, 1985). If learning is a process, then understanding may be defined as the product of that process. White (1988) describes a person's understanding in a particular area as a network of six different types of elements of memory: propositions, episodes, images, strings, intellectual skills, and motor skills. These elements are operated upon by a seventh type of element — cognitive skills. White's model provides a useful explanation of why one student's understandings are different than another's. One student may have constructed links between a proposition such as 'when light reflects from a smooth surface the angle of incidence equals the angle of reflection', and many episodes from their life outside of school, while another student may have no such links; a third student may have linked this piece of formal propositional knowledge to a particular school lab experience, while other students will not have done so (Tasker and Lambert, 1981; Tasker and Osborne, 1985). In terms of White's characterization of memory, a rich understanding may be regarded as consisting of many elements of memory, including episodes, each linked to many other mental elements.

White's model is also useful in informing our thinking about teaching. One inference that can be drawn is that the teacher should not worry about finding the single, perfect explanation or activity to teach a particular concept. Instead, they should plan and create multiple and varied situations that would permit students to explore and re-explore the given concept, revisiting the concept regularly in a spiral curriculum. This would assist the learner in constructing multiple links, and thus a richer understanding of the concept. The model also implies that teachers should create opportunities to promote linking between propositional knowledge, classroom episodes, and students' personal experiences. It follows that lessons will need to become more fluid and interactive as the teacher learns to respond to student questions that, on the surface, may appear as 'red herrings', or follows up on students' ideas as they raise examples that the teacher may not have intended to discuss. Inherent in this model is the need for the teacher to be flexible and responsive in the design of lessons, and open to the idea of sharing intellectual control of the agenda with the students. Different instructional skills may be required as teachers depart from set agendas, in order to respond to students' comments, questions, and developing understandings of the curriculum.

We recognize that the knowledge building process we describe as learning is mediated and significantly influenced by the sociocultural setting within which learning takes place. The teacher's classroom strategies, which are part of that milieu, have a substantial influence on the quality of students' learning, with some learning being more powerful and meaningful (i.e., 'better') than others. While these ideas seem straight-forward and self-evident to us, we have found that such notions are not easily communicated to our novice practitioners. A significant issue here is the fact that there seems to be no single, convenient adjective that captures entirely the essence of such learning. Ironically, considering all learning as involving construction creates a communication conundrum for constructivists since this seems to make the term 'constructivist learning' redundant. To manage this conundrum, when speaking with our preservice students we have tended to focus on describing the features of learning we envision as useful and powerful (a.k.a. 'good'). We describe such learning as informed, purposeful, intellectually active, and independent. In contrast, learning we regard as weak (a.k.a. 'poor') is passive and superficial. Our views resonate with other scholars who have used labels such as meaningful, deep processing, conscious, and metacognitive as adjectives for learning consistent with a constructivist perspective. In the course we designed we used the phrase 'quality learning' as a convenient label — recognizing that this had little meaning until we more specifically defined what we meant by 'quality'.

Consistent with our view of understanding, we have found it useful to characterize quality learning in terms of the different linking and monitoring processes the learner engages in. For example, linking may involve: linking content of a current lesson to other recent lessons in the same topic, to work done several weeks or months previously on other topics, to work done in other subjects, to personal life, or to the conceptions and explanations that the learner has at the start of the topic. An intention to promote any of these types of linking processes stimulates different (though compatible) teaching actions. Teaching decisions are similarly influenced and mediated by intentions to promote students to engage in different types of monitoring, such as monitoring one's personal understanding (e.g., 'Is this sentence meaningful to me?'), monitoring one's current conceptions (e.g., 'What view of forces am I using here?'), monitoring the meaning of a communication (e.g., 'What was the main idea in this paragraph?'), monitoring one's progress against instructions (e.g., 'Have I done everything specified?') and monitoring one's progress against one's intentions (e.g., 'Why did I begin this problem by calculating the number of moles of HCI remaining in the flask?'). This last example of monitoring illustrates that quality learning also involves learners engaging in regular analysis of tasks and planning of general strategies rather than diving into memorized algorithms. Characterizing quality learning in terms of such specific metacognitive behaviors provided a basis for group discussions and analyses of teaching episodes during our course. It also established a language that could be drawn upon when examining practicum events and situations in order to link these to theoretical perspectives.

While these perspectives on learning and understanding have many implications for teacher educators involved in preservice programs (ourselves included), we emphasize that among those implications, we do not see, nor would we expect to find emerging, a single, simple answer to the question of 'What is the nature of teaching that is consistent with a constructivist perspective on learning?' We do believe, however, that it is possible to describe features of such teaching. Some of these were mentioned previously, such as sharing intellectual control, encouraging questions that assist students in linking knowledge with their personal lives, and implementing flexible and responsive instructional sequences. Other elements include designing tasks that promote student problem-solving, self-monitoring and self-direction. Copying of notes and rote learning of large numbers of facts and propositions would be minimized, while discussions of principles and their application would be emphasized. Barnes (1976) argues for increasing opportunities for student talk which is more tentative, hypothetical, and exploratory. A number of additional teaching implications emerge from Barnes' suggestion, such as the need for teachers to ask more open and exploratory questions, delay judgment of student responses, and listen and respond to what students are saying, rather than listening for right answers, in order to gain insight into their constructed meanings. Finally, in the classroom that adopts a constructivist perspective, assessment approaches would also need to change in ways consistent with the teaching practices.[2]

When one considers traditional and apparently successful classrooms from these perspectives, then learning appears minimal or at least flawed. The teaching taking place in such classrooms has been described as very transmissive (Barnes, 1976) and the learning identified as superficial and dependent on the teacher (Baird and White, 1982a; Baird and White, 1982b). Students in these classrooms tend to adopt a passive approach to learning and acquire a number of poor learning tendencies that influence their behavior and affect their learning. For example, because of the time-constraints and extensive and superfluous amount of detail and directions included in most science labs, many students suffer from what has been described as cognitive overload (Johnstone and Wham, 1982; Newman, 1985). These students approach labwork as they might approach cooking, following a recipe in a mindless manner, focusing on incidentals, and making few, if any, links to the intended underlying theory (Driver, 1983; Tasker and Osborne, 1985).

Despite the rather bleak description of what takes place there, we recognize and acknowledge that traditional classrooms are far from total failures. Some learning does occur and most preservice teachers (as recent graduates) could be described as successful products of the school and university system where transmissive methodologies are commonplace. Preservice candidates' conceptions of teaching and learning are also products of the traditional system that appeared to succeed with them. This has been born out by numerous research studies (e.g., Richardson, 1996; Wideen, Mayer-Smith and Moon, 1996). Richardson's review (1996) of the roles of attitudes and beliefs in teacher education summarizes studies that portray preservice teachers as entering teacher education programs optimistic about their future as teachers, but believing that they have little to learn from the university-based component of the program, and holding what we would describe as traditional, transmissive views of teaching. These are not encouraging starting conditions for preservice teacher educators, but they are consistent with our personal experiences and expectations at the start of the course. Thus, as we considered issues that would influence the design of our course, we recognized that moving our 'traditional' students to an understanding and acceptance of the constructivist perspectives we held, would involve considerable conceptual transformation, especially since we not only hoped to transform their ideas but also their teaching practice, their professional *modus operandi*. Our challenge was to design a course that would most likely be able to overcome significant barriers to change.

One way of conceiving conceptual change is as a revolution initiated by a number of critical incidents. While we believe that critical incidents may have a role to play, it is our contention that conceptual change is better considered as an evolutionary rather than revolutionary process, with many individual incidents contributing. This view of the nature and process of conceptual change also influenced our course design.

Course Structure

The course we describe is part of a one year post-graduate secondary teacher education program at the University of British Columbia. All of our preservice students were science graduates with no preservice teacher training. Their program begins with thirteen weeks of subject specific and general methods and theory courses, interrupted in week eleven for a short two week school experience. This is followed by a semester long practicum experience. The final semester consists of courses on educational theory, assessment, and electives in subject specific areas. We were responsible only for the design and instruction of the general science and chemistry methods courses taught in the first semester. While we were aware of the content dealt with in other courses in the program, we had no input into their design or implementation. We recognized this as one of the limitations of our instructional situation.

Because we expected most of our science preservice teachers would enter our methods courses with relatively transmissive views of teaching and received views of learning, we planned to focus on these critical teaching and learning issues in our methods course. Through these we hoped to build for our preservice students an understanding of the intimate relationship between learning and teaching, and to lay the groundwork for thinking about non-transmissive ways of approaching classroom instruction. We drew on our own experiences as classroom teachers to provide evidence that when attempts are made to tackle these problems in the classroom, substantial changes in class dynamics and learning can be achieved (Mitchell, 1992).

Our view of conceptual change had a number of implications for the course design. Consistent with our notion of conceptual change as a gradual, evolutionary process and our interest in promoting a reconceptualization of learning and teaching among our preservice teachers, we established constructivism as a theme that ran continuously throughout our course, rather than a topic for a given week.

As mentioned, our goal was to teach about constructivism using approaches informed by constructivism. We attempted to accomplish this in the following ways. First, we dealt with content and issues as we would in a non-transmissive classroom. On multiple occasions we placed our preservice teachers in the position of being a learner of science content and modelled methods that were as self-evidently non-transmissive and non-didactic as possible. On these occasions we probed our preservice teachers' initial understandings in an area of science content and asked them to examine, discuss, and on occasion argue their point of view. After participating in an activity, engaging in a discussion, or obtaining more information, we then asked our 'learners' to reexamine their starting points. We also used this pattern of instruction when we dealt with issues of pedagogy and methodology. For example, we began the methods courses by probing our preservice teachers' views of learning and teaching and asked them to revisit these views on various occasions throughout the semester.

Our second strategy was to debrief our classroom experiences and activities along four dimensions of learning:

1   what science (or other) content was learned;
2   what was learned about learning;
3   what was learned about teaching; and
4   what impact (if any) the experience had on their personal beliefs about learning and teaching.

For example, in one class activity we provided our preservice teachers with an extensive collection of graphs each showing a different set of data on distance vs. time, velocity vs. time, or acceleration vs. time for moving cars. Our preservice teachers were assigned a graph and worked in small groups using a toy car to illustrate to the rest of the class the pattern of the toy car's motion that would result in their graph. During this activity we facilitated the presentation by each group and the subsequent classroom discussion, but did not correct or explain any science content until there seemed to be consensus among the preservice teachers. This exercise was very successful in generating a clear understanding of kinematics (dimension 1). We believed that this success was critical to the preservice teachers' willingness to engage seriously in discussion along the other three dimensions. In our debriefing along dimension 2 (learning about learning) we examined how physics concepts could be learned through discussion, and group construction and reconstruction of knowledge with minimal teacher input. We drew upon their experiences of offering and defending their ideas during the role plays, and their debating their ideas with other groups, to bring out issues such as the value of wrong answers, the importance of tentative, exploratory talk, and the risks perceived by classroom pupils when engaging in these learning activities. In dimension 3 (learning about teaching) we considered the teaching skills needed to successfully run such an activity, including delayed judgment, increased wait-time, and ways of reducing perceived risk for pupils. Finally, we discussed whether and how this experience had affected our preservice teachers' thinking about teaching and learning (dimension 4).

The third approach for teaching about constructivism and its implications for practice was through reflective writing. This happened through the use of journals and as an integral part of all assignments. We used it as a means of promoting thinking at a deeper level about the teaching and learning strategies we had tried and debriefed, and as a gauge of our preservice teachers' understanding. This aspect of our course is similar to that reported by other researchers (Bean and Zulich, 1989; Loughran, 1996; Richert, 1990; Statton, 1988). To promote more freedom of expression the journal reflections were not marked — we responded by writing to the individual preservice teachers about the issues they raised, and communicated to the entire class when concerns of a more general nature were evident in what we read.

Our fourth approach was to provide our preservice teachers with a resource of teaching procedures which were developed to promote a range of cognitive and metacognitive learning behaviors we regarded as consistent with our perspective on learning. For this we used a synopsis of over ninety instructional procedures[3] collaboratively developed and tested by teachers participating in the Project for Enhancing Effective Learning (PEEL) (Baird and Northfield, 1992; Baird and Mitchell, 1987). In planning the activities for our methods courses, we selected and modelled a number of these procedures and subsequently debriefed them in the four dimensions mentioned earlier.

In the introductory chapter Virginia Richardson raises a dilemma concerning the role of formal knowledge and 'correct answers' for teaching from a constructivist view of learning. We concur entirely with her assertion that this dilemma is particularly acute for those who work in teacher education. We hold strong views about the often concealed ineffectiveness of transmissive teaching, yet realize these views are not regarded as universally supported truths; they are not accepted by some of our faculty colleagues, and are not recognized by many of the experienced teachers who supervise our preservice teachers. This left us in a quandary as we set out guidelines for the assessment of our preservice teachers. To what extent should or could we mandate a particular point of view? Would we fail one of our students who, for example, ignored or silenced all student questions and comments that did not match his or her agenda? We recognize this as a dilemma that cannot be solved, only managed. On the one hand, we did not (and do not) believe there is a single 'best' style, and we tried to communicate that our views were ideas we encouraged our preservice teachers to explore, rather than rules that they had to follow. On the other hand, we cannot avoid using the label 'poor' to describe certain teaching approaches and beliefs about teaching or learning that we believe are counterproductive. We have good reasons for these negative judgments arising from concerns about such things as the quality of the learning and effects on the students' self-esteem. It is impossible to articulate clear lines between acceptable and unacceptable practice, yet in the end, we had to pass or fail our preservice students. We have no answers to this dilemma, but we were acutely aware of it and tried to manage it as we worked with our students during our courses and their practica.

Collecting Data

Given the difficulties in achieving conceptual change in preservice teacher education courses and programs, we were interested in exploring the effectiveness of our course in this area. We collected data before the practicum (i.e., during our course), during the extended, second semester practicum, and after the practicum.

Before the Practicum

The preservice teachers' journal entries and the reflection sections of each assignment provided insights as to whether they could use, and whether they would choose to use a constructivist perspective to reflect on events and/or to identify practices that were less likely to generate quality learning. The journal entries were not marked, and the assignments were not evaluated against a criterion of conformity with a course 'party line'. Still, we are aware that because of our role as course instructors and gatekeepers to the profession, our students' writings cannot be taken as certain indicators of their 'beliefs'.

During the Practicum

While about ninety preservice teachers were enrolled in science methods, the structure of the practicum in our teacher education program meant that most of these individuals would be supervised by faculty advisors who had little or no knowledge of our course. There was no feasible way of assisting these staff to build a sufficiently rich understanding of what we had done in our course, for them to validly answer questions such as: To what extent are the preservice teachers you are supervising using our perspective on learning and teaching during their practicum? Accordingly, we decided to focus on the sixteen preservice teachers who were being supervised by the two authors, or by our teaching assistant who had attended our course throughout the semester and had collaborated with us on a number of aspects of its presentation. These sixteen preservice teachers were assigned to us randomly by the university's placement processes and, from our knowledge of our students, they appeared to be a representative sample.

We wanted to know the extent to which our preservice teachers would attempt to implement teaching practices that reflected a constructivist perspective, the level of success of these attempts, the reasons the preservice teachers would give for what they did, and the way they framed their practicum experiences. Our weekly observations of their teaching meant that we had about eleven opportunities to gather data on these questions. We noted general teaching behaviors, such as the type of questions they asked and the way they responded to their pupils' questions, answers, comments and suggestions. We also noted the extent to which our preservice teachers used teaching procedures we had modelled or discussed in classes, or which were included in the resource summarizing ninety-one instructional procedures that we had distributed during the course. In out-of-class discussions we listened to the way they spoke about their intentions and practice, and used this as information to judge the extent to which they had an integrated and coherent view of the ideas we had presented. For example, Did they consistently use a constructivist lens?

An unplanned source of data emerged as we heard a number of unsolicited comments by the faculty advisors of our other seventy-five preservice students, concerning the observation of teaching procedures that these faculty advisors regarded as unusual or original (and which we recognized as related to our course). These comments provided one, albeit crude, form of validation that the practices we were seeing in our group of sixteen students were not restricted to that sample. (Such an outcome might imply that the use of non-transmissive approaches was the result of preservice students wishing to please their faculty advisors [us], rather than the influence of their pre-practicum experiences in our course.)

After the Practicum

In the weeks following the extended practicum, after the preservice teachers had received their satisfactory teaching reports, we interviewed all sixteen of our sample. We wanted information on some questions not yet addressed, as well as data which would triangulate with those from the sources just listed. The interviews were variously done by the first author, our teaching assistant (neither of whom interviewed the students they had previously supervised), and a research assistant who was very familiar with our course. We designed the interview protocol to address six questions:

1 What were the preservice teachers' post-practicum understandings of the ideas presented in the methods course?
2 Were the preservice teachers able to separate the ideas presented in the methods course from the specific content-contexts we had used to present them?
3 How much overlap was there between the methods course activities that we had judged to be successful, and those that our preservice teachers had found useful or influential?
4 How accurate were our judgments concerning the conceptual change and growth we perceived in our preservice teachers?
5 When discussing methods course activities, to what extent did our preservice teachers perceive or recall the four dimensions we had used to debrief them? (During the course we had been explicit about shifting from, say, a learning to a teaching focus, but we had not stated 'there are four dimensions'.)
6 Could we identify causes of success or failure in promoting conceptual change?

Results

Deciding precisely what should be regarded as success in promoting an understanding of constructivism in a preservice teacher education course is a subjective process. As part of that process one must answer the question: What proportion of students should demonstrate acceptance and mastery of the course content and concepts? Many factors affect the answer to this question. A driving instructor who is teaching pupils to execute a handbrake start on a hill will presumably hope for close to 100 per cent success. The rather pessimistic nature of the conceptual change literature summarized earlier, together with our own experiences in this area meant that our expectations were considerably lower than those of a driving instructor. In our view, the data we report here demonstrates a level of success at the optimistic end of our hopes. Overall, we found that eleven of the sixteen preservice teachers in our study were significantly influenced by the constructivist aspects of our course.

While each of our preservice teachers was uniquely different, for the purposes of communicating our interpretations of the data, we have considered each individual in one of four groups along a continuum of course influence ranging from those preservice teachers showing evidence of being deeply influenced to those that appeared to construct limited or negligible understanding. At the most positive end, were a group of six preservice teachers in our study for whom all the available data demonstrated understandings, espoused beliefs, and classroom practices which were coherent and consistent with the ideas that we had been promoting. A second group, of five teachers, frequently took a constructivist perspective and regularly used ideas from our course. However they lacked the consistency and coherency of the first group. Our third group contained four individuals for whom a few parts of our course appeared to have struck a chord, while other aspects were either not understood or ignored, and episodes that we regarded as consistent with an understanding of constructivism were occasional and isolated. At the most negative end of the continuum was a single preservice teacher who demonstrated minimal understanding or acceptance of any aspect of constructivism and its implications for teaching.

The data from journal entries and written assignments completed during the methods course, and the interviews at the end of the long practicum provided evidence that of the sixteen preservice teachers we had followed closely, most (n=13) were able to distinguish between didactic practices and non-transmissive teaching approaches compatible with a constructivist perspective on learning. Furthermore, these teacher candidates demonstrated some familiarity with and comprehension of aspects of teaching for conceptual change.

Julia's journal entry midway through our methods course provides evidence of her developing understanding that the ideas pupils construct may not match what the teacher intends.

> It must be remembered that we as the teacher represent only one perspective. How we view a lesson is not necessarily how the student views it. The lesson may seem very straightforward to us, but not to the students. Or, alternatively, it may seem straightforward to them too, but they may have gotten something totally different out of it, [different] than you [the teacher] intended. (Julia, journal entry, October 25, 1991)

During his interview Phillip speaks about his recognition of the importance of considering pupils' ideas when planning for instruction.

> The major thing that influenced me, was learning how to use knowledge that students' previously had, and incorporating that into lessons. I think that everything we did in the course was built around that and it set the framework for me in terms of what I did in the practicum. I didn't try to go in there and try to fill their heads with everything. I used knowledge they previously had and tried to build on that. (Phillip, interview, June, 1992)

It was also evident that there were preservice teachers in our group that did not develop a deep understanding of constructivism nor a grasp of the elements of teaching to promote quality learning. Mark, who arrived in our course with an exceptional background knowledge of science and a traditional view that excellent teaching was characterized by creativity and clear presentation of content, was the one participant in our study who seemed entirely resistant to changing his beliefs. He wrote in his journal near the end of the semester, 'I regret to say that I wouldn't change to any great degree my original comments on teaching and learning. I might add a few more comments, such as "expect the unexpected" and "know your audience" (e.g., what they know, and the best teaching technique to use, etc.), but otherwise my opinions are more or less the same.' Even after his long practicum where he experienced problems teaching to the level of his junior high school pupils, Mark remained quite steadfast in his views, 'the way I approach this program is trying to dig out all the practical aspects. I'll worry about the theory once I've got my teaching underway' (Mark, final interview, June 1992).

As might be expected, we found a range of interpretations and agreement with the perspectives of the course. Each preservice candidate we worked with constructed their own understanding of what we were attempting to communicate through our various activities. In a manner reminiscent of pupils who integrate science concepts into their own alternative frameworks, Mark selected specific ideas from the course and used these to support his initial views of teaching and learning. He was unable to recognize elements from activities which were designed to help him challenge and reconstruct his ideas.

Other preservice teachers drew from bits and pieces of the course yet spoke about these in a manner that reflected a developing understanding of the messages we had hoped to convey. The 'patchiness' of their understanding was manifest in their focusing on particular aspects of activities, and ignoring or being unaware of other pedagogical issues we had tried to emphasize. This was evident in their discussions of the car graphs activity which we had debriefed along the four dimensions described earlier. When they spoke or wrote about this course activity, most of our preservice teachers focused on issues that related to two or three of the dimensions, but not all four. Still, we regarded this as evidence that the activity had been a success. A subset of our preservice students emphasized the physics content of activity over the learning and teaching issues. Some saw the car graph activity as aiming to teach them or help them review their knowledge of physics, while others suggested the activity was primarily intended as an example of how they should present the concepts of kinematics. For these individuals the content being used to illustrate the procedure or case was seen as the central idea being presented. While the broader issues of teaching and learning that were in the post-discussion that followed were not lost, they were seen to be of lesser significance. The following examples illustrate the range of interpretations that this activity elicited among our preservice teachers.

Saul focused primarily on the physics content of the activity rather than the pedagogical issues. He seemed to be 'stuck' in his role as a student of science although he was able to discuss issues pertaining to learning in more general terms. He didn't tend to view the activity through the teacher's lens.

> This was done because we [student teachers] needed to refresh our understanding of basic physics. This got us to be active learners and not just observers. (Saul, interview, June 1981)

Allison did understand that we were trying to illustrate the value of a particular approach to teaching, but her difficulty with the physics content of the activity frustrated her, and seemed to prevent her from taking away some of the broader messages.

> This showed that role playing the graphs was more practical than just showing the graphs. The kids could see it better and relate it to everyday experiences. But, I personally got nothing from this activity because I didn't understand the physics and felt lost and confused. (Allison, interview, June 1981)

Other students were able to recognize some of the more substantive pedagogical issues raised during our classroom discussion of the events.

> What I took away from the car graphs activity was the idea that a lot of things that you wouldn't normally see as being role-played, can be. For example, there are a lot of concepts in biology that I could role play that wouldn't normally be considered for this strategy. There is a variety of different ways to teach something so kids take it away. The fact is you can use these different, challenging approaches to help kids learn better in the long run. (Phillip, interview, June 1981)

> This [activity] let us see and experience learning from a student's perspective . . . this will give us more power when we work as a teacher setting up these activities. It wouldn't have been nearly as powerful if it had just been explained to us. I think that is why they let us take an hour on that activity. I gained a better understanding that it is not necessary for a teacher to be the source of all information. Letting the student flounder around a bit with some direction, and bounce ideas off each other can be a better way of learning because the ideas they come up with are their own, and so they may trust them more. I realized that this really does work. (Sandra, interview, June 1981)

Both of these preservice teachers were able to separate the science content from the procedure. Phillip was able to see how the activity might be transferable to different instructional contexts. Sandra considered the value of the activity through a learner's eyes, and then reflected on issues that related to teaching, teacher education, and constructivist pedagogy. But, while Sandra enjoyed and learned about teaching when she assumed the role of a student, Ben found this approach distracting and annoying.

> We got bogged down in the science and that frustrated me. I wanted to be treated more as a teacher than as a student, building on prior knowledge. I don't really need to relive the experience . . . I can appreciate it . . . but it was a major sore spot for me. (Ben, interview, June 1981)

As mentioned earlier we were also interested in finding out whether these students could or would choose to implement teaching practices that reflected an understanding of constructivist pedagogy. Thus, during the extended practicum we noted their teaching actions, the procedures they selected, and the manner in which they spoke about their practice. We also considered what events and issues might be influencing their decision to implement a particular procedure.

Our observations of practicum teaching indicated the ability of a significant number of our preservice teachers (n=11) to implement regularly approaches informed by constructivism. In this regard we found students exploring and experimenting with a range of the procedures we had introduced in our course, and some of their lessons were ambitious efforts for beginning practitioners. Prior views of pupils were probed and acknowledged, fluid discussions were undertaken where pupils were asked to consider their beliefs in light of scientific evidence, and role plays and concept mapping tasks were designed to promote linking of science concepts to pupils' personal experiences. Most of these undertakings were successful and none were 'instructional flops', but in certain instances the preservice teachers needed support and guidance as to how to proceed in order to build on their particular strategy. We illustrate this by including some episodes from the practicum. We believe that in these cases it was useful and valuable that the faculty advisor had also been the methods instructor.

Ben decided to begin a unit on digestion by breaking his junior high school class into groups and assigning each group a particular food type (e.g., fats, carbohydrates, proteins). With no additional teacher input on the topic, he then asked the pupils to design a role play that illustrated their group's current ideas about how the body deals with the particular food type they had been assigned. He intended to observe the role plays, and in the subsequent lesson, after a night's reflection and analysis, respond to what emerged. Unfortunately the role plays did not end neatly at the end of a lesson, and he had to begin his response only minutes after seeing the last two groups. He found himself struggling and unclear about how he should or could attend to the wide range of students' entering conceptions (e.g., body fat coming only from fatty foods found in the diet, etc.) that were revealed during the groups' presentations.

Julia developed a short set of open ended questions to begin her unit on junior chemistry. In her probe she asked her pupils to write about and illustrate their initial understanding of various states of matter. In reporting back to her class the following day she found herself face-to-face with the dilemma of how to present scientific explanations without discouraging her pupils from sharing their entering and often alternative views. She chose to delay judgment. In her post-lesson discussion she spoke about how she felt quite uncomfortable in front of the class and realized that she lacked experience and perhaps some pertinent subject matter knowledge that would help inform her pedagogical decision making in such an instructional situation.

The difficulties that Ben and Julia experienced illustrate one of the more complex skills associated with teaching from a constructivist perspective: reacting in ways that are both supportive of student input that reveals unexpected views and interests, while at the same time maintaining some fidelity to the intended curriculum. Knowledge of how best to go about harnessing pupils' questions and ideas on a particular topic is a classic example of what Shulman (1986) refers to as pedagogical content knowledge, the wisdom about teaching a particular piece of content that can only be acquired through the act and practice of teaching it.

Sandra, who successfully implemented a range of approaches consistent with a constructivist perspective, found inexperience wasn't the only stumbling block in the way of getting some of the strategies she learned in our methods course 'to work'. When she initially tried to get her pupils to speak to each other, and to monitor what they understood, she learned this didn't agree with their views of appropriate teaching behavior.

> I tried to get things going . . . to get students to tell the teacher what they understood, where they went wrong. I tried to take me out of the picture, out of the role of being the direct authority. But, when I wasn't giving students direct answers, I had some backlash. They told me 'you're supposed to be the teacher'. Still, I think it started to work. (Sandra, interview, June 1992)

While these preservice teachers experienced some difficulties in their attempts to implement non-traditional teaching strategies, it didn't deter them from continuing their efforts. They felt positive that although they were a bit inexperienced and clumsy in their efforts, they had taken a valuable course of action. In the case of Linda, a non-assertive preservice teacher with a quiet classroom demeanor, adopting non-transmissive classroom strategies turned out to be beneficial in helping her manage what could have developed into a serious classroom control problem.

Linda taught a difficult Science 8 class which contained a boy who was disruptive and aggressive and inclined to loudly interrupt lessons and distract other pupils. Rather than tightening the reins and establishing herself as a rigid authoritarian, Linda opted to give her students more 'voice' and make the class highly interactive. She made use of interpretive discussion procedures, encouraged student discourse, and integrated her pupils' ideas (including those from her 'problem student') into the lessons she taught. The result was startling — she established an excellent classroom atmosphere that was harmonious, supportive and totally non-confrontational.

While numerous instances confirmed that our preservice teachers were able to put into practice the ideas and procedures we had introduced in our course, five of our group of sixteen teachers chose to utilize mostly traditional didactic practices. When these individuals discussed their teaching it became apparent that there were a number of reasons for this. As mentioned previously Mark was untouched by the events of the course and drew most of his ideas from his recollections of teaching he had experienced during his university years. Louise explained that she realized she was being 'traditional', but that her school advisor had pressured her to cover so much content that she felt she couldn't try out many activities. This view was echoed by a number of our preservice teachers, including some who decided to take the risk of ignoring this pressure and continuing to experiment (although, we recognize that our presence, advice, and support may have influenced their decisions). Classroom pupils were also cited as exerting an influence on our preservice teachers' instructional approach — in some cases pupils were uncooperative, unenthusiastic, or outspoken about not liking a particular procedure that was 'different' from what they regarded as appropriate teaching. This led some supervising teachers to counsel our preservice teachers to stick to traditional, safe practices that would 'create fewer waves' and make it easier to control their classes.

Another problem that became apparent was the difficulty that some of our preservice teachers had, once in the practicum, of recognizing *when* a particular teaching procedure modelled in our methods courses could be relevant and applied in their lessons. They could remember our course activities but regarded these as 'embedded' in particular science content and thus not useful for their planning. We also found some of these preservice teachers regarded our approaches and activities as 'add ons' that could be used 'if there was time'. This led to their combining transmissive teaching with concept mapping, discussions of student views, etc., which were being implemented merely to break up the pattern of teacher talk–students write notes.

To summarize, we felt that the data showed our course managed and overcame some of the formidable obstacles to conceptual change in preservice teachers, cited in the literature. The data also illustrated a range of issues that can significantly impact on success or failure in this area. These include:

- the coherency of the understandings constructed by the preservice teacher regarding the ideas presented in university courses;
- the ability of the preservice teacher when planning to teach a particular topic, to draw on ideas that were presented using different topic contexts;

- the degree of development of pedagogical content knowledge;
- the reactions of the pupils and the supervising teachers to new approaches; and
- the presence or absence of timely advice on how to deal with instructional problems from a constructivist perspective. Advice on how to capitalize on a successful lesson is equally important.

Thus, it became evident that the frequency and willingness of our preservice teachers to implement approaches informed by constructivism and the degree of success they experienced were related to a number of complex issues. It is on some of these issues and their implications for those involved with programs of teacher education that we will focus for the remainder of this chapter.

Discussion

In discussions with other university methods instructors, secondary school supervising teachers, and preservice teachers about our course, we became aware of the following three commonly held assertions about learning to teach and teaching science:

- a preservice teacher cannot use 'these approaches'[4] in the practicum.
- a beginning teacher should not attempt 'these approaches' until they have first mastered more 'basic skills'.
- any teacher should spend several weeks with a new class establishing control, and only then can 'these approaches' be contemplated.

As these assertions raise important issues that need to be considered in light of the increasing number of teacher education programs that implicitly or explicitly identify conceptual change as one of their goals, we will consider each of them in turn. We will clarify the arguments made by those who support these assertions and then provide some commentary from our perspective and experience.

Assertion 1   A preservice teacher cannot use 'these approaches'
Proponents of this view offer several arguments to support it. First, they indicate that because the teaching approaches we modelled and advocated were 'less structured', they are more difficult to implement because they require more complex teaching skills and make classroom management more difficult. Second, they point out that 'these approaches' are very different from traditional classroom teaching where the roles of the pupil and teacher are clearly defined. They suggest that the pupils will need to be taught new classroom practices and behaviors *and* that the pupils may not readily accept the new role(s) and responsibilities they are being given. This will create more difficulties for the preservice teacher who is learning to deal with the multiple facets

of learning to teach. Third, they suggest that the supervising teacher may not recognize or accept these 'alternate' approaches as valid teaching and learning practices.

While we have sympathy with these arguments we contend, based on our personal experiences teaching in school classrooms from a constructivist perspective and observations of our preservice teachers, that some of these issues are less problematic than they appear. When considered collectively, teaching approaches consistent with a constructivist perspective may appear less structured than, for example, a traditional lecture or worksheet activity. However, a number of strategies used to promote cognitive and metacognitive learning are highly structured (e.g., concept mapping, Venn diagrams). That these activities are different than the traditional ones does suggest that the teacher will need to explain and provide practice. However, a new procedure often does not require new skills but rather the application of traditional skills in new ways. For example a teaching procedure that requires pupils to translate scientific content into a creative writing piece will require some explanation of the method but will draw on a number of traditional skills including reading and interpreting text, presenting ideas clearly in full sentences, using appropriate punctuation, working quietly, independently, or in groups, etc. Seen in this sense, many (not all) 'non-traditional' strategies do not require new skills but merely build on pieces of previously established classroom knowledge and accepted behaviors essential to the successful use of any classroom procedure.

All teaching procedures, including those regarded as traditional and highly structured, require knowledge and experience with a set of overlapping skills which need to be introduced in a teacher education program. We believe that one should not teach about constructivism without teaching the skills and classroom knowledge associated with it. We also recognize that more 'fluid', less-structured teaching procedures *do* require different teaching skills, however, it is our observation that these have not proved to be more difficult to learn than any other skills. It is also important to distinguish between the skills of running a fluid and highly interactive discussion with a class of students who are used to this approach, and the skills of preparing and teaching this procedure to a group of students accustomed to traditional approaches. The latter situation is significantly more demanding than the former for any teacher, preservice or other, for it integrates promoting pupil change with implementing elements of instruction. Pupil change is a gradual and complex process that requires teacher commitment, stimulation, and support (Mitchell, 1994), and any efforts devoted to changing pupils' learning behaviors must also include planning to change pupils' conceptions of and attitudes to teaching (Baird and Mitchell, 1987).

We understand that the feasibility of implementing any procedure that requires significant pupil change during the practicum depends on both the support of the supervising teacher and the acceptance of the pupils. We also recognize that successful experimentation and innovation by preservice teachers are influenced by a number of other factors including content knowledge, teaching load and responsibilities, and beliefs about teaching, learning, and knowledge (Mayer-Smith, Moon and Wideen, 1994). However, if the supervising teacher supports and permits some exploration by the preservice teacher in their practicum, we contend that the arguments made earlier should not be used as an excuse for transmissive teaching.

Assertion 2   Preservice teachers should first master more basic skills
There are two beliefs implicit in this assertion that we wish to address here:

1   Teaching from a constructivist perspective is a frill or an 'extra' which is not as relevant as the basic skills such as dealing with pupils, explanation, and questioning.
2   These approaches can be add-ons to existing approaches.

We disagree with both of these points. Constructivism is a view of how knowledge is constructed, which in turn has generated a perspective on how learning occurs (von Glaserfeld, 1989). Constructivism is *not* a style of teaching. This suggests that when one embraces a constructivist perspective on learning, then to be consistent with this view one must use teaching approaches that promote cognition, metacognition, student self-monitoring, self-direction, etc. Considering 'these approaches' as add-ons, to be used occasionally in tandem with traditional or didactic teaching would be as inconsistent as lecturing about constructivism. Furthermore, as mentioned in the previous section, we believe many constructivist procedures utilize the 'more basic skills' alluded to in this assertion. Therefore 'mastering basic skills' is accomplished *while* the preservice teacher engages in teaching from a constructivist perspective. We also disagree with those teacher educators that believe assuming a constructivist stance in the classroom is part of series of developmental steps in learning to teach, where the novice teacher would begin with traditional, highly structured approaches and gradually move on to constructivist pedagogy. It is our view that beginning with a transmissive approach would be equivalent to heading off on a long journey down the wrong freeway, in the opposite direction — eventually one will have to turn back and retrace their steps.

Several authors (e.g., Gunstone and Northfield, 1994; Wubbels *et al.*, 1992) have described learning to teach as a process of conceptual change. Mitchell (1994) describes teacher change as the result of a continual interplay between changes in teaching beliefs, attitudes, trusts, and behaviors — changes in each area influence the other. We contend that it is not possible for a teacher education course to achieve changes in preservice teachers' beliefs about teaching and learning without influencing attitudes and promoting behaviors consistent with such beliefs. However, since we regard conceptual change as gradual and evolutionary, it would be illogical to suggest that change begins and ends with a single methods course. If conceptual change is to continue we contend that the practicum experience must provide a supportive environment and multiple opportunities for preservice teachers to explore and experiment with the ideas and procedures presented in methods courses. These ideas and procedures are neither frills nor extras but rather the 'basic skills' that our preservice teachers need to master.

Assertion 3   Any teacher (preservice included) should begin by establishing control before implementing 'these approaches'

Implementing 'less traditional, less structured' teaching procedures does not necessarily lead to poorly managed classes. Even more fluid teaching approaches have structure and, as mentioned previously, build on traditional skills that pupils are familiar with. We recognize that classrooms must be orderly and that teachers must have control if learning is to take place in an intended manner. However we do not agree that establishing orderly classes is synonymous with implementing tightly structured tasks where the teacher dominates and prescribes every action. For example, in many humanities classes, pupils regularly participate in very loosely structured tasks within an orderly classroom environment in which the teacher plays a facilitative role (Mayer-Smith, Moon and Wideen, 1994). Thus, we contend that it is not the degree of fluidity that determines whether a class remains manageable and whether students engage in learning in an orderly manner, but rather whether the teacher has fully thought through his or her intentions and design for a given learning task. This would be the same regardless of whether a traditional or constructivist classroom was being considered.

We find it useful to distinguish between management control (which teachers must have) and intellectual control, and assert that the latter can be 'shared' with pupils without compromising, and in fact, often enhancing the former. Consider here the case of Linda working with her difficult Science 8 class. Much misbehavior stems from a lack of pupil interest, and providing pupils with an opportunity to negotiate and provide input into the class procedures generates a sense of shared ownership. This has been identified as a key component of high levels of interest in student science classes (Mitchell, 1993).

Will preservice teachers adopt and use a constructivist perspective? Posner *et al.* (1982) suggested that for a new idea to be accepted and implemented it must be seen to be intelligible, plausible, and fruitful. Northfield *et al.* (1987) added a fourth criteria, namely, that it must also be feasible in the context where its use is being considered. Using the model of Posner *et al.* (1982) to examine our attempts to promote conceptual change and an understanding of a constructivist perspective on learning and its implication for teaching, highlights the importance of the practicum experience in teacher education. University experiences such as those designed and included in our methods course can make constructivism intelligible: preservice teachers can build a satisfactorily detailed meaning from a range of activities, and plausible: the preservice teachers recognize that they can learn difficult content without didactic explanations. Such experiences may also contribute to some aspects of fruitfulness. For example, many of our preservice teachers enjoyed activities such as the car graphs and said that they would like to use similar activities in their classrooms. However, only the actual practicum setting provides evidence for whether constructivist-based approaches are fruitful — e.g., are the lessons participatory and does significant learning occur? Moreover, only the practicum experiences can answer questions of feasibility such as whether the curriculum can be taught in the time allowed using these approaches.

Conclusion

Through our experiences as instructors teaching methods courses and as faculty supervisors observing practica experiences we have learned a great deal about helping our preservice teachers understand and make sense of a constructivist perspective and its implications for classroom practice, and we have developed a richer understanding of the complexities of this task. Much of what we have learned supports what other researchers have found, namely that conceptual change in preservice teachers is possible, and that some, but not all, preservice candidates will be receptive to, and develop, a deep understanding of constructivist pedagogy. We also have gained some specific insights from trying to illustrate the application of constructivist theory in practice. Here we have learned how easy it is for theoretical ideas to become embedded and lost in the specific content contexts used to exemplify these ideas. Attempting to solve this problem leads to a dilemma. If one introduces the application of constructivist ideas within a specific context, say, as part of a physics example, then many preservice teachers will only think of those ideas when considering that particular instructional context. But, if one introduces or describes the same ideas in general terms only, the ideas are regarded as too theoretical, and thus inaccessible or useless. To manage this dilemma we believe it is essential to introduce ideas using multiple contexts whenever time permits.

Like other teacher educators who work within the constraints of a one year preservice program we recognize there are a number of limitations to what can be accomplished. We believe that some problems can be manipulated by adjusting the timing of program elements — but ultimately this is just a balancing act. We still have no pat answers to some fundamental questions such as, Should we provide exposure to constructivist pedagogy after preservice teachers have some classroom experience, in order that there is some context for discussion? Or, should we engage with constructivist perspectives and instructional procedures congruent with these, first, so that preservice teachers can practice and explore the use of these ideas and procedures in the lower risk setting of the university? Should the practicum be long and uninterrupted to allow for coherence and continuity of the experience, or should it occur in several short sections to provide ample opportunities for discussing the interplay between constructivist theory and classroom practice? How do we share with supervising teachers the pedagogical ideas and practices that we have spent a semester or more working to communicate to our preservice teachers? And finally, how do we support and encourage preservice teachers to try out in their practicum classrooms what they have learned about constructivist pedagogy in their university methods courses?

Notes

1 An earlier version of this chapter was presented at the annual meeting of the American Educational Research Association, New Orleans, 1994.

2 Although the reader may infer at this point that we believe all lessons in a classroom where constructivist pedagogy is featured should involve fluid, interactive discussions, this is not the case. There may be times, for example, when a lecture is appropriate, but we believe that such a teaching practice will need to be accompanied by one or more tasks that promote student processing of new information via some type of linking or monitoring exercise.

3 We use the word procedures rather than strategies to describe classroom tactics such as role play or concept mapping. We reserve the word strategy for longer term series of actions (which usually include a number of procedures) such as a strategy for increasing the proportion of students who regularly contribute to discussions.

4 The term 'these approaches' refers to the collection of constructivist-based strategies and teaching procedures we modelled and debriefed in our methods courses.

References

BAIRD, J.R. and MITCHELL, I.J. (Eds) (1987) *Improving the Quality of Teaching and Learning: An Australian Case Study — The Peel Project*, Melbourne, Australia, The Monash University Printery.

BAIRD, J.R. and NORTHFIELD, J.R. (Eds) (1992) *Learning from the PEEL Experience*, Melbourne, Monash University.

BAIRD, J.R. and WHITE, R.T. (1982a) 'A case study of learning styles in biology', European *Journal of Science Education*, **4**, pp. 325–37.

BAIRD, J.R. and WHITE, R.T. (1982b) 'Promoting self-control of learning', *Instructional Science*, **11**, pp. 227–47.

BALL, D.L. (1990) 'Breaking with experience in learning to teach mathematics: The role of a preservice methods course', *International Journal of Mathematics Education*, **10**, 2, pp. 10–16.

BARNES, D. (1976) *From Communication to Curriculum*, Harmondsworth, UK, Penguin.

BEAN, T.W. and ZULICH, J. (1989) 'Using dialogue journals to foster reflective practice with preservice content-area teachers', *Teacher Education Quarterly*, **16**, 1, pp. 5–13.

DRIVER, R. (1983) *The Pupil as Scientist*, Milton Keynes, Open University Press.

EISENHART, M., BEHM, L. and ROMAGNANO, L. (1991) 'Learning to teach: Developing expertise or rite of passage?', *Journal of Education for Teaching*, **17**, 1, pp. 51–71.

FEIMAN-NEMSER, S. and BUCHMAN, M. (1989) 'Describing teacher education: A framework and illustrative findings from a longitudinal study of six students', *The Elementary School Journal*, **89**, 3, pp. 365–77.

FEIMAN-NEMSER, S., McDIARMID, G., MELNICK, S. and PARKER, M. (1989) *Changing Beginning Teachers' Conceptions: A Description of an Introductory Teacher Education Course* (Research Report 89–1), East Lansing, National Center for Research on Teacher Education, College of Education, Michigan State University.

FOSNOT, C.T. (1992) 'Learning to teach, teaching to learn: The center for constructivist teaching-learning preparation project', Paper presented at the annual meeting of the American Educational Research Association, San Francisco.

GILBERT, J.K., OSBORNE, R. and FENSHAM, P. (1982) 'Children's science and its consequences for teaching', *Science Education*, **66**, pp. 623–33.

GORE, J.M. and ZEICHNER, K.M. (1991) 'Action research and reflective teaching in preservice teacher education: A case study from the United States', *Teaching and Teacher Education*, **7**, 2, pp. 119–36.

GUNSTONE, R. and NORTHFIELD, J. (1992) 'Conceptual change: Approaches in teacher education', Paper presented at the annual meeting of the American Educational Research Association, San Francisco, CA.

GUNSTONE, R.F. and NORTHFIELD, J.R. (1994) 'Conceptual change: Approaches in teacher education', Paper presented at the annual meeting of the American Educational Research Association, San Francisco, CA.

HEWSON, P.W., ZEICHNER, K.M., TABACHNICK, B.R., BLOMKER, K.B. and TOOLIN, R. (1992) 'A conceptual change approach to science teacher education at the University of Wisconsin-Madison', Paper presented at the annual meeting of the American Educational Research Association, San Francisco, CA.

HOLLINGSWORTH, S. (1989) 'Prior beliefs and cognitive change in learning to teach', *American Educational Research Journal*, **26**, 2, pp. 160–89.

JOHNSTONE, A.H. and WHAM, A.J.B. (1982) 'The demands of practical work', *Education in Chemistry*, **19**, pp. 71–3.

KAGAN, D.M. (1992) 'Professional growth among preservice and beginning teachers', *Review of Educational Research*, **62**, 2, pp. 129–65.

LOUGHRAN, J. (1996) *Developing Reflective Practice: Learning about Teaching and Learning through Modelling*, London, Falmer Press.

MAYER-SMITH, J.A., MOON, B.J. and WIDEEN, M.F. (1994) 'Learning to teach within the two cultures of the humanities and the sciences', Paper presented at the annual meeting of the American Educational Research Association, New Orleans, LA.

McDIARMID, G.W. (1990) 'Challenging prospective teachers during early field experiences: A quixotic undertaking?', *Journal of Teacher Education*, **41**, pp. 12–20.

MITCHELL, I.J. (1992) 'The class level', in BAIRD, J.R. and NORTHFIELD, J.R. (Eds) *Learning from the PEEL Experience*, Melbourne, Monash University.

MITCHELL, I.J. (1993) 'Teaching for quality learning', Unpublished PhD, Monash University.

MITCHELL, I.J. (1994) 'School-tertiary collaboration: A long term view', *International Journal of Science Education*, **16**, 5, pp. 599–612.

NEWMAN, B. (1985) 'Realistic expectations for traditional laboratory work', *Research in Science Education*, **15**, pp. 8–12.

NORTHFIELD, J.R., DUIGNAN, P.A. and McPHERSON, R.T.S. (1987) 'Educative leadership for quality learning', *Educative Leader Series*, NSW Department of Education, Sydney.

NORTHFIELD, J.R., GUNSTONE, R.F. and ERICKSON, G. (1996) 'Constructing an approach to science teacher education', in TREAGUST, D., DUIT, R. and FRASER, B. (Eds) *Improving Teaching and Learning in Science and Mathematics*, Sydney, NSW, Falmer Press.

NOVAK, J.D. (1987) *Proceedings of the Second International Seminar: Misconceptions and Education Strategies in Science and Mathematics*, Ithaca, NY.

OLSON, M. (1993) 'Knowing what counts in teacher education', Paper presented at the annual meeting of the Canadian Society for the Study of Education, Ottawa, Canada.

OSBORNE, R.J. and WITTROCK, M.C. (1983) 'Learning science: A generative process', *Science Education*, **67**, 4, pp. 489–508.

OSBORNE, R.J. and WITTROCK, M.C. (1985) 'Generative learning model and its implication for science education', *Studies in Science Education,* **12**, pp. 59–87.

POSNER, G.J., STRIKE, K.A., HEWSON, P.W. and GERTZOG, W.A. (1982) 'Accommodation of a scientific conception: Towards a theory of conceptual change', *Science Education* **66**, 2, pp. 211–27.

RICHARDSON, V. (1996) 'The role of attitudes and beliefs in learning to teach', in SIKULA, J. (Ed) *The Handbook of Research on Teacher Education,* (2nd edition), New York, Macmillan, pp. 102–19.

RICHERT, A.E. (1990) 'Teaching teacher's to reflect: A consideration of programme structure', *Journal of Curriculum Studies,* **22**, 6, pp. 509–27.

SHULMAN, L. (1986) 'Those who understand: Knowledge growth in Teaching', *Educational Researcher,* **15**, 2, pp. 4–14.

SHYMANSKY, J.A. (1992) 'Using constructivist ideas to teach science teachers about constructivist ideas, or Teachers are students too!', *Journal of Science Teacher Education,* **3**, 2, pp. 53–7.

STATTON, J. (1988) 'Contributions of the dialogue journal research to communicating, thinking, and learning', in FARR, M. (Ed) *Interactive Writing in Dialogue Journals: Practitioner, Linguistic, Social and Cognitive Views,* Norwood, NJ, Ablex.

TASKER, R. and LAMBERT, J. (Eds) (1981) *Science Activities: Specific Problems: Some Solutions,* Hamilton, NZ, SERU, University of Waikato.

TASKER, R. and OSBORNE, R. (1985) 'Science teaching and science learning', in OSBORNE, R. and FREYBERG, P. (Eds) *Learning in Science,* Auckland, Heinemann.

VON GLASERFELD, E. (1989) 'Cognition, construction of knowledge, and teaching', *Synthese,* **80**, pp. 121–40.

WHITE, R.T. (1988) *Learning Science,* Oxford, Basil Blackwell.

WIDEEN, M.F., MAYER-SMITH, J.A. and MOON, B.J. (1994) 'The research on learning to teach: Prospects and problems', Paper presented at the annual meeting of American Educational Research Association, San Francisco, CA.

WIDEEN, M.F., MAYER-SMITH, J.A. and MOON, B.J. (1996) 'Learning to teach: A critical review', Paper presented at the annual meeting of Canadian Society for the Study of Education, St Catherines, ONT.

WUBBELS, T., KORTHAGEN, F. and DOLK, M. (1992) 'Conceptual change approaches in teacher education, cognition and action', Paper presented at the annual meeting of the American Educational Research Association, San Francisco, CA.

8 The Lived Curriculum of Constructivist Teacher Education

Francine Peterman

For five years, I enacted a constructivist teacher education curriculum in my classroom at a conservative midwestern teachers college. In response to my beliefs about learning and teaching, to my students' beliefs and expectations, and to my colleagues' critique, the curriculum changed. As written, the curriculum reflected my personal beliefs. When enacted, the curriculum transmuted in response to my students' negotiations with me to reduce the complexity of the tasks I designed. My curriculum challenged institutional norms, as demonstrated by colleagues' critiques of my work in the tenure process at the institution where this study was conducted. In this paper, I examine the personal beliefs, instructional dilemmas, and institutional norms that impacted changes in my written curriculum and curriculum-in-action. In particular, I focus on my grading system, an artifact of my beliefs-in-action.

This study focuses on the two core methods courses I have taught in a teacher education program for five years. Each of these secondary education courses involves students in four weeks of daily, two-hour seminars and four weeks of daily, hour-long participation in local classroom settings. Running concurrently, the first course focuses on senior high settings; the second, on middle school settings. Generally, seminars occur for at least two weeks before students are placed in classrooms, for at least one week in the midst of classroom placements, and for one week at the end of the course. To the degree possible, students are supervised by teachers in their content areas. The supervising teachers engage the students in the daily tasks of teaching, including taking attendance, planning, evaluating students' progress, and teaching for several days, a week, or more.

For this study, I interviewed each student enrolled in my methods courses at least once, maintained a collection of students' weekly reflective journals, secured students' informal evaluations of my teaching, and saved classroom artifacts such as students' classwork, my teaching philosophy, and my course syllabi. The transcribed interviews, reflective journals, informal evaluations, and syllabi served as data sources for a conceptual analysis of the change process. These data sources frame my phenomenological study of changes in my beliefs and practices. Self-reflection and student evaluation provide a means to examine the lived experiences of my students and me in the classroom — the lived curriculum.

Throughout my first year of teaching in higher education, institutional norms and the expectations of my colleagues intrigued me. I arrived in Middle-americus filled with new ideas that challenged current classroom practices. As well, I was prepared by my dissertation chair to remain an ethnographer in my new setting. ('Don't be an action researcher', she warned me.) Immediately, I realized that my beliefs would challenge the current practices in my own college. I began to gather data. What were the college norms, I asked.

One senior faculty member settled into my office during my first week on campus. He simply summarized popular beliefs about the preservice teachers in our program:

1 'They expect a point system.' A point system protects you against students' complaints about fairness in evaluation. From my experience, I inferred, 'Don't stray from the norm.'
2 'They can't write.' I asked more probing questions as he said this. 'Our students can't spell,' he said. Our students needed cognitive coaching, I discovered while working closely with them.
3 'You don't argue with your neighbor unless you're prepared to kill him.' 'Don't expect your students to engage in hearty debate', I thought he meant. 'I do all the talking', I learned as I wandered my college hallways during classes and listened to most of the professors lecture. 'And, when they're ready to argue, they'll go for the jugular', I learned from my own experiences in the tenure process.

These norms framed how I thought about my students and how I planned to teach. The first two norms were consistent with what I knew about high school students' beliefs about teachers and schooling. In action, the first norm represented students' negotiations with the teacher to do as little as possible to receive the desired grade, as aptly described in *Selling Students Short* (Sedlak, Wheeler, Pullin, and Cusick, 1986) and in *The Shopping Mall High School* (Powell, Farrar, and Cohen, 1985). The point system was an explicit treaty, as Powell *et al.* (1985) refer to the arrangements made between teachers and students 'to promote mutual goals' (p. 68). The second norm represented students doing only what was expected — to write. At the end of the first semester, I added another condition to the deal. I required students to present their work in a 'timely, professional, and responsible manner.' This included peer review and cognitive coaching. Over time, my syllabus included a more detailed explanation of 'timely, professional and responsible', including the requirement for peer review.

At first, I misunderstood the third norm. Because several colleagues complained about the difficulty in engaging students in discussions, I thought it meant that students would not engage in hearty classroom discussions. This was never a problem in my classroom. My informant, a senior faculty member, claimed it was based in the rural history of most of my students. Farmers rely upon their neighbors for goods and support. One would not argue with another unless one was prepared to conquer. I learned this one the hard way, as I will explain later.

My first two syllabi were based upon a point system, despite the contradictory implications of my constructivist framework for curriculum design. Early on, I suffered a critical teaching dilemma in which there were contradictory goals. Like the teachers Lampert (1985) described as dilemma managers, I accepted the conflict as useful. The first dilemma arose between my constructivist beliefs and departmental norms. While I believed strongly in authentic assessment, I succumbed to the departmental norm — a point system — to determine students' final grades. I included several authentic assessments such as portfolios and the evaluation of lesson plans as they were implemented in a classroom setting. However, the portfolio and other authentic assessments fit into a larger system based upon the points students could earn. Authentic assessment and point systems are antithetical, I thought. Nevertheless, I determined the cultural norm and expectation for a point system would guide my classroom grading system.

Midway into my first semester, my class and I discussed a variety of classroom assessments and the advantages and disadvantages of each. No sooner did we finish our discussion, one student asked, 'If we value more contextually bound assessments, why a point system in this class?' A classroom discussion ensued. We re-negotiated the grading system, abandoning the point system and settling on a qualitative evaluation of the products resulting from the academic tasks of the course. My students' insights and questions helped me to resolve my teaching dilemma. My second syllabus reflected the negotiated changes in the point system, which focused solely on classroom products such as reflective journals, lesson plans, portfolio, and microteaching sessions.

At the end of my first year, I participated in a workshop in which I developed a professional teaching portfolio. To do so, I was asked to write my teaching philosophy. Writing this philosophy synthesized the new ways of understanding learning and teaching I developed as a graduate student at a large research institution in the Southwest. Several key words framed my philosophy: academic task, constructivism, caring, and studenting. In my teaching portfolio I wrote, 'the following principles guide my teaching:'

1   *Promoting good studenting is more important than promoting good students.* In his review of educational research, Fenstermacher (1986) called for a new genre of research on teaching — one that focused on the student's active, mindful role in the teaching–learning process and on the moral dimensions of teaching. He introduced the notion of *studenting* to mean what the student must do to learn — for instance, think, mindfully engage in activities, question, identify relationships and rules, and remember. Fenstermacher challenged the educational research community to look beyond seemingly simple and implied cause-and-effect relationships that guided effective teaching research and produced an endless list of teaching behaviors that correlated to student achievement. Instead, he asked

researchers and educators to focus on what goes on in the mind of the student who is practicing good studenting, mindfully engaging in the learning process, and to identify normative definitions of good teaching based upon what is good for students to know. To me, while a good student has learned the rules and means that lead to good grades and the teacher's approval, good studenting involves the students in a critical analysis of what is important to know and how they come to know it (Peterman, 1994).

2   *Knowledge is socially constructed.* Since the 1960s, cognitive scientists have engaged in an ongoing dialogue about how learning occurs. Most agree that both prior knowledge and experience play an important role in what and how we learn. They concur with Dewey that important educative experiences involve meaningful activity, questions students raise about the activity, and rich mental schemata which represent what students already know. Through social interaction and mindful engagement in activity, students construct knowledge, building more complex, abstract schemata representing their understandings of their world.

3   *An ethic of caring guides a good teacher's actions, encouraging good studenting and learning.* According to Noddings (1992), an ethic of caring is essential to an educative community. This ethic of caring focuses the teacher on the student in a positive, engaging fashion. An ethic of caring requires that the teacher engage in knowing the student — from the student's perspective and without judgment. It results in affirmations of the student's self, mutual respect, and an open classroom environment in which each individual's knowing and coming to know is valued. But, the ethic of caring requires more. It requires that the teacher know and respect herself in the same way. Therefore, self-knowledge or personal knowledge is as important as practical knowledge.

As I reviewed my course syllabi in light of my philosophy, I found studenting, constructivism, and caring were notably absent from my written curriculum. Yes, I relied heavily upon classroom discussion for the social construction of meaning. Yes, I received abundant student feedback to confirm my belief that I demonstrate an ethic of caring. Yes, studenting framed at least one classroom discussion. But, in comparing my enacted curriculum to my teaching philosophy, I found several contradictions. I struggled with how to promote good studenting. My method of classroom assessment rewarded those who learned to be good students in my class — not necessarily those who practiced good studenting. Yes, students socially constructed knowledge. But, the classroom products provided inadequate evidence of my students' constructions. I determined to examine my beliefs and practices more closely during the next academic year.

The mentor who supervised the development of my teaching portfolio encouraged me to invite a colleague to observe my curriculum-in-action. I hoped a colleague would provide observational data regarding the principles I thought guided my classroom interactions. In my second year, I invited a senior colleague to observe my methods class. I gave him a copy of my philosophy and met with him to discuss how he might help to evaluate my curriculum-in-action, especially in light of my teaching philosophy. My colleague grimaced. 'How can we operationalize caring', he asked. 'That's such a fuzzy concept', he said. 'Are you sure you'd want to include a notion with such soft implications in an evaluation of your teaching?' I selected this colleague as a peer evaluator because he was the most well read of my colleagues. Distraught by his response, I abandoned the task. But I did not abandon my philosophy.

In five years, my philosophy has not changed. Actually, my philosophy is more clearly represented in my written and enacted curriculum. My first several syllabi were two- to three-pages long, including brief course rationale and description, a list of assignments and the points each was worth, and a grading scale. Simple. Students do the work, earn the grade. But I ignored their sense of the world, their questions, their understanding. For the first five semesters, students in my class completed the same basic assignments to earn their grades: participation in a classroom setting, multiple-choice examinations on the textbook, microteaching sessions, teaching autobiography, teaching philosophy, portfolio, interdisciplinary unit plan, and reflective journals. I followed my colleagues' advice and used a point system to determine students' grades. And, after the first semester, not a single student challenged the grading system. It represented school as they knew it, I imagine. And the syllabus provided a simple guide for being a good student, that is, getting a good grade. Good studenting was not necessarily rewarded.

During my third year, 1993 to 1994, a new faculty member was hired to teach the same methods courses I did. He and I held common beliefs about teaching and learning. We planned together and met frequently to reflect upon our teaching. We worked collaboratively to revise our classes. In the spring, we significantly revised the course syllabus. We wanted to engage students in learning, to foster good studenting. In our syllabus, we wrote,

> Personally, you will explore the notion of studenting this semester. Studenting is *learning to learn for learning's sake*. I imagine that most of you want to be teachers because you student well. Throughout the course, however, I would like you to consider the difference between *being a good student and practicing good studenting*. For me, the difference is between *doing what the teacher expects to get the grade I want and doing what I want to do to learn as much as I can*. My aim is to create the classroom conditions for you to student optimally and to reflect continuously on your own studenting so that you can encourage studenting in your own classrooms.

This remains in my syllabus to this date.

Rather than use a point scale to assess students' work, my colleague and I determined that students would need to produce quality work in four areas: reflection, teaching, curriculum design, and professionalism in the senior high methods class and teaching and learning, interdisciplinary curriculum design, middle schooling, and professionalism in the middle school methods class. Rather than accumulate points, students would demonstrate expertise in each area. The quality of their work in each area would determine their grades. To receive a 'C', for instance, a student must demonstrate quality performances in every area and consistently superior performances in at least one area. To receive an 'A', a student must demonstrate quality performances in every area and consistently superior performances in at least three areas. Quality was defined as 'a manner acceptable and workable within the general school culture.' Superior was 'above and beyond that which is acceptable in the culture of the school'. We thought 'quality' would be easy to determine. 'Above and beyond' was simply more than just doing the work, we thought. Our students thought differently, and because these terms were not negotiated in class, a treaty had not been struck. The ambiguity was grounds for conflict — or in our students' words, 'unfair'.

At the end of the semester, my colleague and I met with each student to discuss their portfolios and their grades. We looked forward to reflective conversations with our students about their work. Although we taught our students Doyle's (1983) theory of academic tasks, we forgot the important role of the worth of the task in the grading system. We were not prepared for the battles that ensued and the disparity among our definitions of quality and superior work and those of our students.

As we met with students to discuss their work, my colleague and I were surprised by our students' definitions. We soon discovered, 'just doing the work' meant it was 'quality' work to many students and 'doing more work' meant it was 'superior'. Several students told us, 'I did the work, what more did you want?' Another told me, 'My father's a teacher and he said, "All they expect you to do is to show up and have a good attitude." I have a good attitude. Isn't that quality?' As in the past, only a few students demonstrated good studenting. The negotiations for grades were tough. 'What do you mean I'm getting a "C?"', one student asked me. 'I did all the work. And, look how much stuff I brought in my portfolio', she said pointing to a plastic crate filled with handouts, lesson plans, and probably all of the work she'd completed in her education classes. This student later wrote a letter to my department chairperson, claiming I was 'unfair' and 'unprofessional'.

After our end-of-semester conferences, my colleague and I were exhausted, disillusioned, and disturbed. In conflict, negotiations are far more difficult. The negativity of several students in our end-of-the semester conferences tired us. Although we discussed the negotiation for grades as part of our curriculum, we failed to predict the consequences of ambiguous criteria on those negotiations in our lived curriculum. And, we still hadn't figured out how to promote good studenting.

My course evaluations plummeted that semester. In informal and formal evaluations, students asked for more clarity and fairness. I responded with a more detailed syllabus, outlining criteria and expectations for each assignment. Rather than return to the point system, revered by my senior colleagues, I gave students grades on each assignment. Students' grades reflected the average of their grades in each of the four areas covered in the class.

While I had previously been ranked among the top faculty in merit pay awards, during my fourth year of teaching, I endured a professional flogging in the promotion and tenure process. While I paid close attention to the culture of my classroom, I overlooked the political nature of my department. Upset with the results of their negotiation for grades, four students didn't argue with their neighbor — me; they prepared to kill my career. Students dissatisfied with their negotiated grades had complained to my department chairperson. Rather than discuss their complaints with me, the chair presented four anonymous, written complaints to my colleagues. Given this information, my department registered its concern about my teaching. I was granted a year's unsatisfactory progress toward tenure and denied merit pay for the first time in my twenty years of teaching. After hearing my department's discussion of my record of teaching, my colleague withdrew from our collaborative planning process. 'I did walk away', my colleague wrote as he reviewed this manuscript. 'It wasn't because I believed the discussion but from fear of being included in it. In either case, a gutless move.'

To survive the promotion and tenure process, I dedicated myself more astutely to my classroom. I reviewed my teaching philosophy and revised my syllabus to reflect my beliefs. I determined to enact my philosophy that included promoting studenting, engaging in socially constructing the curriculum, and fostering an ethic of care in my classroom. But, how might my grading system reflect this renewed concern for my constructivist practices and the enactment of my teaching philosophy in the classroom? I struggled.

In my fifth year of teaching, I implemented a revised curriculum. The course was divided into four areas represented in my teaching philosophy: teaching, learning, studenting, and schooling. Four academic tasks and concomitant products framed each area. To receive a 'C' in the class, students needed to receive an average grade of 'C' on the products required in each area. To receive a higher grade, however, students needed to address their own questions, go beyond the minimum expected of students completing these two methods courses. Seven to ten 'advanced assignments' were provided to allow students an opportunity to explore their own questions about teaching and learning. To receive a 'B', students were required to earn at least a 'B' on the core products and a 'B'-average on three advanced assignments. An 'A' required an 'A'-average on core products and 'A'-average on five advanced assignments.

My new curriculum clearly reflected my teaching philosophy, which was included in the course syllabi. As my syllabi changed, my enacted curriculum changed. More mindful of students' constructions of meaning and use of professional language, I refined the teaching strategies I employed. For four years, my class engaged in open-ended, student-centered discussions. I rarely lectured. I was the guide on the side. In guiding discussions, I recorded students' responses to my questions, asked for reasoning, and intentionally withheld my own opinions. Instead, I asked students to respond to each other's ideas. However, in informal evaluations of my class, my students informed me they wanted to know more about what I thought and about how classroom teachers and experts talked about classrooms. 'I'd like to know more about what you think', several students told me. 'You have taught for more than twenty years', a student told me after class one day. 'I wish you'd share your experiences with us.' 'You write what everyone says on the board', one student said. 'If you don't tell me, it's difficult for me to tell what's the right answer.'

In response to my students' evaluations, I paid closer attention to transitions and connections, making my personal and theoretical knowledge more explicit. While I still used a variety of student-centered strategies, I frequently summarized what we had learned in a cognitive map I drew on the board as students responded to questions I strategically structured. Each semester, I noticed that during the first two weeks of class, every student seemed to copy each word I wrote on the board. However, by the third week of class, only a few students copied my maps. Why? I speculated that there were no points for recording or knowing what we discussed and mapped. So I thought of ways to highlight what was important to know.

During the last year, I decided to reproduce and distribute the map to students for their records. That seemed to establish which information was important to know. A year after she'd been in my class, a student called me to ask for a copy of all the charts and handouts we developed in our classroom discussions. During the last semester of this study, students noted connections between the maps I drew on the board, the teaching strategies I employed, and their own teaching. We used these maps to discuss ways in which to frame classroom discussions and what series of questions they might ask in questioning strategies. Students in this class produced outstanding lesson plans and detailed questioning strategies, far superior to those of students in other classes.

During the last year, my teaching evaluations improved significantly. There were no complaints to my department chairperson. Several students commented on the relevance of course content to the National Teachers Exam, they were required to take. 'At one point', one student told me, 'I just closed my eyes and imagined you taking the test for me. I heard your voice and saw you writing on the blackboard.'

More importantly, my students engaged more independently in the learning process. They were studenting, not just being good students. Interestingly, the principals of schools where my students were placed noticed, too, and recorded their observations of my students' professionalism in letters to my dean. Most important, the quality of students' products improved significantly.

Doyle defines academic tasks as the products, processes, resources, and worth of the task in the grading system. His definition captures the dynamic nature of tasks as they are enacted. An important artifact of the curriculum-in-action, the grading system serves a pivotal function, implicitly linking students' learning and the teachers' beliefs about teaching and learning. Examining the relationships between my grading and my belief systems allowed me to construct a better understanding of my enacted curriculum. The incongruence between my written and enacted beliefs created teaching dilemmas I was forced to address. As my written and enacted curriculum more closely reflected my constructivist beliefs about teaching and learning, my students' products and learning improved.

Each semester, I revisited my plan in light of my students' comments and evaluations. I invited feedback to assist me in reflecting upon and reforming my practice. Planning integrated what I learned from my students' and my reflections on my teaching and their learning. For instance, each semester students were required to develop an interdisciplinary unit. My curricular goals for the task were to have students critique this cooperative learning strategy, produce concept-based curriculum, and create challenging, academic tasks for their students. When I first assigned this task, I required students to work outside of class. Therefore, I had little opportunity to interact with students as they designed their units, and the students found it difficult to schedule time to work together. To critique the cooperative learning experience, I asked students to write recommendations or guidelines a teacher should follow in developing effective cooperative learning strategies. Consistently, students remarked, 'The teacher should structure class time to allow students to work together.' So, I did.

During the last three semesters, I scheduled class time for students to compose their interdisciplinary unit plans. Like teachers in their lounge, we met in the cafeteria at the student center. As I circulated among cooperative groups, I listened to my students as they were collaboratively engaged in meaningful activity. Their conversations about curriculum were focused on what, how, and why they would teach specific content. Further, their products were more creative and detailed. Most of all, they experienced collaborative planning among colleagues. During my fifth year teaching, my students remarked that the unit plan was one of the most important learning experiences.

Questions of causality elude me. I am more concerned with the complex ecology in which changes in my teaching and my students' learning occurred. I am certain that the barter system and the grades for which students barter are keys to understanding the complexities of teaching and learning. Further, what students must do to earn the grade — simply be good students by figuring out what they need to do to earn the grade they want or be more engaged by practicing good studenting — impacts how we teach and what our students learn.

The lived curriculum I have described emerged as a result of interactions among my students and me in a college classroom and in school settings within the community. More than my beliefs, my reflections and personal experiences and those of my students impacted the changes I implemented. I wonder consistently about the contradictions between what I believe and know about teaching and learning and what my students have come to know and believe before arriving in my classroom. My constructivist practices require studenting not just being a good student. One student who challenged my practices and wrote several letters calling for my dismissal was accustomed to being a good student. Until she entered my classroom, she knew how to figure out what the teacher wanted and what right answer was desired. The complex, ambiguous nature of my classroom tasks challenged her, made her uncomfortable. She responded by saying I was 'unfair' and 'unclear'. I'm beginning to see these descriptors as signs of tough negotiations that emerge as students figure out the grading scale. Those who are in education to be good students may be frustrated by constructivist practices. My role must be to help them reconstruct their notions of being students, practicing good studenting, and encouraging the same for their own students.

Classroom research afforded me an opportunity to improve my teaching and my students' learning. Through this reflection, I regained my conviction to classroom research, despite my mentor's warning. I tried to change the system. During the last year, it seemed to work well. However, by trying to change the norms, I riled four too many students and provided fuel for a political vendetta. My constructivist beliefs and practices provided one avenue for a professional assault on my achieving tenure at my first college. I've moved on to another institution, one where the norms seem more like my own values and beliefs — hopefully, where colleagues and students may argue with their neighbors without killing them.

References

DOYLE, W. (1983) 'Academic work', *Review of Educational Research*, **53**, pp. 159–99.

FENSTERMACHER, G.D. (1986) 'Philosophy of research on teaching: Three aspects', in Wittrock, *Handbook of Research on Teaching* (5th Ed,) NY, MacMillan, (pp. 37–49).

LAMPERT, M. (1985) 'How do teachers manage to teach? Perspectives on problems in practice', *Harvard Educational Review*, **55**, pp. 178–94.

NODDINGS, N. (1992) *The Challenge of Care in Schools*, NY, Teachers College Press.

PETERMAN, F. (1994, April) 'Caring and studenting: Essential principles for university teaching', in MAGNUSSON, J. (Chairperson), *Studenting, Caring, and Teaching as Research: Challenging Perspectives on College Teaching*, Paper presented in a symposium at the annual conference of the American Educational Research Association, New Orleans, LA.

POWELL, A.G., FARRAR, E. and COHEN, D.K. (1985) *The Shopping Mall High School*, Boston, MA, Houghton Mifflin.

SEDLAK, M.W., WHEELER, C.W., PULLIN, D.C. and CUSICK, P.A. (1986) *Selling Students Short*, NY, Teachers College Press.

9 Meeting Student Teachers on Their Own Terms: Experience Precedes Understanding

John Loughran and Tom Russell

Introduction

Preservice student teachers enter their teacher education programs with differing perceptions of what they think their course should do for them in 'teaching them to teach'. These perspectives may make it difficult for some to recognize that preservice education is only a starting point in learning about teaching, not an end unto itself. But these individuals all hold significant views about the nature of teaching and learning, and we believe it is essential to 'meet them on their own terms'. We share a view that our practices as teacher educators must acknowledge, develop and challenge the various perspectives that preservice teachers bring to the task of learning to teach. We also believe that experience precedes full understanding, so that part of meeting new teachers on their own terms involves showing them how experience extends their understanding and enables them to use it to guide future teaching.

For both student teachers and their teacher educators, it is important to recognize that learning about teaching extends far beyond a preservice program. A teacher education course can not fully 'equip' student teachers with all the skills and understandings necessary to teach; many skills need to be developed and refined throughout a teaching career. We believe that one role of preservice education is to help student teachers develop their 'thinking about teaching skills' so that they are encouraged to learn through and from their experiences.

Learning from experience is an important teaching trait that is highlighted by Schön (1983; 1987) in his descriptions of reflective practice. In accord with his views, many teacher education courses attempt to focus on teaching teachers to reflect (Korthagen, 1985; Zeichner and Liston, 1986 and 1987; Hillkirk and Dupuis, 1989; Valli, 1989; and Richert, 1990). As a consequence, many of the structural features of teacher education programs have been questioned and recast in an attempt to foster the development of student teachers' reflective practice. In order to fully realize the outcomes of structural changes, we believe that such changes need to be coupled explicitly with an understanding of student teachers' learning about teaching, so that student teachers are offered opportunities to make better sense of their own learning about teaching.

This chapter portrays our approach to teacher education through both the structural features of our respective programs and our understanding of student teachers' learning about teaching. *Learning is therefore a prime focus* and the data we offer in this chapter demonstrate how our student teachers learn from, and through, the opportunities presented to them and how they reconsider these over time as they embark on their teaching careers. We seek to illustrate how experience also precedes understanding in our understanding of our own work as teacher educators.

This chapter arises from several shared experiences. Tom Russell visited Monash for four weeks in June 1993, and John Loughran visited Queen's for the last four months of 1995. Tom sat in on several of John's classes, and then John sat in on an entire term of Tom's classes. The result has included the discovery of many shared perspectives on the *pedagogy of teacher education,* despite the fact that the program at Monash has much more explicit coherence at the level of pedagogical principles. While the data we include here come from very different contexts, we select them to illustrate how our shared perspectives appear in the experiences of those we help along the road of learning to teach.

Course Structures

Monash University

The preservice teacher education program at Monash University is a one year post-graduate Diploma in Education. Students enrolled in any of the science teaching methods (General Science, Biology, Physics or Chemistry) are also involved in an integrated Sciences program known as Stream 3. Stream 3 has evolved over a number of years but the program continues to be shaped and influenced by seven important underlying propositions (Northfield and Gunstone, 1983; Gunstone and Northfield, 1992) that, taken together, may be described as a *constructivist approach to teaching and learning.* These propositions (Gunstone *et al.,* 1993) illustrate the value of articulating the principles that guide and direct a teacher education program.

1   Prospective teachers have needs which must be considered in planning and implementing a program and these change through their preservice development.
2   The transition from learner to teacher is difficult but is aided by working closely with one's peers.
3   The student-teacher is a learner who is actively constructing views of teaching and learning based on personal experiences strongly shaped by perceptions held before entering the program.
4   The teaching/learning approaches advocated in the program should be modelled by the teacher educators in their own practice.

5 Student teachers should see the preservice program as an educational experience of worth.

6 Preservice education programs are inevitably inadequate (it is the start of a teacher's career that will involve appreciably more learning over time).

7 Schön's (1983) conception of the reflective practitioner is a vital model for those who teach the preservice program, as well as for those learning to teach.

Understanding these propositions through teacher education practice shapes both the course structure and the pedagogy of the teacher educators involved in the Stream 3 program, which is designed to be responsive to the needs of the student teachers as they prepare for their teaching careers. In preparation for their first school teaching practicum, they begin with a micro-teaching experience followed by a 'one-on-one' activity with a Year 7 student where they teach (and learn) with the student in the student's school setting for a forty-five minute lesson. The student teachers also plan an extended shared teaching episode. This shared group task is organized around a camping experience where, for a morning, they work with a class of Year 7 students from a high school in an outdoor setting. The four-day camp is devoted entirely to developing ways of teaching and learning science in the outdoors. Student teachers are organized into groups of four or five in which they build their working relationships so that the teaching experience with the Year 7s on the last day is supportive, encouraging and challenging. Following the camp, the student teachers embark on their first extended school practicum. This introductory block of the program is designed to build, in increments, student teachers' confidence and skills in teaching for their first three-week school teaching experience.

When the Stream 3 student teachers return to the university, they are involved in a number of 'learning about learning' tasks designed to help them recognize the difficulties associated with learning scientific concepts. This is done by placing them in the role of learner. Physics graduates are challenged by Biology for non-Biologists, Biologists by Physics for non-Physicists, and so on. These programs are designed to highlight for them the difference between 'knowing' scientific concepts and understanding them.

While these learning about learning programs are being conducted, the student teachers are also encouraged to develop portfolio items (Corrigan and Loughran, 1994; Loughran *et al.*, 1994) designed to demonstrate their understanding of the relationship between their learning and their approach to teaching. The production of portfolio items is an ongoing process throughout the year and is an important way for them to begin to articulate their developing professional knowledge as they actively seek ways to make sense of their learning.

The purpose of these experiences is to encourage the student teachers to think about different approaches to teaching and to highlight that although the transmission of propositional knowledge may be an efficient way of working through a syllabus, it does not necessarily lead to learning for understanding. Hence, as they move into their second practicum (3 weeks), the hope is that they are reflecting on the links between their shared teaching and learning experiences such that they attempt, in practice, to better align their teaching with their views of learning.

In the build-up to their third and final school teaching experience (four weeks), the student teachers are encouraged to reflect on their teaching and to question their perception of their students' learning. At this time, the *Project for Enhancing Effective Learning* (Baird and Mitchell, 1986; Baird and Northfield, 1992) becomes a springboard for pursuing ways of teaching that encourage students to be active and responsible learners. PEEL teaching strategies are used to model how different learning styles can be approached through a thoughtful approach to pedagogy. The intent is that student teachers see the acquisition of a working knowledge of a variety of teaching strategies not as a 'bag of tricks' but as a way of enhancing their own professional knowledge. They are placed in learning situations that encourage them to see that teaching strategies should be selected because of the underlying purpose in the learning outcomes anticipated, not simply to break the 'normal routine' of practice.

Through this approach to learning about teaching and learning, their beliefs about assessment are also challenged as they are encouraged to pursue effective ways of gauging their students' learning. In 'unpacking' their students' learning, strategies for 'probing understanding' (White and Gunstone, 1992) are used to highlight the different forms of thinking and knowing that are able to be accessed and assessed. Ultimately, it is up to each individual student-teacher to draw conclusions about the relationship between personal practice, students' learning, and personal ability to assess this in a reasonable and professional manner.

Two common threads pervading the course are the development of portfolio items and Science Techniques. The portfolios offer students ways of reflecting on their developing professional knowledge and their ability to articulate it, while the Science Techniques offer a mixture of pedagogical and science content knowledge. At the start of the year, the Science Techniques are largely organized and run by staff to highlight a variety of approaches to teaching science concepts. After the first practicum, the student teachers take over responsibility for the Science Techniques as they work with their peers to share their specialist content knowledge and to develop appropriate pedagogical approaches to enhance learning within that sphere. This is one way of highlighting *for them and with them* the importance of pedagogical content knowledge (Shulman, 1987) and how that might develop through reflection on experience.

This brief overview of the course structure is designed to demonstrate how the seven propositions that undergird the course influence the way the curriculum is organized so that as student teachers' needs, concerns and experiences shift over time, so the course is responsive to these changes in a constructive and purposeful manner.

Queen's University

Intriguingly, the Bachelor of Education program at Queen's University has no 'basic principles' such as the seven statements that characterize the program at Monash. The program is organized on traditional 'normal school assumptions' about learning to teach, with a series of practices that have become separated from their initial rationales. The program was designed in 1968 and has evolved in modest ways over twenty-five years. As we prepare this chapter, the Faculty of Education has just committed itself to a radically different design, in which teaching experience rather than university courses will be the 'front-end loading' of the program's design. The original program at Queen's, developed at a time of an extreme shortage of teachers, had four two-week practicum periods spread over an eight-month period that began with five weeks of education classes. In recent years, a shift to three three-week teaching placements has resulted in first-hand experiences of teaching coming even later in the program, simply as a result of sending pre-service teachers to schools at 'least inconvenient' times. Program credits can be described in terms of percentages:

Curriculum and instruction	40 per cent
Professional skills	10 per cent
Educational studies	30 per cent
Practicum	20 per cent

Tom's finding himself sharing pedagogical perspectives with John can be traced, in part, to his research over the last twelve years, since the publication of Schön's (1983) first account of 'reflection-in-action'. Tom was struck by the extent to which reflection-in-action, as a process, seemed so much closer to his preservice students' accounts of the tensions they felt between classroom experiences ('the swamp') and their education courses ('the high hard ground'). By joining with his colleague Hugh Munby in a research program on the development of teachers' professional knowledge, Tom was able to develop and maintain, implicitly, a perspective on his teaching of preservice science teachers that is consistent with the seven principles that John describes as explicit in the Monash program. Several publications illustrate this implicit perspective (Munby and Russell, 1994; Russell, 1995).

From this point on, we focus on our shared perspectives, even as we acknowledge their different origins and sources of support within our respective universities.

Teaching about Teaching and Learning

Just as our course structures are based on a philosophy of teaching about teaching and learning, the pedagogical approach we employ must be similarly based. Quality teaching means placing students in an environment that encourages learning. Therefore, teaching needs to be *interactive, challenging and respons-ive* so that individual learning differences, approaches and preferences may be catered for. Teaching and learning are inextricably linked, and quality teach-ing must be guided by the question, 'How does an understanding of learning (particular content) influence the pedagogical approach adopted?' Answering this question involves a recognition that substantive learning occurs not by 'just listening', but by reconstructing understanding through deeds, thoughts and actions. If such learning is to be encouraged, appropriate pedagogy must be employed that challenges and motivates the learner to take the steps to make new meaning from teaching/learning episodes. Understanding the relationship between teaching and learning must go beyond rhetoric to become the shaping force in developing approaches to teaching.

The philosophy that underpins our teaching is that students should be actively engaged in their learning. Their ideas and thinking should be challenged in ways that provoke them to reconsider and better articulate their understand-ing of the subject matter. To do this, a diversity of teaching strategies must be 'on hand', strategies that are appropriate for different situations. *But,* diverse teaching procedures are not simply ways of breaking up the standard routine (Harmin and Simon, 1965). There is a learning purpose related to the use of every strategy, and this understanding is crucial for the value of any strategy to be fully realized. This is highlighted by O'Reilley (1993, p. 34), who appeals to our sense of the importance of pedagogy when she writes:

> We *do* need to examine our teaching practice. Lecturing is an unlikely way to help students attend to the inner music, nor is the tense exchange that often passes for lecture-discussion. While the well-made lecture has an unassailable place in any curriculum, one must be wary of institutions in which lecture develops as the principal means of conveying information. We have a lot to tell our students, but I believe our primary job should be to bring them to asking, by whatever means we can devise, the questions that will elicit what they need to know. Students do not really listen well to the answers to ques-tions they have not learned to ask.

Teaching strategies are both content and context dependent. Also, being able to respond to changes in the teaching and learning environment is vital. Therefore, knowing how to use a strategy is one facet of teaching, knowing why to use it is crucial, *but,* being able to adapt and change, to be responsive to the teaching and learning environment is fundamental to good teaching. If teaching is constrained by 'sticking to what was planned' then no matter how useful a strategy might be, it would be compromised by inflexibility. It is therefore clear that one must be able to adapt to the changing needs of a pedagogical episode. We must be responsive to changes in student learning and be prepared to adapt, adjust and change the pedagogical approach during a session.

Our approach to meeting student teachers on their own terms and enhan-cing their learning opportunities begins with building good teacher–learner relationships. These are developed over time, primarily by *demonstrating that withholding judgment is important in developing mutual trust and respect.* As teachers we always endeavor to show that others' views are important, are actively sought, and are valued in the teaching–learning environment. Meaningful learning is not encouraged if there is not a feeling of 'safety' for individuals to genuinely express their understanding of content/concepts. When learners are able to articulate their views publicly, reconsideration, construction of meaning, and valuable learning are able to occur. Thus there are important personal and social aspects to learning that need to be taken into account in guiding our teaching. In our teaching we develop 'trust' with our students by reinforcing good social behaviors within our classes. This means that all members of the class (teacher and students alike) are encouraged to be supportive of one another because good learning involves risk taking that cannot and will not occur if individuals' ideas or thoughts are ridiculed by others. Recognizing that learners are vulnerable is important. Above all else, it is essential that the expectations we have of our students apply equally to ourselves.

Communication in an active learning environment is enhanced by teaching in ways that do not assume that all dialogue must go through the teacher. In fact, the more students' ideas and responses are used, the more students become involved in group learning. In many instances, we endeavor to decrease our use of 'air time' and thereby increase the opportunities for students to clarify their own thinking and understanding, both publicly and privately.

We use journals (or 'writing folders') and teaching portfolios to encourage reflective thinking. These learning tools offer a chance to understand students as individuals and to have a rich and honest dialogue that is not always possible in the classroom. Writing folders in particular offer opportunities for 'backtalk', and as they are confidential, they offer ways of developing relationships with, and understanding of, individuals that aid both our teaching and their learning. Through both teaching portfolios and writing folders we are able to better meet our student teachers on their terms as we come to better understand their learning about teaching.

Student Teachers' Views

Through our preservice teaching and research we have had the opportunity to follow a number of student teachers as they have embarked on their teaching careers. The data we offer to demonstrate how their views have developed and changed during and after their preservice education programs are drawn from a number of sources. In particular, at Monash University there has been a longitudinal study into the development of science teachers in their first four years of full time teaching (Loughran, 1992) and another involving student teachers' views of the use of portfolio item development (Corrigan and Loughran, 1994; Loughran and Corrigan, 1995). At Queen's there has been a series of studies of classes in the secondary science curriculum area (Munby and Russell, 1994; Russell, 1995a, 1995b).

We do not attempt to tell student teachers what we think they need to know. Rather, we offer our student teachers opportunities to construct meaning through their teaching and learning experiences and to use these to reflect on their teaching practice. As they succeed in constructing meaning from personal experiences, we are able to call attention to the learning processes involved (often 'naming' the process in a memorable way), with a view to encouraging them to understand their own learning and act in similar ways with their own students. To return to 'experience precedes understanding', we want them to understand from personal learning experiences, and then translate their own learning into the particular context in which they find themselves teaching.

Portfolio Item Development

Teaching portfolios are used in the preservice teacher education program at Monash University to help student teachers reflect on their learning about learning and teaching. Through the construction of individual portfolio items, student teachers begin to define for themselves what they consider to be the salient features of their teaching and learning. A teaching portfolio is not simply a collection of a variety of static end products; it is the result of a deliberate process of involvement, engagement and thinking about teaching and learning, from which artifacts are constructed that might convey the reflection on that process to others. Thus there is both a process and a product. The portfolio comprises a variety of artifacts that student teachers can employ as stimuli for articulating their understanding of what it means to be a teacher.

Susan [The teaching portfolio is designed to help me] look at things done in science teaching . . . and pick out various incidents and put [them] in a portfolio under some sort of title and say what I have learnt from it, and indicate what I have done and what I have achieved and what I learnt from it and what it meant to me and how it will impact on my teaching in the future.

Elaine [The teaching portfolio] helped [me] put into words what I thought anyway. I think they gave me words to sort of say what I thought about understanding the way that kids. . . . break down their ideas already before they can take [on] new ones. . . . also I believe that people go through school just compartmentalizing knowledge until there comes the test where they just give it up, well that's my experience so it was good to see that getting some kind of credibility . . . but I guess that in Dip. Ed. [preservice teacher education program] I think I see it more like less of the power to do that sort of thing, to get a kid to the stage where they take responsibility for their own learning and actually try and lead them to things in the real world. There are some strategies you can employ, but basically it comes down to the student taking responsibility and you helping the student to take responsibility. You can't impose correct ways of thinking about science, or even correct ways of thinking about learning, because they've got to make that kind of decision themselves.

Roy   We have got preconceived ideas about what teaching and learning is and they need to be shaken up before we can construct new ones. [I think I] already had some of these ideas percolating around. [I now] understand them a lot more deeply than what I did [before].

These quotations demonstrate how the student teachers are accepting responsibility for their own learning and, in so doing, personally reshaping their views about their teaching. We believe that as this occurs we are also encouraging participants to consider the similarities between themselves as learners and the students who will be learners in their classes in schools. As they come to better understand how they approach their own learning (and accept responsibility for it), they are offered opportunities to relate that understanding to their students' approaches to learning. Therefore, they are challenged to ask whether they also attempt to meet their students on their own terms.

Learning through Writing

Tom always encourages the secondary science student teachers at Queen's to write about their learning, in education courses, in schools, and 'as a package' as the program draws to a close. He recently developed a writing exercise that seemed to work very well, and the results illustrate both our interest in pedagogy and our point about meeting student teachers on their own terms, as they come to understand teaching from experience. During the first class after the first three-week practice teaching placement, he asked each of the twenty-four people in his class to fold a sheet of paper in half and write a paragraph in the top half that described a difficult teaching situation, one in which they wished they could have done a better job. Working in groups of four and five, the paragraphs were then circulated around each table with the invitation that each person write a short response to the situation someone else had described. Two of the twenty-four paragraphs and the accompanying responses are reproduced here, with permission. The content of the paragraphs, taken with the short comments by four other people, reveal a range of views on pedagogy that may not be recognized in preservice programs. We believe that these show that we have no choice but to meet student teachers on their own terms, identifying their existing assumptions about pedagogy, and then working in many different ways to develop those views further, with reference both to teaching that occurs in schools and to teaching that occurs in teacher education courses.

Grade 11 mathematics

I wanted to have my class measure out lengths and angles of triangles and come to some general rules about triangles. These involved SAS, ASA and SSS rules. To my dismay, a procedure that would have taken maybe twenty minutes took more than forty! Of course, not for all of the students. Some students were done in the first ten minutes and remembered the rules, and found it all to be very boring. I had to give them 'extra' work because others in the class couldn't measure an angle with a protractor. I spent about five minutes going over how to use one with them. Anyway, what happened was that I didn't get to the point of the lesson until the last five minutes, and that meant that none of them could really practice any of the things they had discovered. I still don't know what I would do. I like the thought of discovery, and I think it's very important, but what if it takes too long and causes more confusion and stress than simply conveying the information?

We chose to include this paragraph because it seems to touch on most of the major issues any teacher faces, day after day: range of ability, boredom, need for extra work, need for remediation of skills the teacher took for granted, coming to the point only at the end of the lesson, and not having time to practice the central ideas. As always, *time* is a central issue. This paragraph also contains the familiar predisposition to 'discovery', the reservations about time, confusion and stress, *and* the assumption — confirmed in years of university lectures — that it is *possible* to 'convey the information' and do it 'simply', without the bother that always seems to accompany 'discovery' approaches. The only major pedagogical issue not included seems to be that of assessment. This paragraph illustrates the ability of limited teaching experience to stimulate new teachers to ask questions in ways more compelling than 'bringing them up in the methods class'. Now consider the range of responses to this paragraph:

- I struggled with this, too! What if you'd given the five minute demo first? Would it help if you'd had a protractor expert in each group who could lead?
- This is a problem faced in many classes. I tried to move ahead with the lesson, and work with students having difficulty during seatwork. This way the kids who know it could continue with their work and maybe even help the others.
- I think you have to be flexible with your lesson depending on the needs of the majority of the students. If most of the class is done, then go on. If not, you have to wait. Let the few students that are taking a long time practice at lunch, during a spare, or after school.
- If a lesson seems to take too long, as many of mine have, bring their attention back to the experiment the next day to tie in the lab to the theory and attend to any questions that they may have.

The first response recognizes the issues as typical and then offers several practical suggestions. In hindsight, two very relevant suggestions are offered: Do the demonstration early, and ensure that each group has one person ready to act as 'expert'. The second response also suggests drawing on other students to help those having difficulty. The third response describes the familiar idea of moving on when most have finished, and providing help outside of class for those who need more time. The fourth response bridges to the next day's lesson. To us, this paragraph and the range of responses demonstrate that new teachers are 'more than ready' to be met on their own terms. They understand the existing pedagogy of classrooms from personal experiences as students, and they are ready to dig more deeply into the issues that focus on time, ability, and tutoring each other. It also demonstrates the importance of allowing the student teachers the opportunity to actively consider their own practice and to juxtapose their views with those of their peers. This is fundamentally different from student teachers being asked to listen to a professor's approach and 'appear' to act accordingly in future. Student teachers can and do learn from one another and this is something we try to enhance through our pedagogy.

Grade 11 chemistry

The first discussion question following the lab exercise [on Charles' Law and Boyle's Law] was, 'What is the *qualitative* relationship between the temperature/ pressure of a gas and its volume? *Everyone* figured this out and seemed to understand it. When I reviewed the labs, they understood it. When I introduced the actual quantitative relationship, the formal law and formula, they understood it. Then, three or four days later, after doing lots of sample problems using the formulas, I asked them again. And *suddenly* they didn't know, couldn't remember, and started guessing. *Why?*'

This paragraph is intriguing because it suggests the other end of the pedagogical domain: Did they really understand it, so that they can recognize it in different forms? Here again, we see the power of experience as an incentive or challenge that can eventually lead to greater understanding. The closing 'Why?' is an important positive signal, for it does not blame teacher or students. It seems to say, 'Will someone please help me understand what is going on, because I did not expect this result?' Experienced teachers have seen many times the difficulties that emerge on final examinations that ask the student to draw on learning experiences weeks and months earlier. New teachers have been members of groups in which teachers have been presented with similar situations, yet only when they meet it in personal experience are they pushed to probe the issue more deeply. What did the respondents offer? Did they share the question or seek to explain it away?

- Review, review, review — it's lucky you found out then that they had memory problems. The only thing you can really do is review some more and find out if they really did understand in the first place.
- One important thing I learned was the importance of re-introducing previous concepts in each class (where possible — it usually is). The students need to keep these concepts fresh in their minds.
- It's important to continually reinforce ideas, maybe with an intro oral 'quiz' before the class. Repetition is extremely valuable. Imagine how much students actually retain. I mean, often things will be forgotten in my mind without continual reminder.

- That's a tough one! I think you just have to keep drilling the info into their heads through creative reinforcement techniques. It takes some students longer than others to 'truly understand' concepts!

The first person explains the issue in terms of 'memory problems' and emphasizes the importance of 'review', while the second speaks of revisiting ideas in subsequent lessons. The third response introduces terms similar to those in the first response: 'reinforce', 'repeat', 'retain', 'remind'. The final response opens sympathetically, and offers more images: 'drill' and 'reinforce (creatively)' on the path to the teacher's ultimate goal: students who 'truly understand'. In these responses, we see a very powerful set of images and assumptions about how learning occurs and how teaching can and should foster that learning. None of the four responses speaks to the original question, 'Why [do students behave this way]?' We find it important, in our teaching of new teachers, to show them the very powerful images that they bring to both teaching and learning, to accept that reality, and then to challenge them to explore and extend those images as they return to the practice setting.

The excerpts above demonstrate for us how important it is to meet our student teachers on their own terms. Our pedagogy must be such that it acknowledges where the student teachers are and what they perceive their needs and questions to be if we hope to genuinely challenge their assumptions, practices and beliefs about teaching and learning. Clearly, we need to be demonstrating that ourselves, continually, in our own practice. Hence the need for pedagogy that is designed to overtly illustrate the values we believe to be important in enhancing our student teachers' learning about teaching, so that they might reflect on this themselves 'in' their own practice. By offering them opportunities for thinking, reconsidering and reconstructing their understanding through the learning experiences created, we believe the realization that experience precedes understanding can have more meaning for them.

By endeavoring to meet student teachers on their own terms, we believe that we are modelling an approach to pedagogy that genuinely offers participants the opportunity to accept more control and responsibility for their learning about teaching. We believe that this can add the important element of challenge that is so often said to be lacking in teacher education. We challenge them to interpret their own learning in ways that have never been required before, and we stress the importance of the challenge that follows — to translate their insights into their future teaching. If they do come to see us as modelling new approaches to pedagogy, they may then come to create opportunities for their own students to 'accept more control and responsibility for their learning'.

Remembering Preservice Teacher Education

We conclude this chapter by exploring how some of our student teachers have continued to take responsibility for their learning about teaching (from what we consider to be a firm foundation in preservice) as they develop their pedagogy in their initial years of full-time teaching. A familiar myth among experienced teachers suggests that preservice teacher education has little to offer the full-time teacher. We readily acknowledge that preservice education is the start of a career and therefore inevitably inadequate for all the learning that accompanies professional life. However, this does not mean that preservice education must be considered pointless and without merit in its own right. Preservice education offers time and opportunities for thinking and learning about practice, opportunities that may never arise again for some teachers. Accordingly, one of the salient features of our approach to teacher education is that student teachers be sufficiently challenged in their learning about teaching so that their beliefs about practice become clearer to themselves. Then, as they struggle to come to grips with the demands of full-time teaching, the awareness of their personal belief systems may continue to shape their practice as they accumulate and learn from experience. We consider this to be a valid and welcome outcome of any teacher preparation program.

There is little doubt that the memory and impact of the experiences in preservice education will change over time. We argue that if student teachers can see real possibilities in pursuing teaching for understanding through their preservice education courses, then these possibilities might be further pursued (and realized) under appropriate conditions throughout their professional careers. Clearly, then, teachers need to be able to recognize and remember the purpose of preservice education, its aims and intents, while also reconciling these with their own practice. Thus developing and articulating a teaching philosophy is one valuable outcome, one that cannot be transferred in any simple way from teacher educators' minds to their student teachers' minds. A teaching philosophy is something that must be individually cast and recast as it is constructed from and translated into the experiences of practice.

> **Joshua**   Mm, yeah, well I suppose Dip.Ed gave me a year to think about sort of the philosophical approach to pedagogy, to be in a position to decide what I think is important, be in a position to do something with it . . . I think it's infected me positively but if they ever ask me to come back, I would definitely make some changes. But, moments like maths for non mathematicians was fantastic and now I'm teaching maths I think back to those times, physics for non physicists, that was a good learning time too . . .
>
> **Michael**   I thought it [the preservice program] was good as a year, to let me, as a transition year. I certainly needed it before I went out to teach. [It helped me to be] really critical of like what my aims are and if I am achieving them, not if I am appearing to because I have a full exercise book of notes but if I am really achieving my goal which is to get this idea that I had, you know, across to this other person. And that's invaluable I think and it's also pretty rare.

These teachers still recognize the purpose that underpinned their teacher preparation program and we hope that this recognition is allied with a realization that each individual teacher is then able to develop, through this, an approach to teaching that genuinely fosters students' learning for understanding. If this is the case, then these teachers should see that their teaching experiences continually offer them opportunities to reflect on how they approach their teaching.

Gary [It was] to help us think about how students learn and how to best get them to remember stuff and do different things but I rely more I suppose now on what I've seen of kids rather than what I've been told. Like you sort of rely on that for the first little bit but now I think more about the kids that I've seen and how they learn and yeah, so I think more about that than about what I learnt . . . I suppose it more depends on the students and what if I've learnt and how students learn rather than, but I mean it's still, it's the basis that you start with and from that basis you go into your first year and then slowly you build up experience and so you build on that experience.

Matthew Dip.Ed I was probably doing a lot more different things then than I would be doing when I started teaching. Because of the style of school [I'm in], I mean I've said this before, because of the style of school it is here, there's very much pressure on to get through a certain amount of work in a time span, what ever it happens to be. So the pressure's on to do that. And for the first year, in particular I did that. And I worked my arse off so to speak, to fulfill that . . . Just trying to think. I suppose it's a desire to want to do things a little bit differently, compared to what the norm is in the school. Not just because I want to be different but I don't think that's a bad thing. There's quite a lot of other teachers who have been experimenting. Educationally, I'd like to try and break out and do something. So that's a driving force and that's why I've been doing these things in the fourth form this year. So, there you go. Other influences, um syllabus and that's, I suppose, that's almost, you can trace that back to the Dip.Ed influence in the way that we were taught back then and it's a way that I like things. See and I saw the benefits of it and I've just wanted to I suppose to see it for myself, [if I could do it?]

Preservice teacher education is often portrayed as an opportunity to plant seeds, but as a general view we believe this to be far too simplistic. Ideas and practice in teaching and learning should be carefully nurtured and, modelling should be an active process clearly apparent through the experiences in preservice education, so that there is the possibility for germination as the conditions for growth occur during teaching careers. This view of teacher preparation has many features in common with the research on conceptual change in learning science. New ideas need to be 'intelligible', 'plausible', and 'fruitful' (Posner *et al.*, 1982). In learning to teach, the ideas and practice in preservice education need to be intelligible (i.e., they make sense and can be understood), they also need to be plausible (i.e., working with the ideas appears to be a reasonable thing to do) and they most certainly need to be fruitful (i.e., that when using the ideas in practice they deliver as expected).

The approaches to teaching and learning advocated in faculties of education are probably intelligible, plausible and fruitful while individuals are student teachers. So it may well be that the challenge arises for many preservice student teachers when they move into full-time teaching: the change in context challenges these three elements when transplanted into a very different setting. If preservice teacher education is to address this challenge, programs' intents and practices need to be seen as intelligible, plausible and fruitful again in the school setting, as the beginning teachers begin to face the challenges of day to day teaching. It is certainly possible for the program's intents to remain intelligible:

Louise   But you know when you come out of uni, you know, I went through high school I got caught up in HSC [final year of secondary school], and went on to Uni and they talked and talked and that's what I saw teaching as. And so being in Dip.Ed like totally challenged what teaching was and that sort of thing. And so that would stay with me, in a way it changed my thinking of education it was really powerful. And so although when I first got a teaching position, I didn't always teach the way Dip.Ed would have liked me to. Gradually as I get better at teaching I am aiming towards, aiming for that more and more. Does that make sense? . . . It wanted me to teach so to, to make the kids think, to make the kids understand things and understand concepts not just facts. It wanted me to create interest, make teaching interesting, oh learning interesting for the kids and wanted me to enjoy teaching too and it wanted me to enjoy seeing kids learn.

The program may also be something worth doing (plausible);

Interviewer   OK. Well going back to your Dip.Ed again, does that influence how you operate in your teaching?

Angela   Yes, I try and think, like I remember that we learnt those, the way people learn and I always try and, I remember that the episodes was one of the most important things for me and I always try to include episodes in my teaching, that's one of the things I do. I still remember the POEs and concept maps and the problem is I try and always include it in but we have all the subject material done for us, like the course outline already done. So if I want to introduce something I have to kind of put it in myself and I'm always trying to think of ways of including it but yeah, if it's already there for you then you tend to stick to what's there.

Interviewer   You are expected to are you?

Angela   No not really, I suppose, it doesn't matter how you do it as long as you cover that amount of work, so it doesn't really matter how you do it. But if it's there for you, you tend to use it, it's just that, on teaching rounds you were able to use it more because you had more time to think about it and you had more time to be innovative because you only had like two periods a day, so that was really good. So I found that, looking back now on my teaching rounds, I think gosh what brilliant kind of lessons, it was so good I was trying to always make things concrete or always trying and like use those teaching strategies, but now it's always like rush, rush, rush you've got to do this, you've got to do that by period I each day so it's really hard to do that. But it's still there, I still think about oh wouldn't it be good if we could have little discussion groups, wouldn't it be good if we could do concept mapping here, but I don't . . . I suppose, yeah they are still with me, if I have to make up my own unit, like the genetics one I was asked to sit down and fix it up and I did and even the microbiology [unit], I tried to implement things that I had used like concept formation and you know, start the unit off like that. And the students really loved that and yeah I tried to use, when ever I had to design the unit or fix it up, I was asked to do it, that's when I'd try and always think back to those strategies.

The real test is clearly in the program's fruitfulness:

Interviewer Do you think that the experience of that course has influenced the way you're teaching?

Anne It has in many ways. I think looking at the PEEL techniques, something that I am constantly assessing myself, looking at what the kids are learning, whether they're actually learning or just shifting information. And we have a group here which is a PEEL group and we get to sit down and talk every, about twice every three weeks and you do reflect on a lot of your teaching. And just sitting in there and listening to different approaches I'm happy with the way that Monash trained me, in that new way of thinking, whereas a lot of them are having to adjust how they think, that's how I, just come up looking at a situation. So I'm happy in that way. They gave me a good basis to work from.

Over time, from preservice student-teacher education practice to full-time teaching practice, development may be viewed as a gradual change. It is a change in which intelligible, plausible and fruitful approaches to learning to teach, combined with opportunities and experiences that reinforce and support the views being presented, can foster the development of teachers who have a practical foundation that will enhance their understanding of their own teaching and of their students' learning.

Interviewer And what about what you learnt during the Dip.Ed.?

Simon That's hard to hard say. I'm not sure how much I'm relying on that as such or how much that initial teaching and the strategies have just been added to and added to or evolved, so I'm not really sure to what degree my teaching now reflects exactly what I was doing in Dip.Ed. Certainly it's been added to or evolved over time I don't think it's the same thing, it was a start and now, I can't really say, I'm adding to it each year maybe.

Thus we argue that, through our approach to pedagogy in our preservice teacher education programs, we attempt to create opportunities for learning that encourage and challenge participants to reconsider their own developing practice. This is how we take an active approach to meeting student teachers on their own terms — seeking, recognizing and responding to their particular needs and concerns for professional growth, particularly those driven by personal experiences in classrooms, both in schools where they teach and in the university setting of their teacher education courses. We strive to use pedagogy that challenges new teachers to better articulate and understand their beliefs and practices, which are rooted in prior learning experiences as well as recent teaching experiences. In many instances, they are able to accept more responsibility for their own learning about teaching as they actively construct and reflect on their own pedagogy.

References

BAIRD, J.R. and MITCHELL, I.J. (1986) *Improving the Quality of Teaching and Learning: An Australian Case-study — The PEEL Project*, Melbourne, Monash University Printing.

BAIRD, J.R. and NORTHFIELD, J.R. (1992) *Learning from the PEEL Experience*, Melbourne, Monash University Printing.

CORRIGAN, D.J. and LOUGHRAN, J.J. (1994) 'Teaching portfolios: Developing quality learning in pre-service science teachers,' *Research in Science Education*, **24**, pp. 60–7.

GUNSTONE, R.F. and NORTHFIELD, J.R. (1992, April) 'Conceptual change in teacher education: The centrality of metacognition,' Paper presented at the meeting of the American Educational Research Association, San Francisco.

GUNSTONE, R.F., SLATTERY, M., BAIRD, J.R. and NORTHFIELD, J.R. (1993) 'A case study exploration of development in preservice science teachers,' *Science Education*, **77**, pp. 47–73.

HARMIN, M. and SIMON, S. (1965) 'The year the schools began teaching the telephone directory,' *Harvard Educational Review*, **35**, pp. 326–31.

HILLKIRK, K. and DUPUIS, V.L. (1989) 'Outcomes of a teacher education curriculum module that emphasizes inquiry and reflection,' *Teacher Education*, **24**, 3, pp. 20–7.

KORTHAGEN, F.A.J. (1985) 'Reflective teaching and preservice teacher education in the Netherlands,' *Journal of Teacher Education*, **36**, 5, pp. 11–15.

LOUGHRAN, J.J. (1992) 'Becoming a science teacher: First year teachers' approaches to learning about teaching,' *Research in Science Education*, **22**, pp. 273–82.

LOUGHRAN, J.J. and CORRIGAN, D.J. (1995) 'Teaching portfolios: A strategy for developing quality in learning and teaching in pre-service teacher education,' *Teaching and Teacher Education*.

LOUGHRAN, J.J., CORRIGAN, D.J. and BROWN, J. (1994, April) 'Changing conceptions of quality learning in pre-service high school teachers,' Paper presented at the meeting of the American Educational Research Association, New Orleans.

MUNBY, H. and RUSSELL, T. (1994) 'The authority of experience in learning to teach: Messages from a physics method class,' *Journal of Teacher Education*, **45**, pp. 86–95.

NORTHFIELD, J.R. and GUNSTONE, R.F. (1983) 'Research on alternative frameworks: Implications for science teacher education,' *Research in Science Education*, **13**, pp. 185–92.

O'REILLEY, M.R. (1993) *The Peaceable Classroom*, Portsmouth, NH, Boynton/Cook.

POSNER, G.J., STRIKE, K.A., HEWSON, P.W. and GERTZOG, W.A. (1982) 'Accommodation of a scientific conception: Toward a theory of conceptual change,' *Science Education*, **66**, pp. 211–27.

RICHERT, A.E. (1990) 'Teaching teachers to reflect: A consideration of programme structure,' *Journal of Curriculum Studies*, **22**, pp. 509–27.

RUSSELL, T. (1995a, April) 'Giving authority to personal experience: Studying myself as preservice teachers study themselves,' Paper presented at the meeting of the American Educational Research Association, San Francisco.

RUSSELL, T. (1995b) 'Returning to the physics classroom to re-think how one learns to teach physics,' in RUSSELL, T. and KORTHAGEN, F. (Eds) *Teachers Who Teach Teachers: Reflections on Teacher Education*, London, Falmer Press, pp. 95–109.

SCHÖN, D.A. (1983) *The Reflective Practitioner: How Professionals Think in Action*, New York, Basic Books.

SCHÖN, D.A. (1987) *Educating the Reflective Practitioner: Toward a New Design for Teaching and Learning in the Professions*, San Francisco, Jossey-Bass.

SHULMAN, L.S. (1987) 'Knowledge and teaching: Foundations of the new reform,' *Harvard Educational Review*, **57**, pp. 1–22.

VALLI, L. (1989) 'Collaboration for transfer of learning: Preparing preservice teachers,' *Teacher Education Quarterly*, **16**, 1, pp. 85–95.

WHITE, R.T. and GUNSTONE, R.F. (1992) *Probing Understanding*, London, Falmer Press.

ZEICHNER, K.M. and LISTON, D.P. (1986) 'An inquiry-oriented approach to student teaching,' *Journal of Teaching Practice*, **6**, 1, pp. 5–24.

ZEICHNER, K.M. and LISTON, D.P. (1987) 'Teaching student teachers to reflect,' *Harvard Educational Review*, **57**, pp. 23–48.

Notes on Contributors

Kathrene Beasley is a second/third grade teacher at Averill Elementary School. Besides mentoring teachers at all career stages, she is continuously engaged in serious study and development of her own teaching practice. The co-author of several articles on mathematics teaching and mentoring, Kathy Beasley is also a doctoral student at Michigan State University in Teacher Education.

Sharon Feiman-Nemser is a Professor of Education at Michigan State University where she directs a reform-minded, field-based teacher education program. She recently completed a cross-cultural study of mentoring in the US, China and England and continues to work directly with university and school-based mentors.

Don Kauchak is a Professor in the Educational Studies Department at the University of Utah. He writes in the areas of educational psychology and curriculum and instruction. His current research interests are in cognitive approaches to documenting teachers' knowledge growth and in program development in teacher education.

Magdalene Lampert is a Professor of Teacher Education at the University of Michigan. She has been doing research on her own teaching of elementary mathematics since 1984. She co-directed the Mathematics and Teaching through Hypermedia Project with Deborah Ball from 1989 until 1996. Her current work focuses on the development of multimedia archives for the study of teaching and learning in schools.

John Loughran is the Director of Pre-Service Education and Professional Development in the School of Graduate Studies, Faculty of Education, Monash University, Australia. John teaches prospective science teachers in the Graduate Diploma in Education and his research interests include reflective practice, teaching and learning and science education. Recent books include *Developing Reflective Practice: Learning about Teaching and Learning through Modeling*, and a co-authored book with Jeff Northfield, *Opening the Classroom Door: Teacher, Learner, Researcher*, both published by Falmer Press.

Allan MacKinnon is an Associate Professor in the Faculty of Education at Simon Fraser University where he teaches in the area of science education. He is principal investigator of a study of interactive technologies in teacher education, focusing on the use of television conferencing in schools. Allan's interests include the analysis of teaching and learning in professional schools and program development in teacher education.

Jolie A. Mayer-Smith is an Assistant Professor in the Department of Curriculum Studies in the Faculty of Education, University of British Columbia. She teaches courses for secondary preservice science teachers, and her research interests and writings concern preservice teacher education, faculty teaching and development in postsecondary science, and the impact of integrating technologies into secondary science classrooms.

Ian J. Mitchell has been a secondary teacher of Chemistry, Science and Mathematics since 1975 in Melbourne, Australia. Since 1984, he has worked half-time at Monash University as Lecturer in Education. He is currently Facilitator of Teaching and Learning at Eumemmering Secondary College. In 1985, he co-founded the Project for Enhancing Effective Learning (PEEL), a collaborative, action-research project that aimed to develop methods of stimulating metacognitive student learning. His current research interests include the nature of classroom and teacher change, methods of capturing and sharing good teaching practice, and methods of stimulating and supporting teacher research.

Francine Peterman is a Teacher Educator and Assistant Professor of Curriculum at Cleveland State University. Her research focuses on educators' emerging beliefs about teaching and learning, teaching informed by constructivist theories, school reform, and narrative and autobiographical approaches to studying teaching and becoming a teacher.

Virginia Richardson is a Professor of Teacher Education at the University of Michigan. She teaches courses in the Elementary teacher education program, and graduate courses in qualitative methodology and research on teaching. Virginia's recent research has focused on the learning to teach and teacher change process. This involves research on teacher education, staff development, and on the change process itself.

Tom Russell After teaching in Nigeria and America, Tom Russell completed his PhD at the University of Toronto and has taught at Queen's University for 20 years. Courses in science methods and action research are complemented by research with Hugh Munby on the development of teachers' professional knowledge, with special reference to the way in which authority derives from personal experience.

Carol Scarff-Seatter is a doctoral candidate at Simon Fraser University. Her dissertation is an analysis of science teaching and philosophical writings pertaining to elementary science curriculum and instruction. Carol teaches courses in science education at Simon Fraser University and The University of British Columbia.

Jennifer A. Vabeboncoeur is an Instructor with the Roaring Fork Teacher Education Project — a partnership between the University of Colorado-Boulder, the Aspen Educational Research Foundation, and the Roaring Fork and Aspen School Districts. This is a community-based teacher education program that fosters the development of preservice teachers with a vision of education for social justice. She is also a doctoral candidate in the Social, Multicultural, and Bilingual Foundations program at the University of Colorado-Boulder.

Nancy Winitzky is an Associate Professor at the University of Utah, Department of Educational Studies. Her areas of specialization include teacher thinking and teacher education reform. Her work on knowledge growth in beginning teachers is grounded in cognitive approaches to learning. She is also active in teacher education reforms such as professional development schools and interdisciplinary professional education.

Index